ECHOES AND REFLECTIONS

On Media Ecology as a Field of Study

The Hampton Press Communication Series
MEDIA ECOLOGY
Lance Strate, supervisory editor

Mediating the Muse: A Communications Approach to Music, Media, and Cultural Change
  Robert Albrecht

Online Connections: Internet Interpersonal Relationships
  Susan B. Barnes

Bookends: The Changing Media Environment of the American Classroom
  Margaret Cassidy

Walter Ong's Contribution to Cultural Studies: The Phenomenology of the Word and I-Thou Communication
  Thomas J. Farrell

The Power of Metaphor in the Age of Electronic Media
  Raymond Gozzi, Jr.

Perspectives on Culture, Technology and Communication: The Media Ecology Tradition
  Casey Man Kong Lum

An Ong Reader: Challenges for Further Inquiry
  Thomas J. Farrell and Paul A. Soukup (eds.)

No Safety in Numbers: How the Computer Quantified Everything and Made People Risk Aversive
  Henry J. Perkinson

ScreenAgers: Lessons in Chaos from Digital Kids
  Douglas Rushkoff

Echoes and Reflections: On Media Ecology as a Field of Study
  Lance Strate

The Legacy of McLuhan
  Lance Strate and Edward Wachtel (eds.)

The Media Symplex: At the Edge of Meaning in the Age of Chaos
  Frank Zingrone

forthcoming

Biotech Time–Bomb: How Genetic Engineering Could Irreversibly Change Our World
  Scott Eastham

Transforming McLuhan: Critical, Cultural and Postmodern Perspectives
  Paul Grosswiler

Cybermedia and the Ecology of Digital Media
  Lance Strate and Susan B. Barnes (eds.)

ECHOES AND REFLECTIONS

On Media Ecology as a Field of Study

Lance Strate

Fordham University

HAMPTON PRESS, INC.
CRESSKILL, NEW JERSEY

Printed in the United States of America

Library of Congress Cataloging-in-Publication Data

Strate, Lance.
    Echoes and reflections : on media ecology as a field of study / Lance Strate.
        p. cm. -- (The Hampton Press communication series)
    Includes bibliographical references and indexes.
    ISBN 1-57273-725-5
    1. Mass media--Philosophy. I. Title.

P90.S767 2006
302.2301--dc22   2006044370

Hampton Press, Inc.
23 Broadway
Cresskill, NJ 07626

To Neil Postman and Walter J. Ong

CONTENTS

About the Author   ix
Introduction   1

Part One: A Media Ecology Review

1   Introduction to Media Ecology as a Field of Study   15
2   Marshall McLuhan   21
3   Harold Innis and American Cultural Studies   27
4   The Toronto School   31
5   Walter Ong   35
6   Orality-Literacy Studies   39
7   Media History   45
8   Neil Postman   51
9   The New York School and Communication Studies   55
10   Mumford, Technics, and Ecological History   65
11   Ellul and Technological Studies   73
12   Formal Roots   79
13   Conclusion   91

Part Two: Narcissism and Echolalia: Sense and the Struggle for the Self

14   Something from Nothing   95
15   Communication and/as Material Transformation   99
16   Echo and Narcissus   105
17   Autism and the Struggle for the Self   111
18   Theory of Mind   119
19   Conclusion   127

Notes   131
References   135
Author Index   161
Subject Index   167

ABOUT THE AUTHOR

Lance Strate is Associate Professor of Communication and Media Studies at Fordham University, and Director of the Graduate Program in Public Communication. He is president and co-founder of the Media Ecology Association, and a past president of the New York State Communication Association. Editor of the journal *Explorations in Media Ecology* and Supervisory Editor of the Media Ecology Book Series published by Hampton Press, he is the co-editor of several anthologies, including *Communication and Cyberspace: Social Interaction in an Electronic Environment, Legacy of McLuhan,* and the forthcoming *Cybertheory and the Ecology of Digital Media. Understanding Media Ecology,* his next book on this field, is currently in preparation.

INTRODUCTION

I

Echoes and Reflections. Parallels and polar oppositions. Cycles and linear progressions. Concentricities and intersections. Depth and surface. Interiors and exteriors. Emptiness and fullness. The subjective and the objective. The other and the self.

Echoes and Reflections. An audit and a review. Histories and projections. Memory and foresight. The past and the future. Preservation and mutation. Continuity and change.

Echoes and Reflections. The acoustic and the visual. Sounds and appearances. The ear and the eye. Hearing and sight. Music and light.

Echoes and Reflections. Speech and writing. Orality and literacy. Sayings and signs. Oracles and seers. Words and images.

Echoes and Reflections. Tradition and discovery. Faith and reason. Wisdom and knowledge.

II

Echoes and Reflections is a book about differences, about different modes of communication and perception, different modes of action and motion, different modes of experience and existence. It follows that *Echoes and Reflections* is not a book that adopts or advocates a universal and monolithic position along the lines of Platonism, Marxism, Freudianism, and so forth, although it does represent an approach known as *media ecology*. Media ecology is not a system or doctrine, nor any kind of *-ism*, but rather an intellectual tradition, a perspective and a shared sensibility; it can be understood as a network of related literature, a series of conversations and arguments that span the centuries, and also as a family of discoverers, creators, and seekers, to invoke Daniel Boorstin's historic triad (i.e., Boorstin, 1983, 1992, 1998).

Echoes and Reflections is a book about differences, but only the differences that matter, the *differences that make a difference*, to use Gregory Bateson's (1972) resonant formulation. I do not favor the contemporary attempts to turn *difference* into another universal and monolithic theory. Whether it is a fetish or a fad, the insistence that everything is equally different and unique is an insistence that everything is the same in its difference. This may satisfy a political urge for egalitarianism (which is certainly worthwhile in its proper context), but the result is a bland and pointless sameness; it is a chaos and void resulting from philosophical and rhetorical entropy—the heat death of our universes of discourse. Although it is certainly problematic to become lost in a realm of high-level abstractions, disconnected from the concreteness of events and sensory experience, I consider it equally a mistake to reject some of our most important tools of thought, that is, categorizing and generalizing. Without them, all that remains is to describe the particulars - certainly a valid activity, but also a very safe one. When the only thing that is produced is a description of a particular situation in the context of a particular time and a particular place, there is little chance of falsification or even much criticism. It is then possible to hint at generalizations without ever having to defend them, resulting in what Henry Perkinson (1996) calls a risk-free intellectual world. But some risk taking is needed for growth, intellectual or otherwise. Media ecology is made up, in part, of intellectual risk takers. Our field is open to big ideas, to probes and explorations, to grand theories and philosophies, as it is also open to the particulars of ethnographies, histories, and descriptive research. When the two are in conversation with each other, as they are in our intellectual tradition, we get the kind of independent thinking that Camille Paglia (2002) advocates.

Echoes and Reflections is a book about such conversations. It is a book about relationships, the relationship of difference and similarity, the relationship of the universal and the particular, the relationship of the abstract and the concrete; of course, it is also about the relationship between medium and message, sender and receiver, self and other, individual and environment. In this sense, it is a book about dialectics, but not in the Marxian or Hegelian sense, nor in the sense of the medieval university curriculum known as the *trivium*, which consists of rhetoric, grammar, and logic or dialectic. From the standpoint of the trivium, *Echoes and Reflections* may be regarded as a grammar book, in that media ecology is concerned with the structures, rules, and biases governing languages, media, and technologies—governing the world as well as the word. It is concerned with *conjugations*, which in its broadest sense refers to patterns of interaction, bonding and separation, reproduction and change. It is concerned with *tenses*, that is with time in addition to space, with time binding (Korzybski, 1993) and time biases (Innis, 1951), with understanding history and understanding the future, and thereby understanding the present; in addition to tenses, media ecology is also concerned with dynamic *tensions*, and with *tensegrity*, Buckminster Fuller's biomechanical metaphor for the dialectic of tension and compression (Fuller & Applewhite, 1975). *Echoes and Reflections* is also a book about communication, about meaning, and the *meaning of meaning*, to conjure up C. K. Ogden and I. A. Richard's (1923) classic phrase. It is therefore a book about rhetoric, in addition to grammar and dialectic, or put another way, rather than being a book about grammar in isolation, *Echoes and Reflections* is a book about grammar in relation to rhetoric and dialectic.

In the medieval trivium the terms dialectic and logic are interchangeable, and *Echoes and Reflections* is not a logic book in this *trivial* sense, but neither is it illogical. The logics that we associate with Aristotle and his intellectual heirs, including the positive logic of Alfred North Whitehead and Bertrand Russell (1925-1927), and the negative dialectics of Theodor Adorno (1973), represent singular modes of expression and thought. Logic, from Aristotle on, has mostly referred to some form of *monologic*. *Echoes and Reflections*, on the other hand, is a book about *dialogic*, and it is in the sense that *dialectic* is synonymous with *dialogic* (a sense more often than not forgotten) that *Echoes and Reflections* is a book about dialectics. *Monologic* is the logic of universalism (including the universalism of particularism), and it is everywhere expressed in the form of a *technologic*. *Dialogic* is the logic of difference (in relation to similarity), the logic of relationships, and of *mediation*, which monologic by its very nature must deny. *Dialogic* may be a form of *paralogic*, because it bursts the boundaries of *monologic* (paralleling the relationship between paradox and orthodox). *Dialogic* recognizes the presence of dynamic interaction in all things, the presence of mediation surrounding all things, and therefore represents a transition stage between *monologic* and a yet not fully realized *ecologic*. *Echoes and Reflections* is a book about *ecologic*, or at least about our need for one.

Echoes and Reflections is a book about differences and similarities. Echoes are heard and reflections are seen; they activate different sensory organs and constitute different modes of experience. But they are similar in that both involve rebounds and ricochets, the bounce-back of sound and light respectively. Both constitute copies, doubles of an original phenomenon. Both resemble their originals, but are not the things they represent. Both are modes of signification, but more importantly both are *mediations*, situated in between the original phenomenon and the knower who perceives that phenomenon through them. *Echoes and Reflections* is a book about this process of mediation, and the media through which this process occurs. It is a book about the medium as the message, to summon the memory of Marshall McLuhan (2003). It is a book about media as environments, to recall the words of Neil Postman (1970). It is also a book about media as effects, or *blowback* to use the popular parlance, and echoes and reflections are both effects of this nature. In short, *Echoes and Reflections* is a book about media ecology.

III

Echoes and Reflections is specifically a book about media ecology as a field. *Field* is a funny term, in some ways awkward and unflattering. Certainly, *discipline* commands more respect, and a case could be made for media ecology as a discipline (as defined by its disciples); but in contemporary terms, media ecology is best described as being interdisciplinary, or better yet multidisciplinary (as interdisciplinarity sometimes suggests a lack of discipline altogether, another form of risk-free scholarship). Media ecology could also be framed as a *school* (which would be especially appropriate given the historical connection of media ecology scholars such as Neil Postman, Marshall McLuhan, and Walter Ong to the field of education), but that term has been used *within* media ecology to refer to specific subsets such as the Toronto School and the New York School (not to mention the Chicago School and the Frankfurt School, which at least may be considered as overlapping with the field). My friend Casey Lum (2006) has adopted the term *theory group*, but it is not a term that I myself would use given that Postman, McLuhan, and Ong and many others always objected to the use of the term *theory* to describe their work, in part due to its scientific (or scientistic) connotations; they also recognized that the root meaning of *theory* betrays a visual metaphor, and they did not want to identify themselves with the monologic of visualism (the term *system* may be rejected for the same reason). As for *paradigm*, even if the term were not woefully overused, media ecology can neither be said to be dogmatic, nor *paradogmatic*, although it has been described as *preparadigmatic* (Nystrom, 1973).

Media ecology can be understood as a perspective (visual metaphor), an intellectual tradition (suggesting the acoustic metaphor of oral tradition), and an approach (hinting at the tactile and kinetic). It is a family and a network, a genre and a galaxy. Of course, we could also say that media ecology is itself an ecology. But I have chosen *field* because it is an academic term, and this is an academic book. *Echoes and Reflections* may serve as an introduction to media ecology as a field of study, in that it is an introduction to media ecology scholarship (as opposed to an introduction organized by media ecology concepts, methods, or practices).

Despite its inadequacies, *field* is also a fascinating metaphor for academic activity. In agriculture, it is associated with human toil, just as scholars labor to produce food for thought. In sports, it is an arena for play and contests, and intellectual activity is as much about free play, and organized competition as it is about work. In warfare, a field is a battleground, as it all too often is in the ivory tower. In aviation, a field is a launching pad for airplanes, in academia for ideas. In video, a field is a still image, a freeze frame consisting of only half the image (alternate lines of resolution are activated at any given moment), and in *Echoes and Reflections* as in any other attempt to represent a field, what we have is a snapshot, a frozen moment that cannot capture an ever-changing reality, and is also unavoidably incomplete. In other visual arts, the field is the background on top of which various figures may be added, just as an intellectual field provides a much-needed context for understanding individual intellectuals and their ideas. Similarly, in sociology, field refers to a sphere of human activity; in geography it refers to a part of the physical environment; in science it refers to an aura of electromagnetic radiation, and as well to the sum total of the space-time continuum. All of these meanings suggest that *field* is a medium and an ecology, and therefore an entirely appropriate metaphor for media ecology (and also an entirely appropriate object of study for media ecology scholars).

IV

Echoes and Reflection: On Media Ecology as a Field of Study is divided into two parts that may be seen as being in dialogue with one another, constituting a dialectic between the general and the specific, and between the objective and the subjective. Part One, entitled "A Media Ecology Review," provides an objective overview of the field. Chapter One introduces media ecology as a field of study and identifies Marshall McLuhan, Walter Ong, and Neil Postman as the intellectual tradition's most central scholars. Chapter Two focuses on the contributions of Marshall McLuhan, Chapter Three highlights the work of Harold Innis and continues with a discussion of American cultural studies, and Chapter Four consists of a survey of the Toronto School. The essay continues with a discussion of Walter Ong's work in Chapter Five, followed by a look at the relevant research in orality-literacy studies in Chapter Six, and in media history in Chapter Seven. In Chapter Eight the essay turns to a discussion of Neil Postman. Chapter Nine introduces the New York School, and also goes over the contributions of communication studies to the media ecology field. Chapter Ten consists of a review of the work of Lewis Mumford and related studies of technics and ecological history, and Chapter Eleven presents the work of Jacques Ellul and other scholars and critics in technological studies. The essay ends with a discussion of the formal roots of media ecology in the study of language and symbolic communication in Chapter Twelve, and a general discussion of media ecology as an intellectual approach in Chapter Thirteen.

Part Two, entitled "Narcissism and Echolalia: Sense and the Struggle for the Self," presents a subjective personal statement about myself as a communication scholar and how the field of media ecology relates to the discipline of communication for me. I should note here that although media ecology is a communication-centered approach and there is significant overlap between media ecology and communication, the two are quite distinct. Only some of communication scholarship is typically viewed as media ecological, whereas media ecology itself is, as I noted above, multidisciplinary and based on the work of scholars from just about every field imaginable. In Part Two I emphasize the close connection between communication and media ecology for my own scholarship, with no intention to impose the connection on others. The essay also provides a case study on the concept of the self as a specific application of the general approach surveyed in Part One. Chapter Fourteen begins with a story whose theme is *something from nothing*, a theme that I relate to the phenomenon of human communication. In Chapter Fifteen, I proceed to combine media ecology and the study of communication in a discussion of communication and/as material transformation. In Chapter Sixteen, I recount the myth of Echo and Narcissus in order to introduce the topic of the sense of self. I then turn to the topic of autism and the struggle for the self in Chapter Seventeen, drawing on my experiences as the father of an autistic child. I am aware that there are risks involved in combining the personal and the professional in this way, and it is my hope that relating my experiences are relevant rather than self-indulgent. The case study continues in Chapter Eighteen with a discussion of theory of mind as it relates to the formation of a sense of self, and concludes in Chapter Nineteen with comments on coping with the individual difficulties of autism and the larger cultural crises that we face.

V

The story of how this book came to be is not a typical one. It begins with the New York State Communication Association, an organization that has meant a great deal to me over the course of my career. In 1996, I was elect-ed to the office of vice-president elect, with the responsibility for coordinating NYSCA's annual conference in 1998. The theme that I chose for my conference was *Echoes and Reflections*, which seemed to me to be a theme that any communication scholar or student could relate to, but also a theme that would resonate for the field of media ecology. It was not until many years later, when I decided to publish this book, that it occurred to me that my old conference theme would be the perfect title. But back in 1997, I gave no thought to the possibility that I might retrieve and reuse the phrase when I arrived at the annual NYSCA meeting with the call for papers for my *Echoes and Reflections* conference in hand. In those years, the conferences were held at Kutsher's Country Club in Monticello, New York, a venerable Catskills hotel, part of the old borscht belt, and in 1997 my family came with me to enjoy a weekend at the resort. But, as the old Yiddish saying goes, man plans and God laughs. The conference began Friday afternoon, and early the next morning my daughter Sarah, who was a year and a half old, suffered a series of seizures. She was hospitalized for a week, but thankfully she has had no further seizures after that day.

But something was wrong, that much was clear, although it was not until the following May that we learned that Sarah is autistic. Suffice it to say that everything changed as a result of this diagnosis, for myself, for my wife, and for Sarah's older brother Benjamin. Our lives changed, but they did not end. We did everything we could to help our daughter, and we carried on. I ran a successful conference that October, and I was honored to receive NYSCA's John F. Wilson Fellow Award, which recognizes "exceptional scholarship, leadership, and dedication to the field of communication" (their words, not mine). The Wilson Fellows who chose me to join their ranks were Neil Postman, Gary Gumpert, Deborah Borisoff, Dan Hahn, Laurie Arliss, Joyce Hauser, and Susan Drucker, and I remain grateful for the recognition. As a recipient of this award, I was obliged to present a Wilson Fellow Address at the following year's conference, focusing on my scholarship, which would then be printed in NYSCA's journal, the *Speech Communication Annual*. That my address would be about media ecology was clear enough. But the problem was that my scholarly work had been interrupted by the crisis in my personal life. And so, in the year that followed, after much agonizing, I decided to incorporate our family experience into my Wilson Fellow Address. NYSCA had already been a part of Sarah's history, and I decided to make Sarah part of NYSCA's history by integrating what I had learned about autism into my address. I did not make this decision lightly, I should add. Much of what I discovered about autism was of great relevance for the discipline of communication and the field media ecology, but at the same time, it was very painful to talk about my daughter and her disability. Adding to the pressure was the fact that NYSCA vice-president Susan Jasko had asked me to present the address as the Friday night keynote speaker when Kathleen Hall Jamieson dropped out several months before the conference, meaning that I would be talking about Sarah to over two hundred people. But I knew that autism was a subject that needed to be discussed, and so I made my decision to go through with it. I had no idea whether I would be able to perform adequately as a keynoter, nor had I any idea of what the audience's reaction might be. And all I can say is that we shared something very special that night, as hackneyed as that may sound. I have no better words to describe it—you just had to be there.

Looking back to the conference theme I had used the year before, I chose the title "Narcissism and Echolalia: Sense and the Struggle for the Self" for my John F. Wilson Fellow Address, presented on October 8, 1999, at the 57th Annual Meeting of the New York State Communication Association. The following year, Neil Postman asked me to give the address at the 45th Media Ecology Conference, at Rosendale, New York, November 3-5, 2000, and I took the occasion to revise some important revisions to the piece. (Postman's media ecology conferences were organized for the benefit of his students in the media ecology graduate program at New York University, the program through which I earned my doctorate; the conferences and the program came to an end after he passed away in 2003). I also sent a copy of the address to Walter Ong as part of our correspondence over the last few years before his death in 2003, and he strongly encouraged me to continue to speak and write about the topic, which was a great motivator for me. As per the requirements of the Wilson Fellow Award, I published an expanded version of the address in the 2000 issue of the *Speech Communication Annual* (Vol. 14), which was not actually in print until the year 2002 (my own fault, as by that time I had taken over as editor of that journal, and I should add here that the assistance of Associate Editor Susan Barnes was instrumental in getting the issue into print). I included an acknowledgement when I published that article that I will simply reproduce here:

> I want to express my gratitude to the Wilson Fellows for selecting me to receive the John F. Wilson Fellow Award in 1998. It is a great honor to be recognized in this way, and it is especially gratifying to be recognized for scholarship by New York State's Communication Association, because New York State provided all of my education, from the public school system of New York City, including a semester of Communication Arts at Hillcrest High School in Jamaica, Queens; to my undergraduate work at Cornell University, where I was a Communication major studying with Jack Barwind and Njoku Awa; and from the Media Studies MA program at Queens College where I worked with Gary Gumpert, Dan Hahn, Robert Cathcart, John Pollock, and Peter Dahlgren; to New York University's Doctoral

Program in Media Ecology where I studied with Neil Postman, Terence P. Moran, and Christine Nystrom. I want to thank all of my teachers for providing me with an education worthy of the empire state, and I would like to dedicate this article to them. (p. 52)

I later published a shorter version of the article under the title of "Something from Nothing: Seeking a Sense of Self," in *ETC: A Review of General Semantics* in 2003 (Vol. 60, No. 1), and I am grateful to the editor, Paul Dennithorne Johnston, for his willingness to help me disseminate these ideas further, and to the International Society for General Semantics, which published the journal before merging with the Institute of General Semantics. On December 18, 2003, I gave a revised version of the address based on the *ETC* article, to the New York Society for General Semantics, at a meeting held at the Albert Ellis Institute in New York City, and I dedicated that talk to Neil Postman, who had passed away two months earlier.

Part Two of this book is based on the expanded essay that originally appeared in NYSCA's *Speech Communication Annual*, but also incorporating some of the revisions made for the ETC article and entirely new changes made for this volume. In the new version published in this book, I quote in full the text of a children's book by Phoebe Gilman entitled *Something from Nothing*, which Scholastic Canada has allowed me to reprint for a nominal fee.

Part One of this book has a somewhat less complicated history. In 2003, Paul Soukup, SJ, asked me, in his capacity as managing editor of *Communication Research Trends*, if I would prepare a review essay on media ecology for his journal. I agreed, and the result was *A Media Ecology Review*, which was published as a special issue of *Communication Research Trends* (Vol. 23, No. 2) in 2004, and reprinted here with minor revisions. The title is meant as a tribute to a periodical that Neil Postman had put out in the early years of the media ecology graduate program at New York University, *The Media Ecology Review*, as a vehicle for student publication. This was before my time, I might add, and by the time that I enrolled in the program Postman had taken over as editor of *ETC* and was encouraging us to submit our best work to that journal. The essay itself draws on the reading lists used in the media ecology program, prepared by Neil Postman, Christine Nystrom, and Terence P. Moran, which in part are based on reading lists prepared by Louis Forsdale, George Gordon, and Marshall McLuhan; it is, of course, also based on my own reading in the field, which began in my freshman year of college and continues to this day. *A Media Ecology Review* was my attempt to survey the literature in the field of media ecology as thoroughly as possible, but the result is by definition incomplete, and I think it important to make that clear. Moreover, although the review is presented in an objective style, it is in many ways a record of my own path as I have made my way through the field. The passing of Walter Ong and Neil Postman in 2003 lent an exceptional urgency to the essay, and I dedicated the review to them in *Communication Research Trends* and retain that dedication here. When I sent *A Media Ecology Review* to Paul Soukup in 2004, it was long past the deadline he had given me, and the essay was much longer than he had asked for or anticipated. Paul was kind enough not only to publish the piece in its entirety and perform extensive copyediting, but he also went to heroic lengths to format it so that it fit within a single issue rather than be broken up between two. Moreover, Paul was kind enough to make his electronic files available to Hampton Press, for which we both are grateful. I also wish to acknowledge William Biernatzki, SJ, the editor of *Communication Research Trends* and the Centre for the Study of Communication and Culture, the Jesuit institution that publishes this outstanding journal. Additionally, some of the work that appears in *A Media Ecology Review* was adapted from material that I contributed to publications written in collaboration with Susan Barnes (Barnes & Strate, 1996), Casey Man Kong Lum (Strate & Lum, 2000), and Edward Wachtel (Strate & Wachtel, 2005), and I want to recognize their contributions to my own work here.

Hampton Press has published this book as part of the Media Ecology Book Series, of which I am supervisory editor. I first proposed the series to Barbara Bernstein of Hampton Press in 1994, and her approval was a turning point for me personally and for media ecology as a field of study (another turning point came in 2001 when she agreed to publish the journal *Explorations in Media Ecology* in partnership with the Media Ecology Association, beginning in 2002). Over a decade has passed since we launched the book series, and it is a great pleasure to add *Echoes and Reflections* to a series of books written by scholars such as Walter Ong, Douglas Rushkoff, Robert Logan, Frank Zingrone, Henry Perkinson, Susan Barnes, Raymond Gozzi, Jr., Thomas Farrell, Katherine Fry, Robert Albrecht, and Margaret Cassidy, and anthologies edited by Thomas Farrell and Paul Soukup, Casey Man Kong Lum, and Edward Wachtel and myself—and the list keeps growing.

VI

Echoes and Reflections would not be possible without the help, support, and contributions of a great many individuals, some of whom I have already mentioned, all of whom deserve acknowledgement in these pages.

Because the medium is the message, I think it only right to begin by thanking the book publisher, Hampton Press, and Barbara Bernstein, who *is* Hampton Press, for making *Echoes and Reflections* a reality.

The second person that I want to recognize is my colleague, Paul Levinson, who urged me to "just do it," as the saying goes, and get this book in print. Without his prodding, *Echoes and Reflections* would not now exist, and I thank him for that, for his advice and guidance, and also for the example of intellectual activity, productivity, and positive thinking that he sets every day.

Third, I want to extend my gratitude to Paul Soukup, SJ, for convincing me to write *A Media Ecology Review*, which served as the foundation of this book. If not for him, I never would have written that essay, and I also appreciate Paul's support, encouragement, and collaboration in the larger project of establishing media ecology as a field of study.

I want to acknowledge the incalculable influence that the media ecology program at New York University had on my work, and specifically Neil Postman, a mentor and a friend who is sorely missed; Christine Nystrom, who chaired my dissertation committee; Terence P. Moran, who directed the program for many years; Joy Gould Boyum, who also served on my committee; and Henry Perkinson, who taught me to think more clearly and who published the first book in my media ecology book series.

Gary Gumpert, whom I studied under at Queens College, has also been a great teacher, mentor, and friend. And I must include a thank you to Jack Barwind, who introduced me to many media ecological concepts as an undergraduate at Cornell University.

Through our correspondence, and through his writings, I developed a very strong connection to Walter Ong, SJ, and I consider him to be a vital influence and guide. He too is deeply missed.

I am very grateful to the following individuals who have been sources of inspiration and insight, and role models for me: Camille Paglia, James Carey, Frank Dance, James Beniger, Edmund Carpenter, Denise Schmandt-Besserat, Neil Kleinman, Donald Theall, and the late Daniel Boorstin.

Joshua Meyrowitz and Edward Wachtel have been like big brothers to me, personally as well as professionally. I also feel a sense of kinship to Douglas Rushkoff, Dennis Gallagher, and to my Canadian "cousins" Eric McLuhan, Robert Logan, Frank Zingrone, and Paul Heyer.

Special recognition is due to those who have worked with me on the grand adventure of establishing the Media Ecology Association. The MEA's existence ensures that there is an environment, a habitat, a niche for books like *Echoes and Reflections*, and I want to thank Thom Gencarelli and Casey Lum (my original co-conspirators), Sue Barnes and Paul Levinson (who were also present at the moment of creation), and Janet Sternberg, James Morrison, Douglas Rushkoff, Susan Drucker, Ray Gozzi, Paul Soukup, Laura Tropp, Mary Ann Allison, Judith Yaross Lee, Missy Alexander, Elizabeth Fitzgerald, Robert Logan, Corey Anton, Ellen Rose, Stephanie Gibson, James Carey, Gary Gumpert, Christine Nystrom, Joshua

Meyrowitz, and Neil Postman, all of whom played a role in the creation and development of the MEA, its activities and publications. And I am grateful to everyone else who has contributed to the MEA's success. And if you are not familiar with our group, please point your browser to our website: www.media-ecology.org.

As I mentioned above, the New York State Communication Association played an indispensable role in the development of this book and in my professional development. I want to take this opportunity to acknowledge three outstanding NSYCA colleagues who have been very supportive and caring: Susan Jasko, Joseph Coppolino, and Judy Isserlis.

Fordham University has been my base of operations since 1989, and I want to acknowledge the following Fordham colleagues (in addition to those I have already acknowledged above): John Phelan, Ron Jacobson, Margot Hardenbergh, Al Auster, Lewis Freeman, James Capo, John Carey, James Fisher, Dominic Balestra, and Fordham President Joseph M. McShane, SJ. Additionally, over the years, I have benefited from my relationships with many outstanding students at Fordham, NYU, and elsewhere—too many to list by name, so instead please accept my thanks to you all collectively.

I also want to mention my old classmates from the media ecology program at New York University, Robert Albrecht and Paul Lippert, with whom I have shared many a beer and intense conversation. More recently, Pertti Hurme and Fernando Gutiérrez have provided me with opportunities to distill my ideas about media ecology. And I am grateful for the continuation of my childhood friendships with Martin Friedman and Charles Meltzer. Emily Smith has become a family friend, having been my daughter's teacher ever since she was diagnosed, and I want to take this opportunity to thank her for all of her hard work and dedication.

Finally, and most importantly, I am grateful beyond words to my family, to my daughter Sarah who has taught me so much and who is always in my heart, to my son Benjamin who is my right-hand man and my source of pride, to my wife Barbara whose love, generosity, and good nature is a constant source of joy, to my mother Betty Strate whose faith in me has always been a source of strength, and to my father Benjamin Strate, whose memory lives on in everything that I do.

A MEDIA ECOLOGY REVIEW

1

INTRODUCTION TO MEDIA ECOLOGY AS A FIELD OF STUDY

. . . our first thinking about the subject was guided by a biological metaphor. You will remember from the time when you first became acquainted with a Petri dish, that a medium was defined as a substance within which a culture grows. If you replace the word "substance" with the word "technology," the definition would stand as a fundamental principle of media ecology: A medium is a technology within which a culture grows; that is to say, it gives form to a culture's politics, social organization, and habitual ways of thinking. Beginning with that idea, we invoked still another biological metaphor, that of ecology. . . . We put the word "media" in the front of the word "ecology" to suggest that we were not simply interested in media, but in the ways in which the interaction between media and human beings gives a culture its character and, one might say, helps a culture to maintain symbolic balance. (Postman, 2000, pp. 10-11)

Our present fascination with ecology of all kinds is tied in with the information explosion that has marked our age. . . . With the information explosion, we have become more and more conscious of the interrelationships of all the life and structures in the universe around us, and, with our more and more detailed knowledge of cosmic and organic evolution, ultimately of interrelationships as building up to and centering on life, and eventually human life. The human environment is of course not just the earth but the entire universe, with its still incalcu-

lable expanse and an age of around some 12 to 14 billion years. This is
the real cosmos within which human beings appeared and still exist.
(Ong, 2002b, p. 6)

I would like to dedicate this essay to the memories of Walter J. Ong, S.J.
and Neil Postman, who passed away within two months of each other, Ong
on August 12th and Postman on October 5th of 2003. Through their
careers and the body of work they have left us, these two educators, both
of whom achieved the highest possible academic rank, University
Professor, at their respective institutions, Saint Louis and New York
Universities, were instrumental in establishing the foundations of media
ecology as a field of inquiry. Moreover, Walter Ong set the standard and
demonstrated the possibilities for scholarship in the media ecology intellectual tradition, and Neil Postman exemplified the practice of media ecology analysis by a public intellectual engaged in social criticism. Working
parallel to one another, Ong and Postman built upon an intellectual tradition that has its roots in the ancient world, a tradition that coalesced in
response to the revolutions in communication, media, and technology of
the 19th and 20th centuries, and brought it into the 21st century.

In viewing Ong and Postman as twin pillars of media ecology, I do not
mean to deny that there are significant differences between them.
Certainly, it would be possible to contrast their midwest and east coast
backgrounds and their Roman Catholic and Reform Jewish faiths. We
could also differentiate Ong's historical focus from Postman's emphasis on
current affairs, Ong's phenomenological approach from Postman's grounding in linguistics, and Ong's dialectic of the oral and the literate from
Postman's of the word and the image. But what separates the two scholars
is overshadowed by what they hold in common: a shared perspective and
sensibility, and a strong connection to the most celebrated of all media
ecology scholars, Marshall McLuhan. In fact, media ecology can be understood as an intellectual network in which McLuhan, Ong, and Postman
constitute the prime nodes (corresponding geographically to Toronto, St.
Louis, and New York City).

Media ecology is a perspective that embodies what Ong (1977) refers
to as "ecological concern," which he describes as "a new state of consciousness, the ultimate in open-system awareness. Its thrust is the dialectical
opposite of the isolating thrust of writing and print" (p. 324). Ong goes on
to suggest that contemporary questions of ecological concern

echoed earlier thinking culminating in Darwin's work, which has
shown how species themselves, earlier thought of as the closed-system
bases of life and taken to be major elements in philosophical thinking,
are not fixed but develop through natural selection brought about by

open interaction between individuals and environment. The new philosophical attention to openness appears not unrelated to the opening of previously isolated human groups to one another fostered by electronic communications media, telephone, radio, and ultimately television. (p. 324)

Such ecological concern is central to McLuhan's approach to studying media, as he explains in the introduction to the second edition of *Understanding Media* (2003a):

"The medium is the message" means, in terms of the electronic age, that a totally new environment has been created. The "content" of this new environment is the old mechanized environment of the industrial age. The new environment reprocesses the old one as radically as TV is reprocessing the film. For the "content" of TV is the movie. TV is environmental and imperceptible, like all environments. We are aware only of the "content" or the old environment. When machine production was new, it gradually created an environment whose content was the old environment of agrarian life and the arts and crafts. This older environment was elevated to an art form by the new mechanical environment. The machine turned Nature into an art form. (p. 13)

Inspired by McLuhan, Postman formally introduced the term "media ecology" in 1968, in an address delivered at the annual meeting of the National Council of Teachers of English (published under the title of "The Reformed English Curriculum" in 1970). He told his audience that "the first thing to be said about media ecology is that I am not inventing it. I am only naming it" (p. 161). By not claiming the role of founder of a discipline, and not naming anyone else as the inventor, Postman left open the origins of the field, and implied that media ecology has been in existence in one form or another since antiquity. It follows that individuals need not use the term "media ecology" in order to have their work categorized as such. Indeed, they need not have been alive when the term was coined in order to have it identified as media ecological. Postman did, however, provide a definition of media ecology as "the study of media as environments" (Postman, 1970, p. 161), explaining that the main concern is "how media of communication affect human perception, understanding, feeling, and value; and how our interaction with media facilitates or impedes our chances of survival. The word ecology implies the study of environments: their structure, content, and impact on people" (p. 161). These environments consist of techniques as well as technologies, symbols as well as tools, information systems as well as machines. They are made up of modes of communication as well as what is commonly thought of as media (although the term "media" is used to encompass all of these things). Thus, Postman also describes media ecology as "the study of transactions among people, their messages, and their message systems" in *The Soft Revolution* (1971, p. 139), which he co-authored with Charles Weingartner.

Where Postman defines media ecology as a field of inquiry, McLuhan places greater emphasis on praxis when he uses the term. For example, in a 1977 television interview, in response to the question, "what now, briefly, is this thing called media ecology," McLuhan answers:

> It means arranging various media to help each other so they won't can-
> cel each other out, to buttress one medium with another. You might
> say, for example, that radio is a bigger help to literacy than television,
> but television might be a very wonderful aid to teaching languages.
> And so you can do some things on some media that you cannot do on
> others. And, therefore, if you watch the whole field, you can prevent
> this waste that comes by one canceling the other out. (McLuhan,
> 2003b, p. 271)

And in a letter to Claire Booth Luce published in *The Letters of Marshall McLuhan* (1987), he writes: "As for restricting the use of TV, it surely should be a part of a media ecology program" (p. 534). For Postman, praxis first took the form of pedagogy. In "The Reformed English Curriculum" (Postman, 1970) he went so far as to argue for media ecology as an alternative to standard high school English education, a "modest proposal" that did not catch on. In *The Soft Revolution* (Postman & Weingartner, 1971) he reproduced the prospectus for a Ph.D. program in media ecology, stating that "such a program is being contemplated at one university" and extending the invitation, "local catalogues please copy" (p. 138). In point of fact, by the time the book was actually published, New York University had already approved the program, which in 1973 produced the first major treatise to examine media ecology as a formal field of study, Christine Nystrom's doctoral dissertation entitled: *Towards a Science of Media Ecology: The Formulation of Integrated Conceptual Paradigms for the Study of Human Communication Systems*. There she characterizes media ecology as a "perspective, or emerging metadiscipline . . . broadly defined as the study of complex communication systems as environments" and concerned with "the interactions of communications media, technology, technique, and processes with human feeling, thought, value, and behavior" (p. 3).

The first major survey of media ecology as a field was produced by William Kuhns under the title of *The Post-Industrial Prophets* (1971). Although he does not use the term "media ecology," Kuhns makes frequent use of environmental, ecological, and systems terminology as he discusses the work of technology scholars Lewis Mumford, Siegfried Giedion, and Jacques Ellul; media theorists Harold Innis and Marshall McLuhan; and systems pioneers Buckminster Fuller and Norbert Wiener. Kuhns also wrote a short book about technology and contemporary culture, addressed to Christian readers, under the title of *Environmental Man* (1969). While *The Post-Industrial Prophets* emphasizes futurism, media ecology is also concerned with understanding media in a historical context, Ong's area of emphasis. Hence, for example, the four editions of the anthology *Communication in History* edited by David Crowley and Paul Heyer (1991, 1995, 1999, 2003), which represent a somewhat different and more recent attempt at surveying the field as compared to *The Post-Industrial Prophets*. Presenting a sampling of media ecological historical scholarship, Crowley and Heyer emphasize the impact or effects of media, but like Kuhns do not use the term "media ecology." Another anthology, edited by Casey Man Kong Lum (2006), entitled *Perspectives on Culture, Technology, and Communication: The Media Ecology Tradition*, covers a good portion of the theories, key concepts, and development of the field.

Over the past 36 years, use of the term "media ecology" has diffused slowly outside of New York and Toronto, and in some instances was adopted with its original meanings lost or distorted (e.g., Adilkno, 1994; Tabbi & Wutz, 1997). At the same time, other terms were introduced to refer to the same type of perspective and intellectual tradition, such as "Toronto School" (Goody, 1968, 1977), "medium theory" (Meyrowitz, 1985), "American cultural studies" (Carey, 1989), and "mediology" (Debray, 1996). Also, due to its strong association with Ong (1982), "orality-literacy studies" has sometimes been used as a synonym for media ecology. In recent years, however, "media ecology" has come to be widely accepted as the term of choice, especially since the establishment of the Media Ecology Association in 1998. Aptly, Postman (2000) gave the keynote address at the MEA's inaugural convention ("The Humanism of Media Ecology") and Ong (2002b) wrote the lead article for the first issue of the MEA's journal, *Explorations in Media Ecology* ("Ecology and Some of Its Future"). Since the introduction of the term in 1968, "media ecology" has been understood as a perspective or approach, as a field of inquiry or study, and a curriculum. It has also been understood in very basic and concrete terms as a reading list, bibliography, or pattern of citation. Indeed, one way to recognize media ecology scholarship is by the presence of certain sources in the author's reference list (e.g., McLuhan, Ong, and/or Postman).

Media ecology has also come to be understood as an intellectual tradition, one that Camille Paglia (2000) characterizes as particularly North American, as that is the locus of media ecology's historical development in the 20th century. This is not to say that media ecology is only associated with North Americans, or necessarily so, but that the evolution of the field has been influenced by North American pragmatism and openness. Thus, media ecology is a tradition of independent thinkers who "creatively reshaped traditions and cross-fertilized disciplines, juxtaposing the old and the new to make unexpected connections that remain fresh" (Paglia, 2000, p. 22), thinkers such as McLuhan, Ong, and Postman. It is an intellectual tradition based on what Ong (1977) refers to as "open-system awareness" (p. 324).

An open system enhances creativity, freedom, and the process of exploration and discovery, but it is particularly challenging when the goal is to map the system itself. Media ecology is a network of ideas, individuals, and publications, and it is possible to follow the links of the network in any number of different directions. Some links may bring us closer to the core ideas of the field, and others take us further and further away from them, but there is no definitive boundary line or border to cross, just as there is no single point of origination. It is tempting to claim that only the medium of hypertext could adequately represent such an open network, but the benefits of hypertext are traded off against a certain loss of coherence and order, however much that coherence and order may be artificially produced and arbitrary in nature. I will therefore proceed to present a linear journey through the media ecology network, with the understanding that it represents one of many possible pathways, and that at times I may wander into territory that others would consider outside the network, while overlooking points of interest within the network. This review essay will take as its navigational markers the three prime nodes of media ecology: McLuhan, Ong, and Postman.

2

MARSHALL McLUHAN

To begin with McLuhan is not to begin at the beginning of media ecology, but to plunge *in medias res*. Given that the field has no founder and inventor, making it difficult to determine just what constitutes the beginning of the media ecology intellectual tradition, it makes sense to start at the center of the field and work our way outward. Whether McLuhan firmly occupies the center, or is positioned slightly off-center, may be debated, but his importance in establishing the field is generally accepted. As Paul Levinson (2000) puts it

> What did Marshall McLuhan contribute to Media Ecology?
> You might well ask what hydrogen and oxygen contribute to the existence of water.
> Without those elements, there would be no water. Of course, other factors are necessary. Hydrogen and oxygen on their own, in a vacuum, are not sufficient to create water. They are profoundly necessary, but not sufficient.
> Which describes McLuhan's contribution to Media Ecology to a tee. Without his work in the 1950s and '60s, there would be no field of study that sought to explain how the nuances and great sweeps of human history are made possible by media of communication—how media determine the thoughts and actions of people and society. (p. 17)

McLuhan's first book, *The Mechanical Bride: Folklore of Industrial Man*, originally published in 1951, has been reissued by Gingko Press in 2002 after being out of print for many years. Although it is sometimes viewed as a "content book" in contrast to his later emphasis on media, *The Mechanical Bride* is in fact an analysis of how popular culture reflects and promotes the attitudes, beliefs, and values of technological society. Technological man is either a specialist-savant like Sherlock Holmes or an emasculated drone like Dagwood Bumstead, according to McLuhan. Technological woman is mass produced (from the assembly line to the chorus line) with the help of industrial products such as girdles, soaps, and domestic gadgets (or she is replaced by products such as the automobile). Technological children are given baby formula instead of being breast fed (setting up an oral fixation that will later be satisfied by Coca-Cola) and provided a technical education that will allow them to fit into the machine-like organizations of corporate America. Even in death, we are ruled by technology through the sale of coffins that are weather-resistant. In this highly accessible and concrete way, McLuhan provides a multitude of examples of what Jacques Ellul (1964) calls "la technique" and Postman (1992) "technopoly." The new edition of *The Mechanical Bride* is notable for its high quality reproductions of the numerous advertisements, comics, and newspaper and magazine items that are the subject of McLuhan's commentary. As these "exhibits" are over half a century old, they have gained historical value in the place of currency. The distance of time makes it easier to recognize the values, beliefs, and attitudes that they carry, as opposed to contemporary culture, and this makes McLuhan's analysis easier to follow than it might have been in the past.

Insofar as a field is produced by a community of scholars, McLuhan established the interdisciplinary study of media ecology when he joined together with his colleague, the anthropologist Edmund Carpenter, to publish a journal entitled *Explorations*, funded by a grant from the Ford Foundation. Nine issues were produced between 1953 and 1959, followed by an anthology of the journal's best material, entitled *Explorations in Communication* (Carpenter & McLuhan, 1960). Among the contributors were Dorothy Lee, Ray L. Birdwhistell, Siegfried Giedion, David Riesman, H. J. Chaytor, and Gilbert Seldes, in addition to McLuhan and Carpenter themselves. In 1962, McLuhan published what is generally considered his most scholarly work, *The Gutenberg Galaxy: The Making of Typographic Man*. The word "galaxy" in the title functions as a synonym for system, environment, or ecology (or constellation, for that matter). In this book, McLuhan focuses on the role of the alphabet as the foundation of Western civilization, and of the printing press as the agent that shifted the west from medievalism to modernity. He also emphasizes sense perception and the phenomenology of communication, exploring the historical shift from an acoustic orientation in the scribal era to the visual stress that accompanied the printing revolution. At the close of the book McLuhan discusses the transition from a print media environment to an electronic one, and introduces the term "global village," stating, "the new electronic interdependence recreates the world in the image of a global village" (p. 43). This is one of McLuhan's most enduring ideas.

In 1964, McLuhan published his most influential work, *Understanding Media: The Extensions of Man*, which has appe 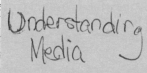 tions, and most recently in a critical edition (McLuhan biographer W. Terrence Gordon. Th a much needed index to the work, as well as tions by McLuhan, a discussion of the critica *Media*, and excerpts from McLuhan's l *Understanding New Media*. (Sponsored by Educational Broadcasters and the U.S. Depar became the basis of both *The Gutenberg Galax* Beginning where *The Gutenberg Galaxy* left off, *Understanding Media* focuses on the contemporary media environment, and in particular, on the transformative powers of television. As in *The Gutenberg Galaxy*, McLuhan considers sense perception primary, and discusses the interplay among the senses in terms of sense ratios and the sensorium. No doubt part of the reason that this book won great popular acclaim for McLuhan during the '60s is the fact that he offers an explanation for the turmoil and upheaval of that era: the changing media environment.

It is in *Understanding Media* that McLuhan settles on, and in turn establishes "media" and "medium" as the field's primary terms, which he presents as synonymous with technology. Media may be most commonly associated with communication technologies, but for McLuhan, all human inventions and innovations are media. His broadening of the meaning of "medium" becomes apparent in the second part of the book, where he devotes chapters to media such as the spoken word, roads, numbers, clothing, housing, money, clocks, the automobile, games, and weapons, in addition to the major mass media and communication technologies. And it is in *Understanding Media* that McLuhan brings together some of his most important themes: that media or technologies extend human beings, human capabilities, and the human body; that such extensions are also amputations, numbing us to the effects of technology; that some media require more sensory processing on the part of the audience than others (hence the categories of hot and cool media); that media function as metaphors, languages, and translators of experience. And it is here that McLuhan introduces his famous aphorism, which is generally considered axial in media ecology: "the medium is the message" (pp. 17 ff.). Simply put, it is the idea that the media or technologies that we use play a leading role in how and what we communicate, how we think, feel, and use our senses, and in our social organization, way of life, and world view.

McLuhan's writing style may be characterized as challenging, especially for new readers, which perhaps explains the success of *The Medium is the Massage*, the 1967 bestseller illustrated by Quentin Fiore and produced by New York writer Jerome Agel. Effective because it summarizes McLuhan's key concepts and shows as well as tells the reader what McLuhan is referring to, *The Medium is the Massage* remains a good introduction to McLuhan's approach. *War and Peace in the Global Village*, again illustrated by Fiore and produced by Agel, was published in 1968 as a follow-up to *The Medium is the Massage*. As a sequel, it is a much more substantial book, advancing McLuhan's probes about perception, communication, and technology into new terrain. Paying particular attention to the interactions between technological innovation and warfare, *War and Peace in the Global Village* has become especially relevant in the post-9/11 era. The late 60s and early 70s were a busy time for McLuhan, as he also collaborated with the artist Harley Parker to produce *Through the Vanishing Point: Space in Poetry and Painting* (1968) and *Counterblast* (1969). The literary essays written earlier in his career were collected in a volume entitled *The Interior Landscape* (1969), and he returned to literary theory in a collaborative effort with the writer Wilfred Watson, *From Cliché to Archetype* (1970). And he produced a sequel to *The Mechanical Bride* with the title, *Culture is Our Business* (1970), and joined together with Barrington Nevitt to write *Take Today: The Executive as Dropout* (1972).Through the remainder of the '70s, McLuhan was working on a new version of *Understanding Media*, and this culminating work was published posthumously as *Laws of Media*, co-authored by his son Eric (McLuhan & McLuhan, 1988). The book introduces the tetrad or four laws of media, which are framed as four questions: What does the medium enhance or extend? What does it obsolesce? What does it retrieve that an earlier medium obsolesced? And what does it reverse or flip into when pushed to its extreme? The tetrad can be used to analyze the effects of any innovation, and in *Laws of Media* the term "medium" is further expanded to include any invention, new ideas, philosophies, and linguistic and rhetorical inventions. (An alternate way to understand the four laws is that they represent the dynamics of a system or ecology as it reacts to disturbances in its equilibrium.) The book also presents McLuhan's thinking on the relationship between brain hemispheres and media (literacy is left-brained, orality/electricity is right-brained). A second introduction to McLuhan's tetrad was completed by Bruce R. Powers and published under the title *The Global Village: Transformations in World Life and Media in the Twenty-First Century* (McLuhan & Powers, 1989).

Several collections of McLuhan's work have also appeared over the past two decades. In *McLuhan: The Man and his Message* (1989) George Sanderson and Frank Macdonald bring together a number of McLuhan's journal articles with contributions from McLuhan's associates, including an essay by Walter Ong on McLuhan as a teacher, and a memoir by John Culkin, the former Jesuit who brought McLuhan to Fordham, on McLuhan's year in New York City. *The Essential McLuhan* (McLuhan, 1995), edited by Eric McLuhan and Frank Zingrone, provides a representative sample of McLuhan's media ecology scholarship from *The Mechanical Bride* to *Laws of Media*, and reprints his famous *Playboy* interview. *Media Research: Technology, Art, Communication* (McLuhan, 1997), edited by Michel A. Moos, brings together many of McLuhan's most important early articles. *The Medium and the Light: Reflections on Religion* (McLuhan, 1999), edited by Eric McLuhan and Jacek Szklarek, collects McLuhan's writing on Catholicism. *The Book of Probes* (2004), designed and illustrated by David Carson and edited by Eric McLuhan, William Kuhns, and Mo Cohen, draws on McLuhan's talent for aphorism and represents the most attractive of many attempts to revisit the style of *The Medium of the Massage*; it includes a section on media ecology and supplemental essays by W. Terrence Gordon, as well as Eric McLuhan and Kuhns. *Understanding Me: Lectures and Interviews* (McLuhan, 2003b), edited by his daughter, Stephanie McLuhan, and David Staines, puts into print for the first time some of McLuhan's most interesting lectures and interviews, including lectures from his year at Fordham.

Understanding Me is based on source material used in the documentary, *The Video McLuhan* (McLuhan-Ortved & Wolfe, 1996). *The Video McLuhan*, a three-part documentary written and narrated by Tom Wolfe, includes a great deal of archival material, including videotaped lectures, interviews, and media appearances, that effectively present McLuhan's personality, career, and ideas. The 2002 documentary *McLuhan's Wake*, directed by Kevin McMahon and written by David Sobelman, provides a stylistic and moving introduction to McLuhan's life and work, emphasizing the relevance of his laws of media in the 21st century; the DVD release contains much supplementary material of interest, including additional interviews with McLuhan's wife, Corinne, his son, Eric, and others such as Neil Postman, Lewis Lapham, and Frank Zingrone.

McLuhan has been the subject of biographies by Phillip Marchand (1989) and W. Terrence Gordon (1997), and numerous books devoted to explaining and/or criticizing his ideas. For example, in *Digital McLuhan*, Paul Levinson (1999) discusses McLuhan's major ideas, indicating how they anticipate and accurately describe the characteristics of digital technology and online communications. Paul Grosswiler (1998), in *Method is the Message*, outlines the common ground between the dialectics of McLuhan and those of Marx, the Frankfurt School, cultural studies scholars, and the postmodernists. Richard Cavell (2002) situates McLuhan within cultural geography in *McLuhan in Space*. And in critical assessments written 30 years apart, *The Medium is the Rear View Mirror* (1971) and *The Virtual Marshall McLuhan* (2001), Donald F. Theall contextualizes McLuhan based on the arts and literature of mid-20th century. McLuhan's influence on French poststructuralism is documented by Gary Genosko's *McLuhan and Baudrillard* (1999), and on the Greenpeace organization by Stephen Dale's *McLuhan's Children* (1996). And an anthology examining the lasting impact of McLuhan on the mass media, new media, journalism, communication studies, cultural studies, literary theory, the arts, history, theology, law, and politics, entitled *The Legacy of McLuhan*, has been published in 2005 (Strate & Wachtel, 2005).

3

HAROLD INNIS AND AMERICAN CULTURAL STUDIES

McLuhan (1962) acknowledged that his work was strongly influenced by Harold A. Innis, his colleague at the University of Toronto until Innis's untimely death in 1952. Innis was an economist who earned his Ph.D. at the University of Chicago, and turned to the study of communication late in his career. He is sometimes considered the first media ecology scholar, and certainly is the first to focus on what is commonly referred to as media, as opposed to technology, language, or symbolic form. McLuhan followed Innis's example in adopting the term "media," albeit broadening its meaning and moving away from Innis's purely materialistic sense of the word. For example, Innis (1951) distinguishes between heavy media, which are durable but difficult to transport, and light media, which are portable but also perishable. Thus, the clay tablets used as writing surfaces in ancient Mesopotamia are heavy media while the papyrus sheets and scrolls used in ancient Egypt are light media. This way of understanding media is derived from Innis's earlier research on economic staples such as fur, fish, and timber.

Between 1948 and 1952, Innis produced a series of essays, addresses, and articles outlining a sweeping theory about the role of media in world history, in which as he put it, "sudden extensions of communication are reflected in cultural disturbances" (1951, p. 31). His most important and best known work is collected in *The Bias of Communication*, originally published in 1951, reissued in 1964 with an introduction written by McLuhan, and in 1991 with a new introduction written by Paul Heyer and David Crowley. In this book, Innis argues that media are used to communicate over time as well as over space, and that the physical properties of different media (e.g., heavy or light) determine their effectiveness at preserving knowledge or transmitting information over distances. Depending on the type of media that a given society has at its disposal, it may remain time-biased, as all traditional societies are, or become space-biased, and driven towards territorial expansion and empire. It follows that the empires of the ancient world struggled to maintain control of papyrus supplies, while modern colonial empires were built on paper, printing, and later telecommunications. On rare occasions a balance between time and space is found, which Innis associated with the flexibility of oral tradition. He also argued that media differ in terms of their scarcity or abundance, the complexity of the symbol systems employed, and the degree to which they make information accessible, and all of these factors may contribute to the development of a monopoly of knowledge. Typically, when a ruling class develops a monopoly of knowledge, those on the margins seek out and eventually find an alternate medium that allows them to break the monopoly, leading to political reform or revolution.

In 1950 Innis published *Empire and Communications*, and a revised edition appeared in 1972 with another introduction by McLuhan. This book makes a chapter by chapter survey of media in the ancient world, covering Mesopotamia, Egypt, Israel, Greece, and Rome. Another set of essays, *Changing Concepts of Time*, was completed shortly before his death in 1952, and has been reissued in 2004 with an introduction by James Carey. This volume represents Innis's attempt, "to elaborate the thesis developed in *The Bias of Communication* and *Empire and Communications* in relation to immediate problems" (p. xxv), with Innis very much concerned with the relationship between intellectuals and politicians. *Changing Concepts of Time* incorporates *The Press: A Neglected Factor in the Economic History of the Twentieth Century*, which was previously published separately (Innis, 1949). Also of interest to media ecology scholars is the posthumous publication of his notes as *The Idea File of Harold Adams Innis* (1980). In all of these works, Innis points to the interrelationships between a variety of factors, including communication, language and culture, knowledge and education, transportation, time-keeping, political economy, military operations, and science and technology, all of which interact to produce both unique historical circumstances and discernible historical patterns. In this, he is both true to his economic roots, and points the way to an ecological approach to understanding human civilization. Innis has been the subject of a brief memoir by Eric Havelock (1982a), who was Innis's University of Toronto colleague before moving on to Yale University. Moreover, Paul Heyer has recently published a definitive biographical study, *Harold Innis* (2003).

Apart from McLuhan's own recognition of his debt to Innis, others tend to connect the two based on their common media ecology perspective. For example, in *History and Communications* Graeme Patterson (1990) presents an innovative integration of Innis's political economy with McLuhan's cliché-archetype dichotomy. In the similarly titled *Communications and History* Paul Heyer (1988) brings together Innis and McLuhan with the French post-structuralist Michel Foucault. Along the same lines, Judith Stamps, in *Unthinking Modernity* (1995), compares and attempts to integrate the Toronto School of Innis and McLuhan with the Frankfurt School as represented by Theodor Adorno and Walter Benjamin. In *Technology and the Canadian Mind* the postmodernist Arthur Kroker (1984) focuses on the common Canadian ground among McLuhan, Innis, and George Grant. And as previously noted, in *The Post-Industrial Prophets* William Kuhns (1971) links McLuhan and Innis together, along with Lewis Mumford, Siegfried Giedion, Jacques Ellul, Buckminster Fuller, and Norbert Wiener.

Against this trend, James Carey cautions against too close an identification between Innis and McLuhan in his influential work, *Communication as Culture* (1989), and a second collection of essays edited by his students and published under the title *James Carey: A Critical Reader* (1997). Favoring Innis's sociological approach, Carey has been particularly concerned with the political and economic consequences of the communications revolution that began in 19th century America. Innovations in telecommunications, starting with the introduction of the telegraph, have resulted in increased control of space, enhancing nationalism, the homogenization of time (in the form of time zones), and social disturbances such as were experienced in the United States during the 1890s. Like Innis (and most other media ecology scholars), Carey is concerned with the preservation of community, which requires greater balance between time and space. Carey refers to a time-oriented (and cultural) perspective as a ritual view, which he contrasts to the transportation view that dominates in the field of mass communication (the transportation view has also been criticized by McLuhan, 1995; Nevitt, 1982; Ong, 1982; and Schwartz, 1974). Carey has referred to his brand of media ecology as American cultural studies, although a recent anthology with the title *American Cultural Studies* (Warren & Vavrus, 2002) indicates that this area is developing a different, albeit closely related identity. Carey's students have followed his lead in producing cultural analyses that emphasize the particular characteristics of specific media environments rather than the larger generalizations put forth by McLuhan, and Innis in the early essays in *The Bias of Communication*. For example, there is Carolyn Marvin's *When Old Technologies Were New* (1988), Kevin Barnhurst and John Nerone's *The Form of News* (2001), Steve Jones's *Rock Formation: Music, Technology, and Mass Communication* (1992), and Fredrick Wasser's *Veni, Vidi, Video: The Hollywood Empire and the VCR* (2001). Others have extended Carey's work on intellectual history, notably Daniel Czitrom who compares Innis favorably to McLuhan in *Media and the American Mind* (1983), and Joli Jensen who critques Neil Postman, Daniel Boorstin, Dwight Macdonald, and Stuart Ewen in *Redeeming Modernity* (1990).

4

THE TORONTO SCHOOL

However the relationship between Innis and McLuhan is viewed, they are generally considered the two key members of the Toronto School, a group that encompasses a number of other significant scholars who have been associated with McLuhan. For example, the anthropologist Edmund Carpenter worked with McLuhan on the *Explorations* journal during the '50s, which for the first time indicated that an interdisciplinary field of study had been identified; together they also published the *Explorations in Communication* anthology (Carpenter & McLuhan, 1960). Carpenter added an intercultural dimension to McLuhan's media ecology, as can be seen in *They Became What They Beheld* (Carpenter & Heyman, 1970), an experimental book along the lines of *The Medium is the Massage*, and *Oh, What a Blow That Phantom Gave Me!* (Carpenter, 1973). The entire text of the latter book is included along with other supplementary material such as an interview with Carpenter on the DVD release of the documentary by John Bishop and Harald Prins also entitled *Oh, What a Blow That Phantom Gave Me!* (2003); the film incorporates footage shot by Carpenter circa 1969 showing the reaction of tribal peoples in New Guinea to their first experience with media such as photography, sound recording, and motion pictures.

Carpenter left the University of Toronto and McLuhan in 1957, but rejoined McLuhan for his year at Fordham University (1967-1968). While in New York City, they met media producer Tony Schwartz, famous for producing the Daisy commercial for Lyndon Johnson's presidential campaign. Schwartz would go on to write two books combining McLuhan's perspective with the experience of a media professional, *The Responsive*

Chord (1974) and *Media: The Second God* (1981). Like McLuhan, Carpenter, and other media ecology scholars, Schwartz was interested in the acoustic sensibility of electronic media, and put forth the concept of resonance as an alternative metaphor to transportation. Rather than trans- ferring information, Schwartz believed that media are most effective when they stimulate the recall of what audience members already have stored in their memories. This emphasis on meaning making on the part of the receiver all but removes content from the equation, leaving the medium as the most significant component in communication. Paul Ryan, who worked as McLuhan's assistant at Fordham and went on to become a well known video artist, published *Cybernetics of the Sacred* (1974), combining McLuhan and Norbert Wiener, and *Video Mind, Earth Mind: Art, Communications, and Ecology* (1993), which also incorporates the semiotics of Charles Saunders Peirce.

Another of McLuhan's University of Toronto colleagues, the physicist Robert K. Logan, published *The Alphabet Effect: The Impact of the Phonetic Alphabet on the Development of Western Civilization* in 1986, based on work that began in collaboration with McLuhan. A new version of the study, under the title *The Alphabet Effect: A Media Ecology Understanding of the Making of Western Civilization*, was published in 2004. Logan has also fol- lowed up on Carpenter's notion that media are our "new languages" (see Carpenter & McLuhan, 1960) in his analyses of the computer and its effects on communication, thought, and behavior, *The Fifth Language: Learning a Living in the Computer Age* (1997) and *The Sixth Language: Learning a Living in the Internet Age* (2000). Logan incorporates complexi- ty theory into his work on media ecology, as does Frank Zingrone, one of McLuhan's students (and co-editor of *The Essential McLuhan*) in *The Media Symplex* (2001). In this book, Zingrone argues that the electronic media provide a simplified image of reality as a counter to the increasing complexity of society brought on by technological innovation. The direc- tor of the University of Toronto's McLuhan Center, Derrick de Kerckhove, has also attempted to update McLuhan with *The Skin of Culture* (1995), *Connected Intelligence* (1997), and *The Architecture of Intelligence* (2001).

Eric McLuhan follows up on his father's work first with his literary analysis, *The Role of Thunder in Finnegans Wake* (1997), and then with his sequel to *Laws of Media, Electric Language: Understanding the Message* (1998), which includes analysis of the internet and applications of the tetrad. McLuhan's *Take Today* co-author, Barrington Nevitt, produced an accessible introduction to the media ecology perspective in *The Communication Ecology* (1982). Similarly, James Curtis's *Culture as Polyphony* (1978) does so by emphasizing the opposition between linear and nonlinear modes, and their relation to sight and sound. Curtis's *Rock Eras* (1987) drafts McLuhan as an aid to understanding popular music.

Composer R. Murray Schafer is generally considered the founder of acoustic ecology, which includes the recording of music, voice, and ambient sound, along with aural performance and other aspects of the auditory environment, and his ties to McLuhan are readily apparent in his 1977 book, *The Tuning of the World.* Graphic designer and curator Ellen Lupton goes to the roots of McLuhan's work in her *Mechanical Brides: Women and Machines from Home to Office* (1993), while museum designer Edwin Schlossberg builds on McLuhan's comments about the active role that audiences take in *Interactive Excellence* (1998). Comics artist Scott McCloud draws heavily on McLuhan in his extraordinary introduction to visual communication in comic book/graphic novel form, *Understanding Comics* (1993); a sequel about comics in the digital age, *Reinventing Comics* (2000), supplements his original groundbreaking work. Visual communication is also the focus of psychologist Robert Romanyshyn's *Technology as Symptom and Dream* (1989), especially McLuhan's insights about the visualism of print culture and perspective in art.

In *Art and Physics* (1991), physicist Leonard Shlain elaborates on McLuhan's insight about the parallel development of the visual arts and theoretical physics in the 20th century, both reflecting a nonlinear, electronic mindset. His second book, *The Alphabet Versus the Goddess* (1999), takes up McLuhan's arguments about the correspondence between left and right brain hemispheres and literate and oral modes of communication. Shlain connects these ideas to the study of gender (males tend to be characterized by left brain dominance, females by the right brain or a balance between the two). Bringing this to bear on the theory that goddess worship was overthrown in ancient Israel and Greece in favor of rule by masculine deities, he interprets this change as a consequence of the introduction of the alphabet. He continues his exploration of gender in *Sex, Time and Power: How Women's Sexuality Shaped Human Evolution* (2003). And, as previously mentioned, Donald Theall (1971, 2001) subjects his former mentor to critical assessment, but also extends McLuhan's arts and letters approach and calls for an "ecology of sense" in *Beyond the Word* (1995) and *James Joyce's Techno-Poetics* (1997).

One of the most comprehensive new extensions of McLuhan, one based in large part on his observation in *Understanding Media* that the content of a medium is another medium, is Jay David Bolter and Richard Grusin's *Remediation: Understanding New Media* (1999). Remediation is in fact the term Bolter and Grusin use to refer to the process whereby one medium takes another medium as its content. This can happen when a new medium remediates an older one (writing remediates speech, print remediates writing, word processing and hypertext remediate print), but also when an older medium remediates a new one (a TV commercial shows us a website, a motion picture displays a computer screen). Bolter and Grusin identify two logics of remediation, the first being immediacy, where the remediation is transparent and gives us the illusion of no mediation at all. The second is hypermediacy, where the remediation is readily apparent and more or less self-reflexive, possibly mixing multiple forms of mediation (as is often the case on a website), making us very aware of the presence of the technology. *Remediation* is divided into three parts, a general introduction to the theory of remediation; a set of case studies of different electronic media such as television, film, computer games, the web, and virtual reality; and a final section on how new media are altering the traditional concept of the self. *Remediation* incorporates postmodern approaches to media ecology, and therefore has something in common with postmodernists influenced by McLuhan such as Jean Baudrillard (1981, 1983), Paul Virilo (1986, 1991, 1997), and Arthur Kroker, who combines McLuhan and Baudrillard in works such as *The Postmodern Scene* (Kroker & Cook, 1987), *Spasm* (Kroker, 1993), and *Digital Delirium* (Kroker & Kroker, 1997).

5

WALTER ONG

As a graduate student at Saint Louis University, Walter Ong was one of McLuhan's students, and McLuhan's influence on Ong is reflected in Ong's M.A. thesis on the Jesuit poet Gerard Manley Hopkins (included in Ong, 2002a; see also Ong, 1986), and his Ph.D. dissertation on the early modern French educational reformer, Peter Ramus, which was completed at Harvard University under the direction of Perry Miller. Ong's Ramus study, published in book form as *Ramus, Method, and the Decay of Dialogue* (1958), established Ong's reputation as an impeccable scholar, and serves as a model for research in media ecology and cultural history; it also influenced McLuhan's own thinking, as reflected in *The Gutenberg Galaxy* (1962). *Ramus, Method, and the Decay of Dialogue* provides a case study documenting the impact of print media on modes of thought, knowledge, and education. Ong documents the shift from the largely oral/aural modes of communication, consciousness, and culture associated with scribal culture, and towards an increasingly more dominant visualism. Like McLuhan, Ong calls our attention to the differences between the visual and the acoustic, and the role of media in altering the balance of the senses.

Ong developed a more sophisticated theoretical framework in *The Presence of the Word* (1967b), which in many ways complements McLuhan's *Understanding Media* (1964). In this book, Ong establishes the primacy of sound and speech in human life, introducing the concepts of primary orality as the orality that existed before writing, and secondary orality as the orality associated with the electronic media (and generally shaped by writing as well). In doing so, he traces the cultural transformations that have accompanied the shift from orality to literacy, from chirography to typography, and from print media to electronic communications. In contrast to McLuhan, who tends to emphasize the revolutionary impact that may accompany the introduction of new technologies, Ong presents an evolutionary model where oral/aural biases persist in residual form in literate cultures. Emphasizing how different media work in the establishment of stable cultures, *The Presence of the Word* helps us to understand media as evolving environments and homeostatic ecologies.

Four collections of essays supplement *The Presence of the Word*. The two earlier ones, *The Barbarian Within* (1962) and *In the Human Grain* (1967a) establish some of Ong's basic themes, such as personalism, the contrast between interior and exterior, and of course the distinctions between various media and modes of communication; many of the chapters in these works are better known through reprints in later collections (i.e., Ong, 1992-1999, 2002a). The later pair, *Rhetoric, Romance, and Technology* (1971) and *Interfaces of the Word* (1977), have been highly influential, bringing together discussions of communication, rhetoric, literary theory, systems theory, and media ecology. Also of interest is Ong's edited anthology, *Knowledge and the Future of Man* (1968), based on a symposium held at Saint Louis University, which includes contributions from both Ong and McLuhan, as well as comparative religion scholar Mircea Eliade.

Orality and Literacy (1982) has been Ong's most popular book, and it stands with *Understanding Media* (McLuhan, 1964) as one of the most frequently cited works in the media ecology literature. Written specifically to review, synthesize, and in many ways establish the field of orality-literacy studies, *Orality and Literacy* downplays the phenomenological approach that Ong employs in his previous works. Instead, the book places greater emphasis on the psychodynamics of orality and literacy, the characteristics of oral and literate communication and cognitive styles, and the vital role that memory and mnemonics play in oral societies. While the focus is clearly on the contrast between oral and literate cultures, Ong also discusses the universality of speech and language, the distinction between the alphabet and other writing systems, the shift from scribal copying to mechanical printing, and the secondary orality of electronic media. The publication of *Orality and Literacy* follows *Fighting for Life* (1981), Ong's media ecological study of masculinity, and precedes *Hopkins, the Self, and God* (1986), Ong's return to the topic of his M.A. thesis; his analysis of Hopkins is based on the orality-literacy perspective, as he shows how his poetry combines a literate mindset and sense of individualism with a romantic retrieval of oral poetic elements. As do other media ecology scholars from a variety of religious backgrounds, Ong examines religion and spirituality on their own terms in a number of these books, and focuses on this topic in early works such as *Frontiers in American Catholicism* (1957) and *American Catholic*

Crossroads (1959). His edited volume, *Darwin's Vision and Christian Perspectives* (1960) brings together his interest in theology and cosmology with his focus on evolution and evolutionary processes. In general, Ong's work on the history of culture, consciousness, and communication is informed by an evolutionary and biological perspective.

Many of Ong's essays have been reprinted in the four volumes of *Faith and Contexts* (1992-1999), and more recently in *An Ong Reader* (2002a), all of which have been edited by Thomas J. Farrell and Paul A. Soukup. *An Ong Reader* is particularly relevant for media ecology scholars as it includes many of Ong's key short works in this area, his later essays on the computer, information, and digital media, as well as his M.A. thesis and the "Why Talk?" interview conducted by Wayne Altree.

Farrell and Soukup also join together with Bruce Gronbeck to edit the first anthology about Ong, *Media, Consciousness, and Culture: Explorations of Walter Ong's Thought* (Gronbeck, Farrell, & Soukup, 1991). A second anthology has since appeared under the title *Time, Memory, and the Verbal Arts: Essays on Walter Ong's Thought* (Weeks & Hoogestraat, 1998). Farrell has also written the first full length study of Walter Ong's scholarship, *Walter Ong's Contribution to Cultural Studies: Phenomenology and I-Thou Communication* (2000), a detailed and definitive discussion of Ong's intellectual career. In this work, Farrell identifies Martin Buber as an important influence on Ong, in that Buber discussed the orality of Hebraic culture in contrast to the highly visual literacy of Hellenic culture; he also discusses the Jungian resonances in Ong's work. A more limited analysis, one that highlights Ong's role as a cultural historian and his use of the interface metaphor, can be found in Betty Youngkin's 1995 work, *The Contributions of Walter J. Ong to the Study of Rhetoric*.

6

ORALITY-LITERACY STUDIES

While most discussions of the Toronto School focus on Innis and McLuhan, Eric Havelock was another foundational media ecology scholar who taught at the University of Toronto. While technically a colleague of Innis, the two had little or no interaction before Havelock left for Yale University, around the time that McLuhan arrived. Havelock's scholarship did influence Innis, McLuhan, Ong, and Postman, and he has frequently been closely linked to Ong as a specialist in orality-literacy studies. As a classics scholar, Havelock explained the transition from Homer to Plato as reflecting a shift from oral to literate culture. He maintains that the introduction of the Greek alphabet was the single most important event in human history, and the basis of western civilization, a position he shares with Innis and McLuhan, having in some ways influenced their thinking on the matter. (Ong, on the other hand, credits the Semites with the invention of the alphabet.)

Havelock's best known work is *Preface to Plato* (1963), much of which is devoted to a discussion of the orality of Homeric epic poetry. He explains how the *Iliad* and the *Odyssey* originated as songs produced and preserved without the benefit of writing, and how the epics' distinctive characteristics, such as use of formulas, meter, concrete imagery, anthropomorphic representations, emphasis on human action, and frequent repetition function as a means to preserve knowledge within collective memory. Thus, he describes Homeric diction as "a total technology of the preserved word," (p. 44), and the epics themselves as a tribal encyclopedia, a means of storing knowledge for the community, functioning in effect as the dominant medium of ancient Greek oral culture. Education, therefore, amounted to the memorization of the songs of Homer and other elements of the oral tradition, as it served as both a record of the past and a set of recommendations for future conduct. And Plato's attack on the poets can thus be understood as involving something much more vital than mere aesthetics: According to Havelock, Plato was advocating a change in the media environment of ancient Greece, from one dominated by oral poetry to one firmly rooted in literacy.

Havelock's *The Greek Concept of Justice* (1978) constitutes an important sequel to *Preface to Plato*, as well as a model of media ecology scholarship. Using the idea of justice as a case study, Havelock engages in philological analysis to trace the transition from the concrete, situational, and personified notion of justice associated with the oral mindset of Homer, to its increasing abstraction as we move through Hesiod and the pre-Socratics, to Plato. Havelock provides a more general discussion of writing and literacy in *Origins of Western Literacy* (1976), based on a series of lectures given at the University of Toronto. In this short book he presents a concise and effective discussion of the differences between orality and literacy, and among the three main types of writing systems (logographic, syllabic, and alphabetic). He also explains that there are different types of literacies, and distinguishes between craft literacy, in which only a select minority know how to read and write, and only use literacy for utilitarian and generally vocational purposes, and social literacy. Social literacy requires a literature (not just written records, but the culture itself encoded in writing), a readership (reading for education and pleasure), an economic writing system (e.g., relatively few characters, like the alphabet, so that it is easy to learn), legible writing style (as opposed to the elaborate writing found in hieroglyphics or the calligraphy of the medieval manuscript), and schools (providing literacy education at an early age).

The four chapters that comprise *Origins of Western Literacy* are incorporated into *The Literate Revolution in Greece and Its Cultural Consequences* (1982b), along with a number of other previously published articles by Havelock on subjects such as Greek oral poetry, philosophy, and the Attic playwrights. Following Ong's publication of *Orality and Literacy*, Havelock summarized his own perspective on the special case of ancient Greece, and on orality and literacy in general in *The Muse Learns to Write* (1986). Also of interest to media ecology scholars is the anthology Havelock co-edited, *Communication Arts in the Ancient World* (Havelock & Hershbell,1978), and his translation of Aeschylus' *Prometheus Bound*, coupled with his commentary and published under the title of *The Crucifixion of Intellectual Man* (1950). Identified with writing, knowledge, and science, the myth of Prometheus speaks to the dialectic between nature and culture as well as orality and literacy. For Havelock, it raised issues concerning the relationship between the intellectual and the production of knowledge on the one hand, and the political leader and the exercise of power on the other. Innis, in *Changing Concepts of Time* (2004) cites *The Crucifixion of Intellectual Man* as an inspiration for his final work.

It should be noted that Havelock was not the first to write about oral cultures: Milman Parry is generally credited with the discovery of primary orality, as Havelock and Ong make clear; moreover, McLuhan begins *The Gutenberg Galaxy* by acknowledging his debt to Parry. Following his premature death, Parry's research was completed by his student Albert Lord, who published *The Singer of Tales* in 1960; Parry's own papers, edited by his son Adam, were published posthumously under the title of *The Making of Homeric Verse* (1971). Parry and Lord's research included textual analysis of the diction and style of the Homeric poems, and field work studying the contemporary oral singers in Serbo-Croatia, which provided a working example of oral composition. Observing that the use of meter in oral poetry influences the content of the poetry, Parry states that

> Homer . . . assigned to his characters divinity, horsemanship, power, and even blond hair, according to the metrical value of their names, with no regard to their birth, their character, their rank, or their legend: except in so far as these things were common to all heroes. Except, that is to say, in so far as these things are interchangeable. If being 'divine', for example, has about the same value as being 'king' or 'horseman' or 'blameless' or 'strong' or any of the other qualities indicated by the generic epithet, then the poet was led by considerations of metre to stress one of these qualities for a given hero more than another. (p. 150)

In other words, Parry was essentially saying that the meter is the message. Havelock in turn used Parry and Lord's understanding of oral composition to establish a broader understanding of primary oral cultures, of how oral poetry functions within oral societies, and therefore of the effects of primary orality on consciousness and culture.

Jack Goody (1968) is generally considered to be the first to make reference to the Toronto School. As an anthropologist, he brings a cross cultural approach to orality-literacy studies, confirming and complementing the historical and literary research of Ong and Havelock. In his 1968 anthology, *Literacy in Traditional Societies* (1968), Goody follows McLuhan and Havelock in emphasizing the invention of the Greek alphabet, but in his best known work, *The Domestication of the Savage Mind* (1976) he broadens his scope to consider the impact of writing in general. He also proposes that orality-literacy makes for a better point of comparison than Claude Lévi-Strauss's traditional dichotomy of the savage or primitive and the civilized, as the latter only labels, while the former provides an explanation for cultural differences rooted in technology, not biology. Goody points to one of the most basic activities associated with writing, the making of lists, as a means of moving thought in the direction of greater abstraction through decontextualization. As writing takes language out of the context of physical presence and interaction, lists take words out of the context of sentences, separating subject from predicate, noun from verb and adjective.

In The *Logic of Writing and the Organization of Society* (1986), Goody mostly draws on historical data in discussing the impact of writing on social institutions. He explains the role of writing in religion, and the shift from oral spirituality that is local and immanent in nature to the transcendence and universalism of literate religions, which also introduce the either/or thinking that goes along with dogma, orthodoxy, conversion, and heresy. Goody also discusses how the invention of writing was associated with the first medium of exchange, the activity of accounting, and the development of the first economic systems; how it made possible the development of centralized government and the state; and how it was necessary for the development of laws and legal systems. In *The Interface Between the Written and the Oral* (1987), Goody reviews the historical development of writing and the gradual shift between orality and literacy, distinguishing between media and modes of communication. Also of relevance to media ecology scholarship is Goody's most recent collection, *The Power of the Written Tradition* (2000).

One of the first anthropologists to discuss the role of orality and literacy across cultures was Dorothy Lee. In her highly influential *Freedom and Culture* (1959), she connects literacy to lineality in thought and perception; she also considers the impact of literacy in *Valuing the Self* (1976). Psychologist David R. Olson emphasizes the cognitive effects of writing and especially reading in *The World on Paper* (1994), and in his co-edited anthology, *Literacy and Orality* (Olson & Torrance, 1991). Philosopher David Abram combines orality and literacy with phenomenology in *The Spell of the Sensuous* (1996). Communication scholar Catherine Kaha Waite draws on Ong and McLuhan and applies the phenomenology of orality-literacy to contemporary media in *Mediation and the Communication Matrix* (2003); her particular focus is on the role of the screen in the continuing transformation of the self. Media arts researcher Robert Albrecht explores the shift from primary to secondary orality in musical experience in *Mediating the Muse* (2004). Rhetorician Kathleen Welch considers the transformations of the word as we move from orality to literacy to electricity in *Electric Rhetoric: Classical Rhetoric, Oralism, and a New Literacy* (1999). And legal expert Ethan Katsh has employed the orality-literacy perspective to explore the impact of electronic communication and digital media on the legal profession and the judicial system in

The Electronic Media and the Transformation of Law (1989) and *Law in a Digital World* (1995).

The orality-literacy approach has proven particularly relevant to investigations into the nature of computer-mediated communication. For example, Jay David Bolter, a classics scholar who turned to the study of new media, incorporates the orality-literacy perspective into his study of hypertext, *Writing Space: The Computer, Hypertext, and the History of Writing* (1991), now in a second edition under the title *Writing Space: Computers, Hypertext, and the Remediation of Print* (2001). Orality-literacy also informs Bolter and Grusin's *Remediation* (1999). Likewise, literary theorist George Landow interprets hypertextuality through orality-literacy and deconstruction in *Hypertext* (1992) and *Hypertext 2.0* (1997). Similarly, English professor Richard Lanham combines Ong's perspective with postmodernism (while critiquing Postman's *Amusing Ourselves to Death*, 1985) in *The Electronic Word* (1993). Michael Heim brings Ong and Havelock together with Heidegger in his study of word processing, *Electric Language* (1987), which he follows up with *The Metaphysics of Virtual Reality* (1993). Brenda Danet draws on the orality-literacy perspective in her research on play and art in online communications in *Cyberpl@y* (2001), concluding that creative expression through e-mail, chat, and websites constitutes a new form of folk art. Orality-literacy perspectives also inform the anthology *The Emerging Cyberculture* (Gibson & Oviedo, 2000).

7

MEDIA HISTORY

While orality-literacy studies cuts across different cultures and time periods, it does not include the full range of possibilities of human communication and mediation. For example, Merlin Donald posits a stage of media evolution prior to orality in *Origins of the Modern Mind* (1991); in this mimetic stage, body movement served as the major mode of communication. Speculation about the origins of language and symbolic communication, for example, Robin Dunbar's *Grooming, Gossip, and the Evolution of Language* (1996) also has its place in the field of media ecology, as there is no absolute distinction between the evolution of media, of language, or that of the human species. Certainly, while orality-literacy studies generally begin with antiquity, they can be extended backwards into the prehistoric world, as John Pfeiffer does in *The Creative Explosion* (1982). His title refers to the sudden appearance of cave art and other forms of visual expression and technological innovation some 20-30,000 years ago. Pfeiffer argues that this marks the first appearance of mnemonics, and that the cave paintings represent the first form of memory theater. Pfeiffer draws on Frances Yates's book, *The Art of Memory* (1966), an important work that presents the cultural history of visual mnemonic systems from ancient Greece to early modern Europe.

The history of writing is also a subject of great relevance for media ecology, and this includes the groundbreaking work of archeologist Denise Schmandt-Besserat, who unearthed the origins of writing in ancient Mesopotamia. Schmandt-Besserat has explained how writing developed through a series of innovations involving accounting procedures used by the ancient Sumerians, from clay tokens to clay envelopes to cuneiform, in a series of books and articles: *An Archaic Recording System and the Origin of Writing* (1978), *Early Technologies* (1979), "The Origins of Writing" (1986), the impressive two volume set *Before Writing* (1992), and the abridged version, *How Writing Came About* (1996). In demonstrating the common origins of writing, numerals, and coins, Schmandt-Besserat also confirms the arguments of Dorothy Lee, McLuhan, Carpenter, and others about the inherent linearity of writing.

Other scholars have produced surveys and taxonomies of the various writing systems that have been developed and evolved over the past 6,000 years. I. J. Gelb's classic work, *A Study of Writing* (1963), adds a developmental theory of writing that suggests a natural progression from logographic to phonetic writing, and from syllabic to alphabetic writing systems. Gelb coins the term "grammatology" to refer to the study of writing, which in turn inspires the deconstruction of writing initiated by Jacques Derrida, hence *Of Grammatology* (1976). Henri-Jean Martin has produced the definitive work on the subject, *The History and Power of Writing* (1994), which covers the impact of printing as well as writing. As noted above, Robert Logan's *The Alphabet Effect* (in press) traces the diffusion of alphabetic writing from ancient Israel, Greece, and Rome to India, Arabia, and the modern western world. Logan is particularly interested in the connection between the alphabet and the historical development of law and science.

Along with the study of writing systems, scholars such as Innis, McLuhan, and Ong have been interested in the unique characteristics of handwritten documents, scribal copying, and manuscript culture, as contrasted with the familiar world of print media. H. J. Chaytor set the mark for scholarship in this area with *From Script to Print* (1950), which emphasizes the study of scribal culture. Research on the printing press and print media generally incorporates some discussion of chirography for purposes of comparison, for example Lucien Febvre and Henri-Jean Martin's key contribution, *The Coming of the Book* (1976). S. H. Steinberg's *Five Hundred Years of Printing*, originally published in 1955, has gone through a series of new editions and revisions, some posthumous, the most recent in 1996. Steinberg's study is particularly valuable for its account of the technological development of the Gutenberg press, its survey of the varieties of print media, and the role of print in establishing vernacular literature and fostering nationalism.

Elizabeth Eisenstein provides an exhaustive study of the printing revolution in her two volume *The Printing Press as an Agent of Change* (1979), in which she grapples with McLuhan's arguments about the effects of typography, moving from a skeptical position to one that ultimately confirms McLuhan's insights. Eisenstein details the development of printing and its effects in early modern Europe, and includes major case studies of

the role of printing in preserving the Renaissance (which immediately precedes Gutenberg and is encoded and in effect enshrined in print) as a permanent historical break, in promoting the Protestant Reformation and
establishing a permanent schism in western Christianity, and in allowing
for the development of modern science (for example, the Copernican revolution began before the invention of the telescope, and was based on the
new availability of printed astronomical records). Eisenstein's research has
also been published in an abridged form under the title *The Printing
Revolution in Early Modern Europe* (1983). David Kaufer and Kathleen
Carley offer a communication and media ecology perspective on printing
in *Communication at a Distance* (1993), arguing that the changes discussed
by Eisenstein were more evolutionary than revolutionary.

Print media and literacy are not just a matter of historical research, as
can be seen from Jonathan Kozol's study, *Illiterate America* (1986), and
Daniel Boorstin's report, *Books in Our Future* (1984), in which he identifies a growing problem of aliteracy (referring to literates who choose not to
read, an option made possible by the presence of electronic alternatives to
print media). Certainly news and journalism are topics that once were
exclusively associated with print media, and now cut across all manner of
electronic media. Mitchell Stephens considers the entire range from orality to electricity in *A History of News* (1988), while Michael O'Neill discusses the impact of television news in promoting democracy in *The Roar
of the Crowd* (1993). Friedrich Kittler addresses media history in a series of
books, *Discourse Networks 1800/1900* (1990); *Literature, Media,
Information Systems* (1997); and *Gramophone, Film, Typewriter* (1999).
Anthony Smith considers how the development of mass communications
in the west dominates global news coverage in *The Geopolitics of
Information* (1980a), and discusses the impact of the computer on newspapers in *Goodbye, Gutenberg* (1980b), on knowledge in *Books to Bytes*
(1993), and on identity in *Software for the Self* (1996). Similarly,
Argentinian theorist Alejandro Piscitelli draws on the historical perspectives of Ong, Innis, McLuhan, Goody, and Eisenstein in arguing that the television era has come to a close, rendered obsolescent by the internet, in
Post/Televisión: Ecología de Los Medios en la Era de Internet (1998). One of
the most significant recent studies of the changing media environment has
been produced by Ronald Deibert, a political scientist specializing in international relations. Deibert's *Parchment, Printing, and Hypermedia:
Communication in World Order Transformation* (1997) is very much in the
tradition of Harold Innis's studies of social organization, empire, and
nationalism. Deibert use the terms medium theory and ecological holism
to describe his media ecology of world order, tracing the changes as we
move from medieval scribal theocracy to modern print-based nationalism
to our emerging postmodern, electronically mediated world order.

Walter Benjamin is often associated with the Frankfurt School (see, for example, Stamps, 1995), although he was very much on the margins of that group, socially and politically. His own brand of Marxist criticism contains numerous media ecology insights, such as the following:

> During long periods of history, the mode of human sense perception changes with humanity's entire mode of existence. The manner in which human sense perception is organized, the medium in which it is accomplished, is determined not only by nature but by historical circumstances as well. (Benjamin, 1968, p. 222)

This quote is taken from Benjamin's often cited essay, "The Work of Art in the Age of Mechanical Reproduction," which was originally published in 1936 and is frequently reprinted. In this article, Benjamin's main concern is with printing, but specifically with lithography rather than typography. The mechanical reproduction of art, he argues, calls into question the concept of authenticity; continued innovations in image technology, i.e., photography and film, blur the distinction between original and copy, making authenticity even more problematic. He uses the term "aura" to refer to the sense of authenticity that is lost through the media of reproduction, at the same time maintaining that mass reproduction is ultimately democratizing.

Daniel Boorstin provides a conservative spin on Benjamin's argument in *The Image: A Guide to Pseudo-Events in America* (1978a), a revised edition of *The Image: Or What Happened to the American Dream* (1962). Rather than mechanical reproduction alone, Boorstin's agent of change is what he calls the Graphic Revolution, the series of innovations in communications that begins in the 19th century with the steam powered printing press and photography, and includes the invention of sound recording, the motion picture, radio, and television. According to Boorstin, our technologies have given us extravagant expectations about the world, and led us to replace reality with our now easily manufactured illusions. For example, in journalism the emphasis shifts from the gathering of news, based on real events, to the manufacture of news by journalists and public relations specialists, through interviews, publicity stunts, press releases, leaks, and other forms of pseudo-events (otherwise known as media events). Along the same lines, Boorstin argues that genuine heroes have been replaced by celebrities whose fame is artificially produced; this idea is further explored in Susan Drucker and Robert Cathcart's anthology, *American Heroes in a Media Age* (1994). Boorstin also discusses the distinction between the traditional activity of travel and the modern notion of tourism, and the dissolution of forms (a line of argument that anticipates such current phenomena as docudrama and edutainment). A similar critique is put forth by Christopher Lasch in *The Culture of Narcissism* (1978), where he diagnoses image culture as a psychoanalytic symptom denoting a surfeit of self-love; Lasch follows this with critical discussions of progress and liberalism in *The True and Only Heaven* (1991) and *The Revolt of the Elites* (1995). Kevin DeLuca's *Image Politics* (1999) provides a more sympathetic view of the use of publicity in the service of media activism, specifically environmentalism. Drawing on rhetorical criticism as well as McLuhan's media ecology, DeLuca details how groups like Greenpeace learned from McLuhan how to generate media coverage.

Jean Baudrillard gives Benjamin and McLuhan a postmodern turn in publications such as *Simulations* (1983) and *Simulacra and Simulation* (1994), arguing that our technologies have progressed so far that we now are able to create hyperreal simulations, artificial creations that are more real than real. Gary Gumpert provides a more concrete discussion in *Talking Tombstones and Other Tales of the Media Age* (1987), where he analyzes the ambiguities of electronic media in regard to the perception of time and space, and of perfection. Similarly, Steve Jones examines the question of authenticity in relation to sound recording technology, digital sampling, and computer-generated music in *Rock Formation* (1992). Susan Sontag also draws on Benjamin and McLuhan in *On Photography* (1997), a meditation on the effects of the medium in which she comes to the following conclusion:

> Images are more real than anyone could have supposed. And just because they are an unlimited resource, one that cannot be exhausted by consumerist waste, there is all the more reason to apply the conservationist remedy. If there can be a better way for the real world to include the one of images, it will require an ecology not only of real things but of images as well. (p. 158)

Sontag's call for an ecology of images has been answered by Julianne Newton in her wide-ranging work, *The Burden of Visual Truth* (2000), which considers the new technology of digital photography, in Ann Barry's *Visual Intelligence* (1997), and in Scott McCloud's *Understanding Comics* (1993) and *Reinventing Comics* (2000). Sontag herself has recently returned to the subject with *Regarding the Pain of Others* (2003). The issues originally raised by Benjamin are also reflected in critques such as Postman's *Amusing Ourselves to Death* (1985), Ian Mitroff and Warren Bennis's *The Unreality Industry* (1989), Mitchell Stephen's *The Rise of the Image, the Fall of the Word* (1998), Neal Gabler's *Life the Movie* (1998), and Arthur Hunt III's *The Vanishing Word* (2003). Michael E. Hobart and Zachary S. Schiffman emphasize information rather than images in their take on the history of media, *Information Ages: Literacy, Numeracy, and the Computer Revolution* (1998). Finally, it is important to note that media history in turn influences the study of history itself, a point made by media ecologists such as Innis (1951), Eisenstein (1979), and Terence Ripmaster in *The Ecology of History* (1978).

8

NEIL POSTMAN

As a doctoral student in the 1950s, studying about language and communication under Louis Forsdale at Columbia University's Teachers College, Neil Postman was introduced to Marshall McLuhan, who Forsdale frequently invited down to New York City to lecture. Postman wrote about McLuhan's relevance for English education as early as 1961 in a book commissioned by the National Council of Teachers of English, entitled *Television and the Teaching of English*. He also advocated language education as an alternative to traditional approaches to grade school English, the latter prescribing proper grammar, spelling, and elite culture, the former emphasizing the communication process or medium over content. Collaborating with his classmate from Teachers College, Charles Weingartner, Postman elaborated on this argument in *Linguistics: A Revolution in Teaching* (Postman & Weingartner, 1966). With the understanding that media constitute our new languages (Carpenter & McLuhan, 1960), Postman and Weingartner integrated the two arguments to produce their highly successful *Teaching as a Subversive Activity* (1969), which was particularly popular within the educational reform movement of the '60s. This book reflects McLuhan's criticism of print-based schools as outmoded and obsolescent, and calls for new modes of education better suited to the age of electronic media. In particular, Postman and Weingartner call for a curriculum based on the "Sapir-Whorf-Korzybski-Ames-Einstein-Heisenberg-Wittgen-stein-McLuhan-Et Al. Hypothesis . . . that language is not merely a vehicle of expression, it is also the driver; and that what we perceive, and therefore can learn, is a function of our languaging processes" (p. 101). *Teaching as a Subversive Activity* had a dramatic impact on the educational reform movement during the early '70s, and remains influential to this day. Postman and Weingartner produced two additional books on education, *The Soft Revolution* in 1971 (which included a prospectus for a graduate program in media ecology) and *The School Book* (which includes a discussion of McLuhan's relevance for educational reform) in 1973.

In addition to education, Postman emphasizes linguistics, semantics, and the study of interpersonal communication to a much greater extent than either McLuhan or Ong, as can be seen from his 1976 book, *Crazy Talk, Stupid Talk*. That same year, he began a 10 year term as editor of *ETC.: A Journal of General Semantics*, publishing a number of significant pieces on media ecology by scholars such as McLuhan, Eric Havelock, Gary Gumpert, Joshua Meyrowitz, and Paul Levinson. Postman's reputation as a media critic was established after 1979, the year he published *Teaching as a Conserving Activity*. Reversing himself from the position he had taken with Weingartner in *Teaching as a Subversive Activity* (1969), Postman concludes that schools need to counter the effects of television and the electronic media by preserving the values and methods associated with print-based literacy. His primary point of comparison is the school as opposed to television, arguing that they are competing forms of education. But it is in this book that Postman also identifies the key opposition between the word (both oral and literate, but reaching its highest form in print culture) and the image (which television makes predominant). This argument can be contrasted to McLuhan and Ong's emphasis on sense perception and the contrast between the ear and eye, as Postman instead stresses language and symbolic form. This line of inquiry is then continued in *The Disappearance of Childhood* (1982), in which Postman argues that the concept of an extended childhood is a construction of print culture that has been destroyed by the leveling effect of the televised image. Postman opens *The Disappearance of Childhood* with a memorable remark on the human medium: "Children are the living messages that we send to a time we will not see" (p. 1). The same line of inquiry culminates in *Amusing Ourselves to Death* (1985), which is one of the most frequently cited works in the media ecology literature, along with McLuhan's *Understanding Media* (2003a) and Ong's *Orality and Literacy* (1982). In *Amusing Ourselves to Death* Postman argues that our image culture trivializes serious discourse, e.g., news, politics, religion, and education. Each of these three books contains basic summaries of the media ecology perspective (although usually without using the term), under headings such as "the medium is the metaphor" and "media epistemology."

For the remainder of his career, Postman continued to be an outspoken critic of television (e.g., Postman, Nystrom, Strate, & Weingartner, 1987; Postman, 1988; Postman & Powers, 1992), but he also became known as a neo-Luddite after the publication of *Technopoly* in 1992. In this book, Postman distinguishes between three different types of culture, tool-using where technology is limited, technocracy where technology is on the rise but still in competition with other social institutions, and technopoly where technology monopolizes the culture. Although he does not make the connection here, these three cultures roughly correspond to the oral, print, and electronic media environments. Criticizing the uncritical acceptance and worship of technology in contemporary America, Postman argues that we tend to consider only what innovations are supposed to do, and never take into account what they will undo, that is, their negative effects. And noting that the problem that we face today is not scarcity of information but information overload, he suggests that we think about whether the "problem" that a new technology is supposed to solve is really a problem in the first place. If not, he believes that we ought to consider that the innovation, whose full effects will not be known until after it is widely adopted, may in fact be unnecessary. The reason why it is hard to say no to technology is that in a technopoly there are no other values, no competing system of beliefs, no ruling idea to set against the technological imperative. In *The End of Education* (1995), Postman suggests that without such values, beliefs, ideas, myths, or narratives, there is no basis for a public school system. He provides suggestions for new narratives, one being the history of communication, media, and technology. In his final book, *Building a Bridge to the Eighteenth Century* (1999), Postman advocates the retrieval of another narrative and set of values, that of the Enlightenment and print culture. In her book, *Redeeming Modernity*, Joli Jensen (1990) has criticized Postman as being an anti-modernist. It would be more accurate, however, to view him as opposing the postmodern and in favor of the conservation of the modern (Strate, 1994, 2003; see also Gencarelli, 2000).

9

THE NEW YORK SCHOOL AND COMMUNICATION STUDIES

It is possible to refer to a New York School both in the specific terms of Postman and his New York University colleagues and students, and in the more general terms of the New York City area academics and intellectuals who have been influenced by McLuhan. This more general and geographic notion of a New York School might begin with Louis Forsdale at Columbia University's Teachers College during the 1950s. (We could reach even further back to include Susanne Langer and Lewis Mumford, but they are discussed in other sections instead). One of the distinguishing characteristics of the New York School is its strong connection to the field of communication, either by way of adoption, as was the case for Postman, Forsdale, and many others, or by specialization.

Henry Perkinson, a colleague of Neil Postman at New York University, was introduced to media ecology and communication studies through his interactions with Postman. Taking issue with Postman's pessimism about media and technology, Perkinson developed an approach to media history that placed greater emphasis on human agency and defended the notion of human progress. Best known for his work on the history and philosophy of education, Perkinson emphasizes Karl Popper's philosophy of fallibalism, which stresses that we improve our situations through criticism, which leads to the recognition and correction of error. In his three books on communication, Perkinson argues that the introduction of a new medium provides new ways of encoding reality, which in turn allows us to recognize inadequacies and sources of error that had previously been ignored. By recognizing and addressing these problems, human life improves, progress occurs, and things get better. In *Getting Better: Television and Moral Progress* (1991) Perkinson argues that the introduction of television gave us a dominant medium that encodes the world audiovisually and analogically, and therefore emphasizes relationships. With our new found sensitivity to human relationships, situations that seemed tolerable when encoded in print, such as racial and gender inequalities, stand revealed as morally inadequate, leading to demands for change, protest movements, and ultimately a more moral society. The result is a new postmodern morality characterized by egalitarianism. In *How Things Got Better: Speech, Writing, Printing, and Cultural Change* (1995) Perkinson reviews media history to show how each major innovation in communication led to improvements in the human condition. In *No Safety in Numbers: How the Computer Quantified Everything and Made People Risk-Aversive* (1996), Perkinson's argument changes somewhat. Arguing that the computer encodes the world in numerical terms, he concludes that this has led to the identification of new risks, which people then try to eliminate. Due to the ascendancy of postmodern egalitarian morality, however, Perkinson believes that we unreasonably require the elimination of any risk that is identified, making us a risk-aversive society, a characteristic that extends beyond our concerns for health and safety, influencing politics, economics, and education and scholarship in negative ways.

Paul Levinson, a student of Neil Postman's, is also influenced by Karl Popper's philosophy, and the editor of a festschrift for Popper, *In Pursuit of Truth* (1982). Developing a theory of media evolution that he first presents in *Mind at Large* (1988), Levinson argues that human beings function as technology's environment, selecting out characteristics that most resemble our experience of the world. Based on this view, which he terms "anthropocentric," Levinson champions technological progress and media innovation in two collections of essays, *Electronic Chronicles* (1992) and *Learning Cyberspace* (1995). He continued to substantiate his ideas about media evolution in his study *The Soft Edge: A Natural History and Future of the Information Revolution* (1997). McLuhan is another of Levinon's major influences, and his *Digital McLuhan* (1999) surveys many of McLuhan's major concepts, showing how they apply to the internet, digital technologies, and the contemporary electronic media environment. While maintaining his positive evaluation of cyberspace technologies, Levinson warns against neglecting other technologies devoted to the physical world, especially transportation technologies, in *Realspace* (2003). His latest work is a case study of mobile telephony, entitled *Cellphone* (2004).

Gary Gumpert was based in Queens College of the City University of New York for many years, where he was, for a time, a colleague of Charles Weingartner. As a communication scholar, Gumpert has long advocated bridging the gap between interpersonal and mass communication as areas of study. Traditionally, the study of media was exclusively the province of mass communication scholars, while specialists in interpersonal communication limited themselves to researching face-to-face to communication. McLuhan and other media ecology scholars represent a third alternative, as the study of media transcends its specific use for mass communication or interpersonal purposes. Gumpert championed McLuhan's third way, and pioneered the study of mediated interpersonal communication, collaborating with his Queens College colleague Robert Cathcart on three editions of the *Inter/Media* anthology (1979, 1982, 1986), and with Sandra Fish on *Talking to Strangers: Mediated Therapeutic Communication* (1990). James Chesebro, who also taught at Queens College, follows up on the interpersonal media approach in *Computer-Mediated Communication* (Chesebro & Bonsall, 1989) and *Analyzing Media* (Chesebro & Bertelsen, 1996), as does Susan B. Barnes in *Online Connections* (2001) and *Computer-Mediated Communication* (2003).

Gumpert explores the topic further in *Talking Tombstones* (1987), and has gone on to collaborate with his former student and colleague Susan Drucker in the study of communication and social space, with the understanding that media generate a new kind of space while traditional physical places function as media in their own right. Thus, the introduction of the electronic media constitute a shift from physical space to electronic space. They have applied this approach in a series of anthologies covering the study of gender and public space in *Voices in the Street* (Drucker & Gumpert, 1997), communication and immigration in *The Huddled Masses* (Gumpert & Drucker, 1998), the regulation of cyberspace in *Real Law @ Virtual Space* (Drucker & Gumpert, 1999), and communication and baseball in *Take Me Out to the Ballgame* (Gumpert & Drucker, 2002). The coupling of media ecology and communication and social space can also be found in the two editions of *Communication and Cyberspace: Social Interaction in an Electronic Environment* (Strate, Jacobson, & Gibson, 1996, 2003).

The study of social space was pioneered by the anthropologist Edward T. Hall, who introduces the term proxemics in *The Hidden Dimension* (1966), referring to the human use of space, from the distance we maintain in interpersonal interaction to our use of furniture, our architecture, and our urban development. He also studies the human use of time in *The Dance of Life* (1983), differentiating between monochronic time in which the preferred mode of activity is doing one thing at a time in sequence (which McLuhan associates with print media and mechanical culture), and polychronic time, which allows for what we today call multitasking (which McLuhan associates with orality and electronics). In paying special attention to space and time, Hall's work parallels that of Innis and Mumford, and his first book, *The Silent Language* (1959) is an important building block in the media ecology intellectual tradition. Here, in addition to considering space and time, he discusses the idea that organisms extend themselves through technology, like Mumford (see below) framing this as an activity found in the animal kingdom rather than exclusive to human beings:

> In order to exploit the environment all organisms adapt their bodies to meet specialized environmental conditions. A few examples: the long neck of the giraffe (adapted to high foliage of trees), the teeth of the saber-toothed tiger, toes of the tree sloth, hoof of the horse, and man's opposable thumb. Occasionally organisms have developed specialized extensions of their bodies to take the place of what the body itself might do and thereby free the body for other things. Among these ingenious natural developments are the web of the spider, cocoons, nests of birds and fish. When man appeared with his specialized body, such extension activities came into their own as a means of exploiting the environment.
>
> Today man had developed extensions for practically everything he used to do with this body. The evolution of weapons begins with the teeth and the fist and ends with the atom bomb. Clothes and houses are extensions of man's biological temperature-control mechanisms. Furniture takes the place of squatting and sitting on the ground. Power tools, glasses, TV, telephones, and books which carry the voice across both time and space are examples of material extensions. Money is a way of extending and storing labor. Our transportation networks now do what we used to do with our feet and backs. In fact, all man-made material things can be treated as extensions of what man once did with his body or some specialized part of his body.
>
> Materials and the rest of culture are intimately entwined. . . . The relationship between materials and language is particularly close. Not only does each material thing have a name, but language and materials are often handled by man in much the same way. It is impossible to think of culture without language or materials. (pp. 56-57)

Hall's discussion of technology, language and culture moved McLuhan to adopt the notion that media are human extensions in *Understanding Media* (2003a). Hall also states that "culture is communication" (p. 97), which parallel's McLuhan's "the medium is the message" and is echoed by Carey's (1989) "communication as culture." Moreover, Hall examines three types of cultural communication, the formal, the informal, and the technical. Based on the understanding that culture encompasses both verbal and nonverbal communication, he goes on to compare culture to language, setting out a structure of culture that parallels the structure of language. In *Beyond Culture* (1976), Hall returns to the topic of extensions, stating that "all of culture is a complex system of extensions" (p. 40); in other words, all of culture is a complex system of technologies or media. Along the same lines, he argues

The study of man is a study of his extensions. It is now possible to actually see evolution taking place, an evolution that takes place outside the organism and at a greatly accelerated pace when compared to intrinsic evolution. Man has dominated the earth because his extensions have evolved so fast that there is nothing to stand in their way. The risk, of course, is that by enormously multiplying his power, man is in the position of being able to destroy his own biotope—that part of the environment that contains within it the basic elements for satisfying human needs. Unfortunately, because they do have a life of their own, extensions have a way of taking over. (p. 38)

Hall stresses the role of both environment and context in cultural and intercultural communication in *Beyond Culture* (1976), distinguishing between high context and low context cultures. In high context cultures, less is communicated by the source, more is expected of the receiver in terms of prior knowledge, and it is considered inappropriate to ask questions; such cultures parallel McLuhan's concept of cool media, Ong's orality, and Mumford's organic ideology (see below). In low context cultures, the source tends to spell everything out, the receiver is not expected to know or pick up what is going on, and asking questions is not out of line; such cultures parallel McLuhan's concept of hot media, Ong's literacy, and Mumford's machine ideology (see below). The role of context in culture and nonverbal communication is also addressed in Ray Birdwhistell's *Kinesics and Context* (1970), and media ecology itself has been characterized as eschewing the popular research method of content analysis in favor of *context* analysis.

Paralleling the notion that culture is communication, members of the Chicago School of sociology introduced the idea that communication is the underlying basis (or medium) of society and our sense of self. This perspective, known as symbolic interaction, can be traced back to George Herbert Mead, whose lecture notes were published posthumously under the title *Mind, Self and Society* (1934). These ideas were elaborated by Hugh Duncan in works such as *Communication and Social Order* (1962), and *Symbols in Society* (1968), and notably by Erving Goffman. In his best known work, *The Presentation of Self in Everyday Life* (1959), Goffman argues that communication is a matter of playing a role, which requires us to project a definition of the situation. The effectiveness of our role-playing, which in turn determines whether other individuals (who are also playing roles) accept our definition of the situation, depends in part on our ability to maintain a barrier between what Goffman terms the front and back regions. The front region is the equivalent of the stage on which the performance occurs, while the back region is the equivalent of the backstage area where performers can rest and act out of character; it is also the equivalent of rehearsal time where performers can work on their performances. When the barrier is not maintained, the performance is undermined if not destroyed. As Joshua Meyrowitz points out in *No Sense of Place* (1985), situations, like social space and cultural contexts, can be viewed as a type of medium. Goffman's work focuses on face-to-face situations in publications such as *Asylums* (1961), *Behavior in Public Places* (1963), *Interaction Ritual* (1967), and *Frame Analysis* (1974), but he also considers traditional forms of mediated communication such as print and broadcasting in his later work, such as *Gender Advertisements* (1979) and *Forms of Talk* (1981).

In addition to being a symbolic interactionist, Goffman is also linked to Hall, Birdwhistel, and other scholars collectively known as the Palo Alto Group, a "school" inspired by Norbert Wiener's (1950, 1961, 1964) cybernetics. The central figure in the Palo Alto Group is Gregory Bateson, whose work cuts across cybernetics, systems theory, ecology, biology, anthropology, psychiatry, communication, and semantics. In his collected essays, entitled *Steps to an Ecology of Mind* (1972), Bateson proposes "a new way of thinking about ideas and about those aggregates of *ideas* which I call 'minds.' This way of thinking I call the 'ecology of mind,' or the ecology of ideas" (p. xv, emphasis in the original). He goes on to explain:

> The questions which this book raises are ecological: How do ideas interact? Is there some sort of natural selection which determines the survival of some ideas and the extinction or death of others? What sort of economics limits the multiplicity of ideas in a given region of the mind? What are the necessary conditions for stability (or survival) of such a system or subsystem. (pp. xv-xvi)

This clearly anticipates Richard Dawkin's concept of the meme, a self-replicating idea, based on an analogy with the gene, introduced in *The Selfish Gene* (1989), and further explored by Douglas Rushkoff in *Media Virus* (1994b), Richard Brodie in *Virus of the Mind* (1996), and Susan Blackmore in *The Meme Machine* (1999). Bateson also anticipates the study of neural networks pioneered by neurobiologist Gerald Edelman and presented in books such as *Neural Darwinism* (1987) and *Bright Air, Brilliant Fire* (1992), which has been the subject of a movement within computer science and artificial intelligence. Bateson's approach is indeed rooted in information theory, as put forth by Wiener's colleagues at the Massachusetts Institute of Technology, Claude Shannon and Warren Weaver in *The Mathematical Theory of Communication* (1949). Bateson (1972) famously defines information as "a difference which makes a difference" (p. 453), which is a good way of describing media ecology's main concern as well, occupying a middle ground between the universalism of modernist theoretical formations and the particularism of many contemporary cultural theorists. Bateson continues to explore the common ground between psychology and biology as systems in the recently reprinted *Mind and Nature: A Necessary Unity* (2002), while his coauthored book *Communication* (Ruesch & Bateson, 1951) remains influential in both the field of communication and the practice of psychotherapy.

Bateson was associated with the Mental Research Institute in Palo Alto, California, founded by Don Jackson in 1959, and whose early staff included Don Weakland, Richard Fisch, and Paul Watzlawick. Watzlawick, alone and in collaboration with others, built upon Bateson's foundation new approaches to therapy (e.g., brief therapy, family therapy), and established a number of key concepts in communication theory. The major work produced by Watzlawick is *Pragmatics of Human Communication* (1967), co-authored by Janet Bavelas (née Beavin), and Don Jackson. It is here that the first axiom of communication, "one cannot not communicate," is put forth. Here too, the important contrast is drawn between digital and analogic codes of communication, a binary opposition derived from computing that allows for a broad division between means or media of communication: digital would include most forms of language as well as all forms of number, while analogic encompasses most types of nonverbal communication, including pictures and music. Moreover, the authors distinguish between two levels of communication, the content level, on which plain communication occurs, and the relationship level, which involves communication about communication. The distinction between content, which we generally pay attention to, and relationship, which we tend to ignore and therefore becomes an invisible environment, can be understood as another aspect of the distinction between content and medium. In other words, relationships are a type or aspect of media, and different media represent different types of relationships. Experimental psychologist Stanley Milgram's famous obedience to authority experiments illustrate the power of the relationship level. Along with the book *Obedience to Authority* (1974), the Milgram anthology *The Individual in a Social World* (1992) is relevant to the field of media ecology, as is his collaboration with R. Lance Shotland, *Television and Antisocial Behavior* (1973). For Watzlawick, the study of relationships is based on systems theory, and he presents his perspective on systems, which he associates with group theory in mathematics, in *Change* (1974), co-authored by John Weakland and Richard Fisch. Watzlawick also argues for the social construction of reality in *How Real is Real?* (1976), and has returned to many of these same themes in subsequent works, *The Situation is Hopeless, But Not Serious* (1983), *Ultra-Solutions* (1988), and *Münchhausen's Pigtail* (1990).

In *Towards a Science of Media Ecology* (1973), Chistine Nystrom draws a parallel between the development of media ecology on the one hand, and cybernetics and systems theory on the other, as both represent holistic, ecological approaches. Joshua Meyrowitz, who studied under Gumpert, Postman, and Nystrom, uses the concept of information systems to bridge the media ecology of McLuhan and the symbolic interactionism of Goffman in his influential work in theory building, *No Sense of Place* (1985). Meyrowitz explains that media of communication and face-to-face situations in real physical places are both information systems that can be analyzed in terms of patterns of access to information, and barriers that prevent information from being disseminated. Concentrating on the shift from the typographic to the electronic media environment, Meyrowitz argues that whereas print media requires varying degrees of literacy, and therefore imposes various barriers to information access, television and other electronic media have broken down the barriers and created a vast shared information environment. This in turn has led to changes in social roles and relationships that were based on particular pattern of access. Thus, while barriers to information about the opposite sex helped differentiate gender roles during the print era, the high degree of access to such information in the electronic age has led to a blurring of the boundaries in a variety of ways. It has also resulted in the paradox of all sorts of minority groups demanding the equal right to be recognized as a minority. Along the same lines, the strong distinction between childhood and adulthood that developed within print culture has been undermined by the electronic media, and the inability to maintain an effective back region has broken down hierarchies and undermined political leadership and authority as we move from typography to television. Meyrowitz introduces the term medium theory here, which can be understood as referring to the theory that the medium is the message. Medium theory is therefore best understood as the adaptation of media ecology to a social scientific framework.

Meyrowitz is not alone in combining symbolic interaction with media ecology. Other sociologists trained in the symbolic interactionist tradition have explored the areas of communication and media, notably Carl Couch in *Constructing Civilizations* (1984), *Social Processes and Relationships* (1989), and *Information Technologies and Social Orders* (1996); David Altheide in *Creating Reality* (1976), *Media Power* (1985), *An Ecology of Communication* (1995), and *Creating Fear* (2002); Robert Snow in *Creating Media Culture* (1983); and Altheide and Snow together in *Media Logic* (1979) and *Media Worlds in the Postjournalism Era* (1991). Mark Poster adapts medium theory to poststructuralism, applying Baudrillard, Derrida, Lyotard, and Foucault to computers and television in *The Mode of Information* (1990), and following up with *The Second Media Age* (1995). Psychologist Kenneth Gergen focuses on the impact of interpersonal media such as the telephone and e-mail in *The Saturated Self* (1991). Following Watzlawick, Gergen argues that we define ourselves through our relationships, and within each relationship we form a distinct role or self. As electronic technologies have led to a sharp rise in the number of interpersonal contacts we make and keep up with, and the frequency of our interactions, the number of roles and selves that we maintain increases as well. This results, Gergen argues, in the postmodern breakdown of the self or decentering of the subject (a development that Poster emphasizes as well).

Systems theory offers another building block for media ecology, one rooted in Norbert Wiener's (1950, 1961, 1964) cybernetics, and established by Ludwig von Bertalanffy in works such as *Robots, Men, and Minds* (1967) and *General System Theory* (1969), and by Ervin Laszlo in a work originally entitled *The Systems View of the World: The Natural Philosophy of the New Developments in the Sciences* (1972); a revised edition is published under the title *The Systems View of the World: A Holistic Vision for our Time* (1996). Jeremy Campbell has produced a popular summary of cybernetics, information theory, and the systems approach that incorporates media ecology's emphasis on communication, entitled *Grammatical Man* (1982). The systems concept of autopoiesis or self-organization was introduced by the Chilean biologists Humberto Maturana and Francisco Varela in *Autopoiesis and Cognition* (1980), and explained for the general reader in *The Tree of Knowledge* (1992). Their view that self-organization involves closure against the system's environment supports Watzlawick's position on the social construction of reality. Maturana and Varela's approach to systems theory provides the basis for the work of the German sociologist, Niklas Luhmann. In studies such as *The Differentiation of Society* (1982), *Ecological Communication* (1989), *Social Systems* (1995), *Art as a Social System* (2000a), and *The Reality of the Mass Media* (2000b), Luhmann puts forth a view of society as a system whose parts are not individuals or institutions, but acts of communication. Drawing on Ong, Havelock, and Eisenstein, Luhmann sees media history as a process that generates increasing amounts of information, which in turn leads to the development of an increasingly more complex society. Complexity, in this instance, refers to the process by which systems generate their own internal subsystems (e.g., legal, political, economic, and educational subsystems), each of which becomes relatively autonomous within the context of the larger system. Emphasizing the role of binary coding in maintaining the boundaries of the subsystems, and the social system as a whole, Luhmann sees the mass media as constructing a simplified and self-referential conception of the environment.

Parallel to the work of Maturana and Varela, the Nobel Prize-winning chemist and physicist, Ilya Prigogine provides the groundwork for the new study of complexity, emphasizing that order emerges out of chaos, at least in systems far from equilibrium, which Prigogine terms dissipative systems. (From a media ecology perspective, chaos would be the medium, and order the message.) Prigogine discusses his theories in works such as *Order Out of Chaos* (1984) and *The End of Certainty* (1997), both of which are collaborations with Isabelle Stengers. The study of complexity has been further elaborated upon by many others, notably the biologist Stuart Kauffman, whose books include *The Origins of Order* (1993), *At Home in the Universe* (1995), and *Investigations* (2000). Kauffman emphasizes evolution as a natural outcome of complex systems. The phenomenon of emergence as a characteristic of complex systems is the subject of a popular book by Steven Johnson entitled *Emergence: The Connected Lives of Ants, Brains, Cities, and Software* (2001); Johnson has also written on computers in *Interface Culture* (1997). Two recent books link complexity with the study of social networks, including Stanley Milgram's famous Small World Theorem: *Sync: The Emerging Science of Spontaneous Order* (2003) is written by mathematician Steven Strogatz, and *Six Degrees: The Science of a Connected Age* (2003) is written by his former student, sociologist Duncan Watts. And Fritjof Capra has produced a synthesis of the concepts of systems, complexity, networks, and ecology in *The Web of Life* (1996) and *The Hidden Connections* (2002), following up on his earlier work on the nonlinear worldview of contemporary physics, *The Tao of Physics* (1975) and *The Turning Point* (1982).

Some of the preliminary work of integrating these ideas into the mainstream of the media ecology intellectual tradition has already been undertaken by physicist Robert Logan in *The Fifth Language* (1997) and *The Sixth Language* (2000), and by Frank Zingrone in *The Media Symplex* (2001). N. Katherine Hayles has also made major contributions in this area with *How We Became Posthuman* (1999) and *Writing Machines* (2002).

10

MUMFORD, TECHNICS, AND ECOLOGICAL HISTORY

Kuhns makes Lewis Mumford the first futurist that he discusses in *The Post-Industrial Prophets* (1971), Carey (1997) identifies Mumford (along with Innis) as a major influence on McLuhan, and Nystrom (1973) goes so far as to single out Mumford's *Technics and Civilization* (1934) as media ecology's "founding work" (p. 10). This is despite the fact that Mumford did not foreground communication or media in his writings, although neither did he ignore them as he addressed topics such as culture, art, architecture, the city, and of course technics or technology. Given the fact that McLuhan and many other media ecology scholars treat the terms "technology" and "technics" as more or less equivalent to "medium" and "media," it is quite possible to refer to Mumford as a media theorist, or medium theorist (Meyrowitz, 1985). Also of no small significance is the fact that Mumford had quite a bit to say about ecology and environments, and described his work as "ecological history" according to Donald Miller's (1989, p. 84) biography. This theme runs through the approximately 30 books he published between 1922 and 1982 (see Strate & Lum, 2000).

Whether or not it is considered the founding work, *Technics and Civilization* (1934) has been very influential, having set the stage for subsequent media ecological inquiry. For one, it is a pioneering work in the history of technology. But beyond providing a detailed account of the evolution of technology, Mumford puts forth a theory of history in which different ages or epochs are defined by different technological ecologies or complexes. Rather than the more popular conception that posits a great divide brought on by the Industrial Revolution, Mumford emphasizes the evolution of the machine and machine civilization over the course of "three successive but *over-lapping and interpenetrating phases*" (Mumford, 1934, p. 109; emphasis in the original). Each phase is defined by its characteristic tools, techniques, materials, and sources of energy. The first, which he refers to as the eotechnic phase (about A.D. 1000 to 1750), is described as a water-and-wood complex, during which machine technology did not upset the ecological balance, while allowing for a relatively high degree of creativity, versatility, and autonomy among craftsmen. The second era, which he refers to as the paleotechnic phase (after 1750 and into the 20th century), is described as a coal-and-iron complex, during which industrialization caused major ecological damage, and created the most inhuman of working conditions (Mumford singles out coal mining in this regard). Workers in the factories were transformed into interchangeable human parts of the machine in this most dehumanizing of cultures, and all aspects of life, including art, came to be patterned after the machine. The third epoch, which he refers to as the neotechnic phase (beginning in the 20th century), is described as an electricity-and-alloy complex, and in 1934 Mumford was cautiously optimistic about its potential to restore ecological balance and reverse the effects of the previous phase. He wrote at length about electricity's decentralizing characteristics, about its organic nature and, with it, the possibility that the machine can be made to follow the pattern of life, to serve human beings rather than be served by them. Overall, he viewed the history of technology as one in which a mechanical ideology had replaced an organic one, and would hopefully be replaced in turn by a retrieval of or reversal back into organic ideology via electricity.

While Mumford's early optimism dissolved following the Second World War, his initial assessment served as the basis for McLuhan's discussion of electricity and the electronic communications in *Understanding Media* (2003a; see Carey, 1997). Moreover, various other ideas popularized by McLuhan can be found in *Technics and Civilization,* such as the idea that technologies are extensions of the biological, that communication media are extensions of our sense organs and that they can alter our perceptions, that the content of a medium is another medium, that the printing press played a key role in the mechanization of the west (although Mumford argued that it played a secondary role, amplifying the effects of the mechanical clock), and that technology is an invisible environment (see Carey, 1997; Kuhns, 1971). In this book, Mumford anticipates systems theory, introducing the term "technical syncretism" (p.107) which is akin to the concepts of synergy, emergence, or the idea that the whole is greater than the sum of its parts. And he anticipates cybernetics in his discussion of the mechanical clock, a technology that he identifies as mainly being used to control and coordinate human activity. Mumford traces the invention of the clock back to the Benedictine monks of the 12th and 13th centuries, where it was driven in part by the desire to maintain regularity in the routine of the monasteries, to keep track of or signal the canonical hours. Ultimately, it became a means to impose order on human conduct and to regulate human actions within the monastic walls. This invention, Mumford observed, "helped to give human enterprise the regular collective beat and rhythm of the machine; for the clock is not merely a means of keeping track of the hours, but of synchronizing the actions of men" (pp. 13-14). And as it diffused outside of the monastery walls, it became the center of urban life, so that "the regular striking of the bells brought a new regularity into the life of the workman and the merchant. The bells of the clock tower almost defined urban existence. Time-keeping passed into time-serving and time-accounting and time-rationing" (Mumford, 1934, p. 14). Thus Mumford sees the clock as the technology that set the stage for all subsequent mechanization, industrialization, the rise of capitalism, modern science, and the shift to the paleotechnic period.

In *Art and Technics*, a short book based on a Columbia University lecture series and published in 1952, Mumford argues that our tendency to see art and technology as very different, and perhaps opposite areas of activity is both recent and mistaken. Looking back to the original meaning of *tekhne* as relating to both arts and crafts, he in effect suggests that the separation between technics, aesthetics, and semiotics is a false one. Invoking such authorities as George Herbert Mead, Ernst Cassirer, Susanne Langer, and Johann Huizinga, Mumford argues that what makes our species unique is not tools, industry, or labor, but rather language, art, and play. And he acknowledges the close relationship between technology and biology: "Man's technical contrivances have their parallel in organic activities exhibited by other living creatures: bees build hives on engineering principles, the electric eel can produce electric shocks at high voltage, the bat developed its own radar for night flight long before man" (p.17). Mumford's interest in the arts extended to literature, as can be seen in his early works, *The Golden Day: A Study in American Experience and Culture* (1926), and *Herman Melville* (1929). But it was in the study of architecture in particular that he gained distinction, writing for *The New Yorker* magazine for over 30 years as their architectural critic, and publishing books such as *Sticks and Stones: A Study of American Architecture and Civilization* (1924), *The Brown Decades: A Study of the Arts in America, 1865-1895* (1931), *The South in Architecture* (1941), and *From the Ground Up* (1956a). Architecture exemplifies the wedding of art and technology, and by extension so does the city, a point that Mumford made early on in *The Culture of Cities* (1938), and in subsequent works such as *City Development* (1945), *The City in History* (1961), and *The Urban Prospect* (1968). In fact, Mumford was a pioneer of urban studies as well as technology studies and media ecology.

In *The City in History* (1961), Mumford argues that in studying technology we tend to focus on tools, weapons, and the like, overlooking the container as technology. For Mumford, this reflects a gender bias, as he suggests that tools and weapons are phallic extensions while containers are extensions of the feminine:

> in woman the soft internal organs are the center of her life: her arms and legs serve less significantly for movement than for holding and enclosing, whether it be a lover or a child; and it is in the orifices and sacs, in mouth, vulva, vagina, breast, womb, that her sexually individualized activities take place.
>
> Under woman's dominance, the neolithic period is pre-eminently one of containers: it is an age of stone and pottery utensils, of vases, jars, vats, cisterns, bins, barns, granaries, houses, not least great collective containers like irrigation ditches and villages. The uniqueness and significance of this contribution has too often been overlooked by modern scholars who gauge all technical advances in terms of the machine. (pp.15-16)

Thus, the agricultural revolution is also a revolution in container technology, one that leads to further advancements in human dwellings and settlements, and ultimately to the city. Mumford (1961) refers to the city as the "maternal enclosure" (p. 15), and "a container of containers" (p. 16). Urban enclosure and centralization made possible forms of control and coordination inconceivable in tribal cultures, leading to what Mumford argues is the original machine:

> The many diverse elements of the community hitherto scattered over a great valley system and occasionally into regions far beyond, were mobilized and packed together under pressure, behind the massive walls of the city. Even the gigantic forces of nature were brought under conscious human direction: tens of thousands of men moved into action as one machine under centralized command, building irrigation ditches, canals, urban mounds, ziggurats, temples, palaces, pyramids, on a scale hitherto inconceivable. As an immediate outcome of the new power mythology, the machine itself had been invented: long invisible to archaeologists because the substance of which it was composed—human bodies—had been dismantled and decomposed. The city was the container that brought about this implosion, and through its very form held together the new forces, intensified their internal reactions, and raised the whole level of achievement. (p. 34)

Thus, Mumford argues that the first machines were organic, consisting of the centralized organization and coordination of human labor; only later would their fallible and fragile human parts be replaced by more reliable artificial ones. This is a theme that Mumford would expand on in *The Myth of the Machine* (1967, 1970).

In many ways, Mumford's two-volume history of technology and culture, *The Myth of the Machine: I. Technics and Human Development* (1967), and *The Myth of the Machine: II. The Pentagon of Power* (1970) is his magnum opus, although some find it overly polemical in its critique of technology (and its criticism of McLuhan). Here we find Mumford elaborating on his arguments about containers as technology, and the biological roots of technical activity:

> In any adequate definition of technics, it should be plain that many insects, birds, and mammals had made far more radical innovations in the fabrication of containers, with their intricate nests and bowers, their geometric bee hives, their urbanoid anthills and termitaries, their beaver lodges, than man's ancestors had achieved in the making of tools until the emergence of *Homo sapiens*. In short, if technical proficiency alone were sufficient to identify and foster intelligence, man was for long a laggard, compared with many other species. The consequences of this perception should be plain: namely, that there was nothing uniquely human in tool-making until it was modified by linguistic symbols, esthetic designs, and socially transmitted knowledge. At that point, the human brain, not just the hand, was what made a profound difference; and that brain could not possibly have been just a hand-made product, since it was already well developed in four-footed creatures like rats, which have no free-fingered hands. (p. 5)

In *The Myth of the Machine* (1967, 1970) Mumford also uses the term megamachine to refer to the invisible machine based on the control and coordination of human activity in the ancient world, under the direction of an autocratic ruler such as a pharoah, and achieved through the use of communication technology:

> If one single invention was necessary to make this larger mechanism operative for constructive tasks as well as for coercion, it was probably the invention of writing. This method of translating speech into graphic record not merely made it possible to transmit impulses and messages throughout the system, but to fix accountability when written orders were not carried out. Accountability and the written word both went along historically with the control of large numbers; and it is no accident that the earliest uses of writing were not to convey ideas, religious or otherwise, but to keep temple records of grain, cattle, pottery, fabricated goods, stored and disbursed. (Mumford, 1967, p. 192)

In the second volume of *The Myth of the Machine, The Pentagon of Power* (1970), Mumford argues that modern megamachines have emerged in the 20th century, first in totalitarian societies such as the Soviet Union and Nazi Germany, but also in the United States due to the coupling of the military-industrial complex with communications technology. To counter this, Mumford (1970) continued to call for a return to the organic: "If we are to prevent mega-technics from further controlling and deforming every aspect of human culture, we shall be able to do so only with the aid of a radically different model derived directly . . . from living organisms and living complexes (ecosystems)" (p. 395). Mumford was a social critic and activist who opposed nuclear weapons (see, for example, *In the Name of Sanity*, 1954) and uncontrolled urban expansion and highway construction (see, for example, *The Highway and the City*, 1963). And, much like Ong, Postman, and other media ecology scholars, he was a devoted humanist and personalist (see, for example, *The Condition of Man*, 1944, and *The Transformations of Man*, 1956b).

Mumford credited Patrick Geddes with being his major intellectual influence (Carey, 1997; Miller, 1989; Novak, 1995). A Scottish biologist, Geddes's work ranged from botany, ecology, and paleontology to sociology, demographics, economics, anthropology, religious studies, and urban studies; his publications include *City Development* (1904) and *Cities in Evolution* (1915). For Mumford, the power of Geddes's ideas stemmed from his biological, evolutionary, and ecological perspective:

> Trained as a biologist in the laboratory of Thomas Huxley, Geddes became interested in relationships existing throughout the natural environment—plant, animal, and human. Geddes' notion of a "human ecology" was important in shaping both Mumford's method of historical analysis and the scope of his interests. In fact, Mumford claims that Geddes went further than any other philosopher "in laying the ground for a systematic ecology of human culture." (Novak, 1995, p. 25)

Geddes's human ecology was picked up by members of the Chicago School of sociology, notably Robert E. Park, Earnest W. Burgess, and Roderick D. McKenzie, and he also had a major influence on the work of Harold Innis (Carey, 1989). Geddes's also engaged in technological history (he introduced the terms "paleotechnic" and "neotechnic" which Mumford adapted for his own history of technics), and he was one of the first to argue for the revolutionary potential of electric technology (Carey, 1989). The economist Thorstein Veblen was another scholar who influenced both Mumford (Miller, 1989) and Innis (Stamps, 1995). Veblen went beyond economics to draw on linguistics, folklore, history, philosophy, anthropology, and sociology in *The Theory of the Leisure Class* (1899) and lesser known works such as *The Engineers and the Price System* (1921). Veblen combined technology studies with a search for socialist alternatives to Marxism, but Karl Marx too can be seen as putting forth some of the first theories about technological development and history in the 19th century, in *The German Ideology* (Marx & Engels, 1972) and *Capital: A Critique of Political Economy* (1967), for example.

Whatever the contributions of Marx, Veblen, and Geddes to the development of the media ecology intellectual tradition, Mumford's importance is clear; as noted above, he influenced McLuhan's thought in significant ways (e.g., 2002, 2003a), and the same is true for Innis (1950, 1972) and Postman (e.g., 1979, 1982, 1985, 1992). Mumford's influence also can be seen in the works of Siegfried Giedion (another one of Kuhn's post-industrial prophets), in books such as *Space, Time and Architecture* (1947) and *Mechanization Takes Command: A Contribution to Anonymous History* (1948). Similarly, there is Lynn White, Jr.'s historical study of technics, *Medieval Technology and Social Change* (1962) and *Medieval Religion and Technology* (1978). Mumford's ecological approach to technology is also reflected in the historical studies produced by the late Librarian of Congress Emeritus Daniel Boorstin, such as *The Republic of Technology* (1978b), and his trilogy, *The Discoverers* (1983), *The Creators* (1992), and *The Seekers* (1998). Jay David Bolter's *Turing's Man* (1984) picks up on Mumford's historical approach in its argument that each era has a particular "defining technology," and Bolter extends Mumford's analysis by discussing the clock as a technological ancestor of the computer. David Landes' book, *Revolution in Time: Clocks and the Making of the Modern World* (2000) expands on Mumford's analysis of the clock. William Mitchell addresses the familiar Mumfordian themes of technology and the city in his trilogy, *City of Bits* (1995), *e-topia* (1999), and *Me++: The Cyborg Self and the Networked City* (2003); he also discusses art and visual communication in *The Reconfigured Eye: Visual Truth in the Post-Photographic Era* (1992). And Scott Eastham combines Mumford and McLuhan, along with Buckminster Fuller, in *The Media Matrix* (1990), emphasizing the concept of container technology; recently he has also come out with a critical analysis of genetic engineering entitled *The Biotech Time-Bomb* (2003).

11

ELLUL AND
TECHNOLOGY STUDIES

The most radical of Kuhns's (1971) post-industrial prophets is the French social critic Jacques Ellul. Ellul rarely addresses the effects of individual technologies, instead focusing on technology at the highest level of abstraction, as a system, worldview, and way of life; the term he uses in this context is *la technique*. In what many consider his major work, *The Technological Society* (1964), Ellul argues that we have entered a historical phase in which we have given up control over human affairs to technology and the technological imperative. According to Ellul, technology has become autonomous and automatic, self-augmenting or expanding at an ever increasing rate, and encompassing every sector of human society. It dominates the natural world and has replaced religion and even science as our governing ideology. Except that technology is not really an ideology, he argues, in that it represents no set of ideas or values other that itself. Efficiency is the only thing that matters in a technological system, so all other considerations are subordinated to efficiency, if not eliminated outright. Ellul continues his argument in *The Technological System* (1980), where he refers to technology as an environment and ecology, and like Mumford (1970) is critical of McLuhan's stance on technology. And he returns to it once again in *The Technological Bluff* (1990), where he critiques computers and technological networks.

Apart from his three major technology books, Ellul also followed up *The Technological Society* with *Propaganda: The Formation of Men's Attitudes* (1965), focusing on propaganda as a particular type of technology or technique, one whose aim is to control human behavior so that we are integrated into the technological system. Here he discusses different categories of propaganda, including the propaganda of integration (which aims at keeping the individual satisfied with the status quo) and agitation (whose purpose is to move the individual to action); sociological propaganda (a subtle form that works through entertainment, advertising, schools, the arts, religion, etc.) and political propaganda (the most obvious type of propaganda); and horizontal propaganda (through peer groups) and vertical propaganda (coming from authorities). Ellul notes that literacy and mass communications technologies are vital for propaganda, for without a means of delivering the messages, there is no way for propaganda techniques to influence populations. This line of inquiry continues into *The Political Illusion* (1967), where Ellul discusses the need to maintain the illusion that public opinion controls political decision making in order to maintain legitmacy. He argues that this illusion is used to counter the reality that government decisions need to be based on the technical criterion of efficiency, which in turn requires the use of propaganda techniques to direct public opinion to support those decisions and maintain the illusion of popular support and sovereignty.

In *The Humiliation of the Word* (1985), Ellul argues that our audiovisual technologies and the image culture they have given rise to also contribute to the technological society and the degradation of the human condition by undermining the role of verbal communication. Much like Postman, Ellul defends the word against the image, and criticizes the loss of rational discourse. But Ellul also combines sociology here with theology, as he works from a Christian perspective as a member of the French Reformed Church. Ellul has published numerous works on theology and ethics in addition to being a religious activist. Among the most significant theological works translated into English are *The Presence of the Kingdom* (1951), *The Meaning of the City* (1970), *The Ethics of Freedom* (1976), and *Anarchy and Christianity* (1991). Moreover, several interview books have been published where Ellul explains his sociological and religious perspectives, *Perspectives on Our Age* (1981), *In Season, Out of Season: An Introduction to the Thought of Jacques Ellul* (1982), and the posthumously published *Jacques Ellul on Religion, Technology, and Politics* (1998). Also posthumously published is a collection of articles entitled *Sources and Trajectories: Eight Early Articles by Jacques Ellul that Set the Stage* (1997). Clifford Christians, who is associated with James Carey and American cultural studies, has written about Jacques Ellul from a communication perspective in *Jacques Ellul and Democracy's "Vital Information" Premise* (1976) and is co-editor of, *Jacques Ellul: Interpretive Essays* (Christians & Van Hook, 1981).

Along with Mumford, Giedion, Ellul, Innis, and McLuhan, Kuhns (1971) also includes two other post-industrial prophets, Buckminster Fuller and Norbert Wiener. Fuller was an inventor and architect as well as a scholar and critic, and unlike Mumford was generally a proponent of technology. He coined terms such as "synergy," which refers to the systems theory concept that the whole is greater than the sum of its parts, and "tensegrity," a contraction of tension and integrity. Tensegrity represents the combination of push and pull forces that serve as an alternative to typical methods of construction, and Fuller's geodesic dome is an example of tensegrity at work. These concepts are discussed in *Synergetics: The Geometry of Thinking* (Fuller & Applewhite, 1975). Fuller also coined the term "spaceship earth," often used as a synonym for McLuhan's "global village," and devoted a book to the topic, *Operating Manual for Spaceship Earth* (1971). And following McLuhan, Fuller joined with Jerome Agel and Quentin Fiore to produce a book along the lines of *The Medium is the Massage*, entitled *I Seem to Be a Verb* (Fuller, Agel, & Fiore, 1970).

Wiener, who coined the term cybernetics as the science of control, finds common ground between electronic technology and biology in that both can be viewed as information systems based on feedback loops. He has written about cybernetics in a more technical volume entitled *Cybernetics: Or Control and Communication in the Machine and Animal* (1961), and a more popular variation, *The Human Use of Human Beings: Cybernetics and Society* (1950); he also takes up the subject of science and religion in *God and Golem, Inc.: A Comment on Certain Points Where Cybernetics Impinges on Religion* (1964). Wiener and his fellow pioneers in information theory, Claude Shannon and Warren Weaver (1949), form the basis of James Beniger's history of 19th and early 20th century technology and techniques, *The Control Revolution* (1986). Beniger argues that the increasing complexity of industrialization led to the development of numerous information technologies to control and coordinate human and machine activity, long before the current information age began. N. Katherine Hayles has also drawn on information theory to examine *How We Became Posthuman* (1999), as well as how writing has been transformed in *Writing Machines* (2002), another book patterned after *The Medium is the Massage*.

Along with Mumford and Ellul, Peter F. Drucker is one of the most prolific media ecology scholars, whose work ranges across philosophy, political science, economics, sociology, and management, the latter a field he invented. Although Kuhns (1971) does not include him in his survey, Drucker is most certainly a futurist and post-industrial prophet. For example, he was one of the first to identify the fact that assembly line production was being obsolesced by electronic technologies, in works such as *The Future of Industrial Man* (1942), and *Landmarks of Tomorrow* (1959). He continued to discuss the impact of new technologies and identify effects such as the creation of knowledge industries and knowledge workers in *The Age of Discontinuity* (1968), and later in *The New Realities* (1989) and *Post-Capitalist Society* (1993). Drucker considers the impact of technology on business in *Technology, Management & Society* (1970), but looks at the corporation as essentially a technology in its own right in *The Concept of the Corporation* (1946). He refers to his approach as social ecology in *The Ecological Vision* (2000), a collection of essays on technology, business, economics, government, and culture. And Drucker discusses his relationship to McLuhan in *Adventures of a Bystander* (1979), a semi-autobiographical work.

Ivan Illich represents one of the more critical voices in technology studies in works such as *Tools for Conviviality* (1973) and *H2O and the Waters of Forgetfulness: Reflections on the Historicity of "Stuff"* (1985). Like Postman and Weingartner, Illich was part of the educational reform movement of the '60s and '70s, through works such as *Deschooling Society* (1971), and he also took a leadership position in the environmentalist movement with *Energy and Equity* (1974). His radical critique extended to medical establishment, i.e., *Medical Nemesis* (1975), and professional specialization in general, i.e., *Disabling Professions* (1977). And he has collaborated with Barry Sanders to provide a sustained critique of the alphabet, the basis of schooling, in *ABC: The Alphabetization of the Popular Mind* (Illich & Sanders, 1989); in a subsequent work, *A is for Ox: Violence, Electronic Media, and the Silencing of the Written Word*, Sanders (1994) has advocated a balance between orality and literacy in response to the electronic media. Like Drucker and Illich, Jeremy Rifkin also combines technological criticism with economic analysis in works such as *Time Wars* (1987), *Beyond Beef* (1992), *The End of Work* (1995), *The Biotech Century* (1998), *The Age of Access* (2000), and *The Hydrogen Economy* (2002). Jerry Mander's *Four Arguments for the Elimination of Television* (1978) offers a polemical critique specifically directed at televison as a medium, and a more general one aimed at modern technology in *In the Absence of the Sacred: The Failure of Technology and the Survival of the Indian Nations* (1991). Also, postmodernist Jean-Francois Lyotard has written about the impact of technology, specifically in undermining common culture in *The Postmodern Condition* (1984), and more generally in *The Inhuman* (1991). Edward Tenner provides a more measured approach in surveying the unanticipated and negative effects of innovations in *Why Things Bite Back* (1996), and the sequel, *Our Own Devices* (2003).

Political scientist Langdon Winner follows Ellul's lead in arguing that technological innovation is not neutral, but rather constitutes an invisible form of political decision-making, in *Autonomous Technology* (1977), *The Whale and the Reactor* (1986), and *Democracy in a Technological Society* (1992). Similarly, Donald Wood, in *Post-Intellectualism and the Decline of Democracy* (1996) and *The Unraveling of the West* (2003) has built on Postman's concept of technopoly, arguing that we have moved into a postmodern period characterized by technological determinism and what Wood terms post-intellectualism. This in turn has threatened and undermined democracy in the U.S. and western civilization in general. Educational policy likewise has surrendered to the technological imperative, despite a record of broken promises about revolutionizing pedagogy, as Margaret Cassidy reveals in her historical study, *Bookends: The Changing Media Environment of American Classrooms* (2004), based on a dissertation completed under Postman. Likewise, Paul Thaler argues that television technology has altered the dynamics of the legal system and undermined our system of justice in *The Watchful Eye* (1994), based on research conducted under Postman, and his study of the O. J. Simpson trial, *The Spectacle* (1997). Cheryl Pawlowski, another of Postman's former students, critiques the impact of television on the family in *Glued to the Tube* (2000). Arthur Hunt III extends Postman's arguments about visual technology from the perspective of a conservative evangelical Christian in *The Vanishing Word* (2003). Critiques similar to Postman's have also been produced by Neil Gabler, *Life the Movie* (1998), and Mitchell Stephens, *The Rise of the Image, The Fall of the Word* (1998). Katherine Fry discusses the mythic frame that broadcast journalists use to interpret natural disaster reporting in *Constructing the Heartland: Television News and Natural Disaster* (2003). Jack Lule discusses this same tendency as it applies to news in general in *Daily News, Eternal Stories: The Mythological Role of Journalism* (2001). To counter the negative effects of electronic and audiovisual media on the journalism profession, Jay Rosen advocates an activist, public journalism in *What are Journalists For?* (1999), in an argument that parallels his mentor, Neil Postman's proposals for schooling in *Teaching as a Conserving Activity* (1979).

The computer has been the focus of a number of technological critiques, from Joseph Weisenbaum's early warning, *Computer Power and Human Reason* (1976), to Theodore Roszak's neo-Luddite treatise, *The Cult of Information* (1994). Stephen Talbott's *The Future Does Not Compute* (1995) warns against the computer's capacity for abstraction from reality, a trend that he traces back to Renaissance art in an argument reminiscent of Ong's and McLuhan's discussions of visualism. Drawing on Postman, Mark Slouka also warns about the divorce from reality brought on by the computer and the internet in his *War of the Worlds* (1996). Technorealist David Shenk uses an ecological metaphor to talk about information overload in *Data Smog* (1997), which was followed up by *The End of Patience* (1999). Alternately, some media ecology scholars have studied how people interact with technology, such as Sherry Turkle in *The Second Self* (1984) and *Life on the Screen* (1995), and Susan B. Barnes in *Online Connections* (2001) and *Computer-Mediated Communication* (2003). Likewise, Casey Man Kong Lum provides an ethnography of how groups interact with karaoke technology in *In Search of a Voice* (1996), in which he uses media ecology theory to interpret his data.

Many of the issues regarding the interaction between individuals and technologies are examined by Don Ihde, who engages in the philosophy of technology from a phenomenological approach in works such as *Technics and Praxis* (1979), *Existential Technics* (1983), *Technology and the Lifeworld* (1990), *Instrumental Realism* (1991), and *Bodies in Technology* (2002). Ihde also shares Ong's and McLuhan's emphasis on sense perception, as can be seen in *Sense and Significance* (1973), *Listening and Voice* (1976), and *Expanding Hermeneutics: Visualism in Science* (1998). Ihde's approach is based, in part, on the philosophy of Martin Heidegger, who addresses the topic directly in *The Question Concerning Technology* (1973). Carl Mitcham is another contemporary scholar specializing in the philosophy of technology, whose *Thinking Through Technology* (1994) examines in detail various conceptions of technology and its effects. Also, David Rothenberg in *Hand's End* (1993) mixes philosophy with ecology in pondering the relationship between technology and nature.

Popular writer Howard Rheingold has explored the effects of technology, and especially the computer, in a series of books, *Tools for Thought* (1985), which explores the personal computer revolution, *Virtual Reality* (1991), which focuses on computer-generated media environments, and *The Virtual Community* (1993), which surveys the use of online communications to establish a sense of community within the internet environment. His most recent work, *Smart Mobs* (2003), looks at personal communications technology, such as the cell phone, as devices for the coordination of group activities, such as protests. Similarly, former *Wired* magazine editor Kevin Kelly looks at the computer and related technology's growing autonomy in *Out of Control: The Rise of Neo-Biological Civilization* (1994). Rand Institute analysts John Arquila and David Ronfeldt have also contributed to the scholarhsip on networks, with an emphasis on their role in war, terrorism, crime, and politics, in a series of books, including *The Advent of Netwar* (1996), *In Athena's Camp* (1997), *The Emergence of Noopolitik* (1999), *Swarming and the Future of Conflict* (2000), and *Networks and Netwars* (2001), as well as Ronfeldt's case study, *The Zapatista "Social Netwar" in Mexico* (1998). And Douglas Rushkoff has produced a series of highly original works in media ecology, including *Cyberia* (1994a), an exploration of cyberculture; *Media Virus* (1994b), a discussion of how media spread ideas using the biological metaphor of the virus or meme; and *Playing the Future* (1996), an examination of youth culture in the digital age. While these three studies take an optimistic view of new media, in *Coericion* (1999) Rushkoff warns against the use of longstanding persuasive techniques coupled with information technologies employed to manipulate consumers and citizens. Rushkoff champions the notion of open source technology, both as a technology and an approach to religion in *Nothing Sacred* (2003a), his proposal for reform Judaism, and to politics in *Open Source Democracy* (2003b).

12

FORMAL ROOTS

It is possible to trace the roots of the media ecology intellectual tradition back to antiquity, and thereby to begin at the beginning after a fashion, with the *Book of Genesis*: "In the beginning God created the heaven and the earth. Now the earth was unformed and void, and darkness was upon the face of the deep; and the Spirit of God hovered over the face of the waters. And God said: 'Let there be light.' And there was light" (1:1-3). In this way, the first form or medium to be introduced into the unformed world is God's speech act, which precedes and announces the second form, light. Language is presented as the original and ideal form, which is reflected in turn in the New Testament's *Gospel of John*: "In the beginning was the Word, and the Word was with God, and the Word was God" (1:1). And sound takes precedence over light, just as orality precedes literacy. That the ear is given precedence over the eye is consistent with the criticism of the image in favor of (and accomplished through) the word that recurs throughout the Jewish *Holy Scriptures*. For example, the *115th Psalm of David* (2-8) reads:

> Wherefore should the nations say:
> 'Where is now their God?'
> But our God is in the heavens;
> Whatsoever pleased Him He hath done.
> Their idols are silver and gold,
> The work of men's hands.
> They have mouths, but they speak not;
> Eyes they have, but they hear not;

Noses have they, but they smell not;
They have hands, but they handle not;
Feet have they, but they walk not;
Neither speak they through their throat.
They that make them shall be like unto them;
Yea, every one that trusteth in them.

And the Second Commandment of Moses states: "Thou shalt have no other gods before Me. Thou shalt not make unto thee a graven image, nor any manner of likeness, of any thing that is in heaven above, or that is in the earth beneath, or that is in the water under the earth" (Exodus 20:3-5). This general iconoclasm is strongly linked to a critique of technology, "the work of men's hands," a theme that also appears, for example, in the story of the Tower of Babel and the description of Egyptian bondage in Exodus.

What is probably the first secular discussion in the media ecology intellectual tradition appears in Plato's *Phaedrus* (1973), where Socrates presents a brief criticism of technological innovation through the parable of the Egyptian God Theuth and the Pharoah Thamus. In this dialogue, Socrates also provides a concise critique of writing (which is compared unfavorably to speech and memory), and a sustained critique of rhetoric (which is the product of writing). Similar commentary also appears in Plato's *Seventh Letter* (see Plato, 1973), where he suggests that the motives for writing as opposed to speaking have much to do with the desire for honor and renown, what we would today refer to as publicity, rather than knowledge and understanding.

Aristotle too adds a building block with his *Rhetoric* (1954), where he defines rhetoric as "the faculty of observing in any given case the available *means* of persuasion" (p. 24, emphasis added), insofar that *means* is synonymous with *medium*, and rhetoric refers to the study of a category of technique. Artistotle's *Physics* (1969) is also of importance, as it discusses the four types of causes: efficient cause (which we think of as the only real type of cause, as in the cause-and-effect of modern scientific thought), material cause (the material basis that is at the root of economics-trained theorists such as Marx and Innis), formal cause (based on pattern or "blueprint," which is very much in line with McLuhan's thinking, especially in *Laws of Media*), and final cause (the oak as the final cause of the acorn, a biological approach that Campbell, 1982, associates with a systems view).

Media ecology also has roots in literature, which should come as no surprise given that McLuhan, Ong, and Postman all were English professors originally. It follows that they and others have found media ecological insights in modern fiction, from Shakespeare and Cervantes to Mary Shelley, Samuel Butler, Edward Bellamy, George Orwell, and Aldous Huxley (see, for example, McLuhan, 1964; McLuhan & Watson, 1970;

Ong, 1986, 2002a; Postman, 1970, 1985). In particular, media ecology scholars such as Marshall McLuhan (1969; McLuhan & Fiore, 1968), Eric McLuhan (1997), and Donald Theall (1995, 1997) have cited and studied James Joyce, with particular attention given to the word play in *Finnegans Wake*. Along with literature, literary criticism constitutes a portion of the field's roots, with the New Criticism of I. A. Richards of particular influence on McLuhan, Ong, and Postman. Richards collaborated with Charles Ogden, the inventor of Basic English (a version of the language stripped down to 850 words in order to facilitate international communication) on *The Meaning of Meaning* (Ogden & Richards, 1923), where they discuss the structure and function of language and symbolic communication. Symbols, they argue, may reflect some aspect of reality, but they may also refract what is real due to the inherent bias of the symbolic form or medium involved:

> We have spoken . . . of reflection and refraction by the linguistic medium. These metaphors if carefully considered will not mislead. But language, though often spoken of as a medium of communication, is best regarded as an instrument; and all instruments are extensions, or refinements, of our sense organs. The telescope, the telephone, the microscope, the microphone, and the galvanometer are, like the monocle or the eye itself, capable of distorting, that is, of introducing new relevant members into the contexts of our signs. And as receptive instruments extend our organs, so do manipulative instruments extend the scope of our motor activities. When we cannot actually point to the bears we have dispatched we tell our friends about them or draw them; or if a slightly better instrument than language is at our command we produce a photograph. The same analogy holds for the emotive uses of language: words can be used as bludgeons or bodkins. But in photography it is not uncommon for effects due to the processes of manipulation to be mistaken by amateurs for features of the objects depicted. Some of these effects have been exploited by experts so as greatly to exercise the late Sir Arthur Conan Doyle and his friends. In a similar fashion language is full of elements with no representative or symbolic function, due solely to its manipulation; these are similarly misrepresented or exploited by metaphysicians and their friends so as greatly to exercise one another—and such of the laity as are prepared to listen to them. (p. 98)

In referring to language as an instrument, Ogden and Richards are categorizing "the linguistic medium" as a technology. Their early reference to media as extensions of the senses no doubt had an effect on Richards's student, McLuhan. In this book with Ogden, and on his own in works such as *Practical Criticism* (1929), and *The Philosophy of Rhetoric* (1936), Richards stresses the value of rhetorical criticism and metaphor analysis, the role of the reader or audience in interpreting messages, and the centrality of context in determining the meaning of content.

Through the literary criticism of I. A. Richards, we can trace the roots of media ecology back to the pragmatism and semiotics of Charles Saunders Peirce (1991). Peirce's emphasis is on the pragmatics of communication, and specifically on how meaning is made. In his semiotics, he identifies three different types of signs, i. e., index, icon, and symbol, and with them the concomitant notion that different signifiers are associated with different signifieds. This prepares the way for McLuhan's focus on different types of media, and the idea that each medium has its own bias or message, as Aquiles Esté explains in *Cultura Replicante* (1997). Along the same lines, Paul Ryan presents an applied synthesis of Peirce and McLuhan in *Video Mind, Earth Mind* (1993). Also influential are the studies of symbolism, language, and logic carried out by Alfred North Whitehead and Bertrand Russell, notably in their three volume *Principia Mathematica* (1925-1927). Of particular relevance for both symbol systems and general systems is the theory of logical types, which distinguishes between different levels, i.e., the members of a group and the group itself—these two levels correspond to the content and relationship level of communication discussed by Watzlawick et al. (1967), and to the levels of content and medium or environment. Ludwig Wittgenstein extended Whitehead and Russell's line of inquiry with his *Tractatus Logico-Philosophicus* (1961), and his famous observation, "whereof one cannot speak, thereof one must be silent" (p. 189), is very much a statement about the ways in which a medium defines and delimits its messages. Wittgenstein's struggle with understanding the medium of language is reflected in this early work, and in his *Philosophical Investigations* (1963) where he comes to view language as a game, thereby emphasizing medium over meaning. Douglas Hofstadter returns to the theory of logical types in *Gödel, Escher, Bach* (1979), using the term recursion to refer to self-reference, a concept now commonplace in computer programming.

Certainly in line with Peirce's pragmatism is the practical, and often prescriptive system of general semantics, founded by Alfred Korzybski; his magnum opus, *Science and Sanity: An Introduction to Non-Aristotelian Systems and General Semantics*, was originally published in 1933, with a fifth edition in print as of 1993. General semantics was popularized by S. I. Hayakawa's *Language in Thought and Action*, originally published as *Language in Action* in 1939; a fifth edition co-authored by his son, Alan Hayakawa was published in 1990. Among the numerous other works explaining and elaborating on Korzybski's system are economist Stuart Chase's *The Tyranny of Words* (1938) and speech pathologist Wendell Johnson's *People in Quandries* (1946). Following Whitehead and Russell,

Korzybski is concerned with the relationship between language and the reality it is believed to represent, and argues that there are sources of error inherent in language itself, especially as expressed through Aristotelian logic. Bertalanffy's (1969) general system theory took its name from general semantics, whose departure from Aristotle's linear logic anticipates the nonlinearity of systems and the phenomenon of emergence. Postman incorporated general semantics into his media ecology approach, as he wrote about symbolic ecology, the semantic environment, and language as a medium.

Along with general semantics, the philosophy of Susanne Langer was of great importance to Postman and the New York school of media ecology. Langer represents a key transitional figure, as she broadens the definition of symbol to include art, music, ritual, and even sense perception in her key work, *Philosophy in a New Key* (1957):

> The abstractions made by the ear and the eye—the forms of direct perception—are our most primitive instruments of intelligence. They are genuine symbolic materials, media of understanding, by whose office we apprehend a world of *things*, and of events that are the histories of things. (p. 92; emphasis in the original)

This basic type of symbolism she terms presentational, as opposed to what she calls discursive symbols, a category that includes language and mathematics, and is associated with rationality, the ability to form statements that are propositional (can be evaluated empirically), and broken down into discrete units (e.g., words, numbers). Each type of symbol or medium has its own bias, so that while discursive symbols are well suited for producing logical statements, "language is a very poor medium for expressing our emotional nature" (p. 100). Presentational symbols, on the other hand, cannot be used to form propositions that can be proven true or false, cannot be broken down into distinct units, but are well suited to understanding and conveying feeling and emotion. Presentational and discursive symbols correspond to Watzlawick et al.'s (1967) analogic and digital codes, but Langer goes beyond this polarity to argue that

> there may well be many special regions, to one or another of which the medium of one art is more suited that that of another for its articulate expression. It may well be, for instance, that our physical orientation in the world—our intuitive awareness of mass and motion, restraint and autonomy, and all characteristic feeling that goes with it—is the preëminent subject matter of the dance, or of sculpture, rather than (say) of poetry; or that erotic emotions are more readily formulated in musical terms. I do not know, but the possibility makes me hesitate to

say categorically, as many philosophers and critics have said, that the import of all the arts is the same, and only the medium depends on the peculiar psychological or sensory make-up of the artist, so that one man may fashion in clay what another renders in harmonies or in colors, etc. The medium in which we naturally conceive our ideas may restrict them not only to certain forms but to certain fields, howbeit they all lie within the verbally inaccessible field of vital experience and qualitative thought. (p. 258)

In this tentative and roundabout fashion, Langer is essentially saying that the medium is the message. She more fully and definitively explores the particular meaning of different forms or media in the sequel to *Philosophy in a New Key, Feeling and Form* (1953), and in her three volume *Mind: An Essay on Human Feeling* (1967, 1972, 1982). Alexander Durig produces an interesting application of Langer and Peirce's thought in *Autism and the Crisis of Meaning* (1996). Howard Gardner's theory of multiple intelligences, as discussed in works such as *Frames of Mind* (1983) and *Multiple Intelligences* (1993) is also related back to the distinctions Langer and Pierce make among different symbol systems or codes.

Naturally enough, some of the foundational work on the medium of language comes from linguistics as well as philosophy. In particular it was Edward Sapir and Benjamin Lee Whorf who set the stage for later media ecology scholars with their linguistic relativism, the idea that different languages are associated with different worldviews. Edward Sapir's popular book, *Language: An Introduction to the Study of Speech* (1921), expresses a number of ideas very basic to the media ecology intellectual tradition in his section on language and literature:

Languages are more to us than systems of thought transference. They are invisible garments that drape themselves about our spirit and give a predetermined form to all its symbolic expression. When the expression is of unusual significance, we call it literature. Art is so personal an expression that we do not like to feel that it is bound to predetermined form of any sort. The possibilities of individual expression are infinite, language in particular is the most fluid of mediums. Yet some limitation there must be to this freedom, some resistance of the medium. In great art there is the illusion of absolute freedom. The formal restraints imposed by the material—paint, black and white, marble, piano tones, or whatever it may be—are not perceived; it is as though there were a limitless margin of elbow-room between the artist's fullest utilization of form and the most that the material is innately capable of. The artist has intuitively surrendered to the inescapable tyranny of the material, made its brute nature fuse easily with his conception. The material "disappears" precisely because there is nothing in the artist's conception to indicate that any other material exists. For the time being, he, and we with him, move in the artistic medium as a fish moves in the water, oblivious of the existence of an alien atmosphere. No sooner, however, does the artist transgress the law of his medium than we realize with a start that there is a medium to obey.

Language is the medium of literature as marble or bronze or clay are the materials of the sculptor. Since every language has its distinctive peculiarities, the innate formal limitations—and possibilities—of one literature are never quite the same as those of another. The literature fashioned out of the form and substance of a language has the color and the texture of its matrix. The literary artist may never be conscious of just how he is hindered or helped or otherwise guided by the matrix, but when it is a question of translating his work into another language, the nature of the original matrix manifests itself at once. All his effects have been calculated, or intuitively felt, with reference to the formal "genius" of his own language; they cannot be carried over without loss or modification. Croce is therefore perfectly right in saying that a work of literary art can never be translated. Nevertheless literature does get itself translated, sometimes with astonishing adequacy. This brings up the question whether in the art of literature there are not intertwined two distinct kinds or levels of art—a generalized, non-linguistic art, which can be transferred without loss into an alien linguistic medium, and a specifically linguistic art that is not transferable. I believe the distinction is entirely valid, though we never get the two levels pure in practice. Literature moves in language as a medium, but that medium comprises two layers, the latent content of language—our intuitive record of experience—and the particular conformation of a given language—the specific how of our record of experience. Literature that draws its sustenance mainly—never entirely—from the lower level, say a play of Shakespeare's, is translatable without too great a loss of character. If it moves in the upper rather than in the lower level—a fair example is a lyric of Swinburne's—it is as good as untranslatable. Both types of literary expression may be great or mediocre. (pp. 221-223)

Whereas Sapir created the theoretical framework, Whorf fleshed out the concept of linguistic relativism, particularly through his studies of the languages of Native Americans such as the Hopi and Navajo, as reported in *Language, Thought, and Reality* (1956).

Dorothy Lee also championed this approach in *Freedom and Culture* (1959) and *Valuing the Self* (1976), in addition to exploring orality-literacy distinctions. *They Have a Word For It: A Lighthearted Lexicon of Untranslatable Words and Phrases* (1988), a popular book by Howard Rheingold, is rooted in the Sapir-Whorf Hypothesis (which is also known as the Sapir-Whorf-Lee Hypothesis and the Sapir-Whorf-Korzybski Hypothesis). Linguistic relativism, broadened to include all forms of cultural communication, forms the basis of anthropologist Edward T. Hall's perspective on culture and communication, and that of his fellow anthropologist, Edmund Carpenter.

According to Louis Forsdale in *Perspectives on Communication* (1981), McLuhan's understanding of media is essentially an extension of the Sapir-Whorf Hypothesis, and Forsdale's students, Neil Postman and Charles Weingartner, were trained in linguistics, made it the subject of their first book, and incorporated it into their subsequent work. While the field of linguistics turned its back on relativism due to the influence of Noam Chomsky who in effect argues that all languages constitute a single medium (see, for example, *Language and Mind*, 1972), the two perspectives are not mutually exclusive. We can, after all, consider radio and television to be two different media, but both electronic media. No doubt, given the vagaries of academic fashion, sooner or later linguistics will experience a relativism revival.

Perhaps the contemporary successors to Sapir and Whorf are George Lakoff and Mark Johnson, who specialize in the study of metaphor. Their perspective is that metaphor is much more than a literary or rhetorical device, but rather an intrinsic element of language that has a strong influence on the way we view and experience the world. They established this perspective in *Metaphors We Live By* (1980), and followed up with a study of poetic metaphor, *More Than Cool Reason* (1989), and *Philosophy in the Flesh: The Embodied Mind and its Challenge to Western Thought* (1999). As the title implies, they see the human body as the basis for metaphor (and mind), as it is our primary point of comparison. Johnson also studies this in *The Body in the Mind* (1987), and Lakoff in *Women, Fire, and Dangerous Things* (1987), where he discusses how categories in thought are based on associations rather than abstractions. The study of metaphor figures prominently in the work of Richards, Langer, McLuhan, Postman, and other media ecologists. Raymond Gozzi, Jr. has combined the Lakoff and Johnson approach with McLuhan and Postman's media ecology in *The Power of Metaphor in the Age of Electronic Media* (1999). In addition to presenting numerous case studies of popular metaphor in contemporary American culture, Gozzi argues that metaphor has resurfaced as a dominant mode of communication in the electronic media environment, having been suppressed in literate cultures. This is a positive development in Gozzi's estimation, as he considers metaphor to represent the creative side of language. The same is true of neologism, and Gozzi explores this basic form of linguistic creativity as a reflection of the United States as a technological society in *New Words and a Changing American Culture* (1990). Additionally John Fraim provides an intercultural examination of media and symbolism in *Battle of Symbols* (2003), John McWhorter (2003) critiques the decay of formal language in the television era in *Doing Our Own Thing*, and Marc Leverette adds a study of mythic symbolism in *Professional Wrestling* (2003).

The relationship between language and consciousness, and the extent to which thought is based on the medium of speech, has been explored by Russian psychologists Lev Vygotsky in *Thought and Language* (1986) for example, and by Alexander Luriia in works such as *Language and Cognition* (1981). Frank Dance has championed the role of language and speech as the basis of human communication in anthologies such as *Human Communication Theory: Original Essays* (1967) and *Human Communication Theory: Comparative Essays* (1982), and in the influential text he co-authored with Charles Larson, *The Functions of Human Communication* (1976). Influenced by Walter Ong's writings on orality and paralleling Gumpert and Cathcart's inter/media approach, Dance employs the traditional opposition between mediated and face-to-face communication, but in effect argues that speech is the primary medium for human consciousness and culture, as well as communication. For the French anthropologist, Claude Lévi-Strauss, the structure of our symbolic forms mirrors the structure of our minds, a point he discusses at length in *Structural Anthropology* (1967). In particular, the bilateralism of brain and body is mirrored in the structure of language, which he believes to be based on binary oppositions (e.g., good and evil, life and death, nature and culture). As he explains in works such as *The Raw and the Cooked* (1969), this is also the structure of myth as a symbolic form, whose purpose it is to mediate contradictions. This requires a third term to perform the function of mediation of opposites. While mediation here is used in a somewhat different sense, Lévi-Strauss does deepen our understanding of mediation as the function carried out by a medium. Moreover, his notion that fire is the mediating agent that transforms nature (the raw) into culture (the cooked) suggests the basic unity of fire as *technology*, as *symbol* (mediating term), and as the defining characteristic of *culture*. It is also worth noting that the poststructuralism of literary theorist Jacques Derrida, as put forth in texts such as *Speech and Phenomena* (1973), *Of Grammatology* (1976), and *Writing and Difference* (1978) is based on an understanding of writing as a medium, distinct from speech. Ong is critical of Derrida's deconstruction approach because it universalizes writing as the basis of all signification, rather than attending to the differences between speech and writing, not to mention other forms of communication. Derrida's fellow poststructuralist, Michel Foucault, deals with the rise of visualism, a theme common to Ong and McLuhan, in works such as *Discipline and Punish* (1977), where he emphasizes surveillance and power. Elsewhere, in *The Order of Things* (1971) and *The Archeology of Knowledge* (1972) for example, he discusses the relationship between knowledge and power, as products of discourse.

Regis Debray, the Communist revolutionary turned media theorist, provides an original approach to media ecology, or as he puts it, mediology. Discussed in depth in *Media Manifestos* (1996), he offers mediology as an alternative to semiology, replacing signification with mediation. The concern, then, is less with the medium as a discrete object or phenomenon, and more with its function. In this way, Debray combines the perspective of McLuhan and other media ecology scholars with the French intellectual tradition of Ferdinand de Saussure (i.e., *Course in General Linguistics*, 1983). Debray followed up on his main work in *Media Manifestos* with *Transmitting Culture* (2000), while an earlier book, *Teachers, Writers, Celebrities* (1981) is a study of how the intellectuals of France have been defined by different forms of communication. Much like Boorstin's (1978a) analysis of the hero-celebrity dichotomy, Debray demonstrates that French intellectuals seek out the dominant medium in order to gain and maintain their status, and as that medium changes, they themselves are remade in the new medium's image. Although quite independent of Debray, Bolter and Grusin's (1999) concept of remediation is not unrelated to Debray's mediation, as both refer to processes akin to signification. And along similar lines, Lev Manovich employs a film-based approach in *The Language of New Media* (2001), which echoes Carpenter's call to understand the "new languages of media" (Carpenter & McLuhan, 1960).

Camille Paglia's media ecology approach is highly original, but like McLuhan rooted in literary criticism and art history. In her major study, *Sexual Personae: Art and Decadence from Nefertiti to Emily Dickinson* (1990), she argues for the persistence of paganism within the Christian culture of the west, much as Ong discusses the residual orality present in literate culture. Drawing on Nietzsche, Paglia views this residual paganism as characterized by the binary opposition of Apollo and Dionysus. For example, she writes:

> Art makes *things*. There are . . . no objects in nature, only the grueling erosion of natural force, flecking, dilapidating, grinding down, reducing all matter to fluid, the thick primal soup from which new forms bob, gasping for life. Dionysus was identified with liquids—blood, sap, milk, wine. The Dionysian is nature's chthonian fluidity. Apollo, on the other hand, gives form and shape, marking off one being from another. All artifacts are Apollonian. Melting and union are Dionysian; separation and individuation are Apollonian. (p. 30)

The opposition between Apollonian and Dionysian is one of art vs. nature, and therefore technology vs. biology. It also is one of thing or artifact vs. liquid or medium, matter vs. energy, and Progress and evolution vs. cyclical time. The Apollonian is allied with the visual, while Dionysian is allied with the aural, so that the opposition is one of literacy vs. orality, and of light vs. dark, silence vs. sound, and tragedy vs. comedy. The opposition extends to the sky vs. the earth and the chthonian; the obsessive, the voyeur, and idolatry vs. ecstasy; cold logic vs. emotion; objectification vs. identification; individuation vs. the group; and the aristocratic, monarchist, and reactionary vs. the rabble and the democratic.

In terms familiar within information and systems theory, the Apollonian represents order and the Dionysian chaos. And the Apollonian symbolizes the masculine while the Dionysian stands for the feminine. This last pair is of particular significance, as gender and sexuality are among Paglia's main concerns. Thus she views the recurrence of certain character types, roles, or personae in the history of western art and literature as extensions of our biology, including our sexuality. In this, she draws on both Goffman's symbolic interaction and Freud's depth psychology. Paglia followed up her main work with two collections of essays, *Sex, Art, and American Culture* (1991) and *Vamps and Tramps* (1994), as well as an analysis of Alfred Hitchcock's *The Birds* (1998).

Freud himself addressed the topics of culture and technology as it relates to psyche and self, particularly in his last works, *The Future of an Illusion* (1961) and *Civilization and its Discontents* (1962). Like Paglia, Janice Hocker Rushing and Thomas Frentz combine gender studies and psychoanalysis, in this case employing a Jungian approach, in *Projecting the Shadow* (1995). Analyzing several motion pictures, mostly in the science fiction genre, they argue that the cyborg theme is one in which technology corresponds to the unconscious element Jung called the Shadow. From Rushing and Frentz's perspective, the technological Shadow tends to be rejected and repressed as something artificial and other, whereas it needs to be confronted and ultimately integrated into consciousness in order to achieve psychological growth.

For Johann Huizinga, the essence of human culture, be it art or craft, communication or technics, is play, hence *Homo Ludens* (1955). And art history as much as literary criticism represents one of the building blocks of media ecology. Studies of art and perception have a special significance for the field, notably Ernst Gombrich's *Art and Illusion* (1960) and *The Sense of Order* (1984). Examinations of the biology of sense perception are also of great value, such as can be found in *The Morning Notes of Adelbert Ames, Jr.* (Ames & Dewey, 1960), and R. L. Gregory's *The Intelligent Eye* (1970) and *Eye and Brain* (1973). Based on the psychology and biology of the senses, we can understand that perception is an active process, one that is learned, based on experience with the outside world. It is a process in which we build up a set of assumptions and presumptions about the world, build an instinctive theory about the world, and then use it to interpret subsequent sensory data that we take in. Perception is dependent on the structure of our nervous system and sensory organs, so that the visual world of human beings is different from that of dogs, or bees, for example, and the same would be true of their auditory, olfactory, gustatory, and tactile worlds (see Hall, 1966, for a discussion of different senses of space). Perception is also altered by our technologies, which may play a role in training our senses in certain ways, as reading trains our eyes to focus on a fixed point relatively close in distance (a habit of perception that McLuhan thought connected to perspective in art and other phenomena). Perception occurs internally as well as externally, so that both perception and cognition are functions of the nervous system, which itself can be seen as an evolutionary extension of the circulatory system (which serves as a rudimentary information system in addition to its other functions). This is one of the main points of neuroscientist Antonio Damasio in books such as *Descartes' Error* (1994), *The Feeling of What Happens* (1999), and *Looking for Spinoza* (2003). It follows that internal processing forms the basis of external perception, which in turn provides the basis of consciousness, which Damasio views as a process of displaying images internally. The idea that the mind is entirely a product of biology leads Damasio to echo Langer in placing great emphasis on feeling and emotion in the working of the brain, as opposed to rationality. Through the work of scholars such as Damasio, as well as Edelman (1987, 1992), we can understand the brain, nervous system, and the body itself as a medium.

13

CONCLUSION

Ultimately, we can turn to books such as Albert Einstein's *Relativity, the Special and the General Theory* (1954), and Werner Heisenberg's *Physics and Philosophy* (1958) to understand the physical universe as a medium. Such a course would be entirely in keeping with Postman and Weingartner's discussion of the "Sapir-Whorf-Korzybski-Ames-Einstein-Heisenberg-Wittgenstein-McLuhan-Et Al. Hypothesis" (p. 101), which could be updated to include Stephen Hawking's *A Brief History of Time* (1998). Einstein's physics is as much about relationships, and therefore the process of mediation, as Martin Buber's philosophy, as expressed in *I and Thou* (1970), for example. Farrell (2000) discusses in detail how Buber contributed to Walter Ong's own understanding of media ecology, and it is therefore not surprising to find Ong (2002b) explaining the relationship between these macro and micro level relationships:

> Knowledge of the relationships between the microcosm (the human being) and the macrocosm (the universe), which has for ages been a major concern of philosophy at least in the West, has grown circumstantially as never before. These relationships have become urgent, consciously or subconsciously, so that they are now discussed not only in scientific literature but also through the popular media. The result has been enforcement of a general sense of cosmic holism more detailed and intense than ever before imaginable.
>
> Earlier thought had maximized distinctions; ecological thinking maximizes connections, relationships. The ecological state of mind was rooted initially in biology, but when we speak of our age as the "eco-

logical age" we are referring to its attention to interconnections that are far more generalized than simply biological connections. We live in an age of countless conspicuous interconnections. (p. 7)

The interconnection between the two environments Ong refers to as microcosm and macrocosm is the interconnection between the human medium and the universe as medium, and therefore between moral theology and cosmology.

It is therefore not surprising that Neil Postman (2000) concludes that, "as I understand the whole point of media ecology, it exists to further our insights into how we stand as human beings, how we are doing morally in the journey we are taking" (p. 16). Postman stresses the humanism of media ecology, while Ong emphasizes personalism, the philosophy of the human person, which is also the philosophy of human relationships. Media ecology itself is the product of human relationships, and in this essay I have endeavored to review the field of media ecology by following links through a network of intellectual relationships. In doing so, I have represented the field in broad terms in order to show the range of possibilities that this intellectual tradition encompasses. As a metadiscipline, and in a tradition reaching back to Aristotle's *Rhetoric*, media ecology intersects with all other disciplines and fields of inquiry. Of course, it would be possible to take a significantly narrower view of media ecology than I have here, and many scholars working from this perspective do so. But McLuhan, Ong, and Postman all rejected academic specialization and the hardening of the categories that institutions of higher education are heir to. Their scholarship is characterized by ecological concern and an open-systems approach, imagination and playfulness, and vision and humanity, and these traits, I believe, are exactly what we need as we come to terms with the enormous challenges and complexities of the 21st century.

NARCISSISM AND ECHOLALIA:
SENSE AND THE STRUGGLE
FOR THE SELF

14

SOMETHING FROM NOTHING

The topic that I wish to take up here is the relationship between communication and the sense of self. In doing so, I intend to communicate a little bit about my own sense of self, personally as well as professionally, and will thereby run the risk of narcissism. At the same time, I will also run the risk of echolalia, as most of what I have to say is merely a repetition of what others have said before. I am not at all certain that I will find a happy medium between the extremes of narcissism and echolalia, a happy medium out of which a balanced sense of self can emerge. But it is very much to the point that it is a struggle to achieve and maintain a sense of self, a struggle that can be lost just as easily as won.

Before I elaborate on these themes, though, I want to begin with a story, taken from a children's book that my son Benjamin and I have enjoyed reading together. The book is by Phoebe Gilman, a Canadian author and illustrator who grew up in the Bronx, and it is entitled *Something from Nothing* (1992). The book's original illustrations are novel and enchanting, whereas the text is itself an echo, as it is adapted from a Jewish folktale:

When Joseph was a baby, his grandfather made him a wonderful blanket to keep him warm and cozy and to chase away bad dreams.
But as Joseph grew older, the wonderful blanket grew older too.

One day his mother said to him, "Joseph, look at your blanket. It's frazzled, it's worn, it's unsightly, it's torn. It is time to throw it out."

"Grandpa can fix it," Joseph said.

Joseph's grandfather took the blanket and turned it round and round.

"Hmm," he said as his scissors went snip, snip, snip and his needle flew in and out and in and out.

"There's just enough material here to make . . ."

. . . a wonderful jacket. Joseph put on the wonderful jacket and went outside to play.

But as Joseph grew older, the wonderful jacket grew older too.

One day his mother said to him, "Joseph, look at your jacket. It's shrunken and small, doesn't fit you at all. It is time to throw it out!"

"Grandpa can fix it," Joseph said.

Joseph's grandfather took the jacket and turned it round and round.

"Hmm," he said as his scissors went snip, snip, snip and his needle flew in and out and in and out.

"There's just enough material here to make . . ."

. . . a wonderful vest. Joseph wore the wonderful vest to school the very next day.

But as Joseph grew older, the wonderful vest grew older too.

One day his mother said to him, "Joseph, look at your vest! It's spotted with glue and there's paint on it too. It is time to throw it out!"

"Grandpa can fix it," Joseph said.

Joseph's grandfather took the vest and turned it round and round.

"Hmm," he said as his scissors went snip, snip, snip and his needle flew in and out and in and out,

"There's just enough material here to make . . ."

. . . a wonderful tie. Joseph wore the wonderful tie to his grandparent's house every Friday.

But as Joseph grew older, his wonderful tie grew older too.

One day his mother said to him, "Joseph, look at your tie! This big stain of soup makes the end of it droop. It is time to throw it out!"

"Grandpa can fix it," Joseph said.

Joseph's grandfather took the tie and turned it round and round.

"Hmm," he said as his scissors went snip, snip, snip and his needle flew in and out and in and out,

"There's just enough material here to make . . ."

. . . a wonderful handkerchief. Joseph used the wonderful handkerchief to keep his pebble collection safe.

But as Joseph grew older, his wonderful handkerchief grew older too.

One day his mother said to him, "Joseph, look at your handkerchief! It's been used till it's tattered, it's splotched and it's splattered. It is time to THROW IT OUT!"

"Grandpa can fix it," Joseph said.

Joseph's grandfather took the handkerchief and turned it round and round.

"Hmm," he said as his scissors went snip, snip, snip and his needle flew in and out and in and out,

"There's just enough material here to make . . ."

. . . a wonderful button. Joseph wore the wonderful button on his suspenders to hold his pants up.

One day his mother said to him, "Joseph, where is your button?"

Joseph looked. It was gone!

He searched everywhere but he could not find it. Joseph ran down to his grandfather's house.

"My button! My wonderful button is lost!"

His mother ran after him. "Joseph! Listen to me.

"The button is gone, finished, kaput. Even your grandfather can't make something from nothing."

Joseph's grandfather shook his head sadly. "I'm afraid that your mother is right," he said.

The next day Joseph went to school. "Hmm," he said, as his pen went scritch scratch, scritch scratch, over the paper. "There's just enough material here to make . . ."

. . . a wonderful story. (pp. 1-28)

15

COMMUNICATION AND/AS
MATERIAL TRANSFORMATION

The theme of material is a natural one for a writer and artist like Gilman (1992), who used a folktale as source material out of which to fashion a wonderful children's book. For my part, I am using *Something from Nothing* as material for this essay. Material is a concern for anyone engaged in acts of creation and communication: public speakers need material for their speeches, actors need material to perform their roles, stand-up comics need material to get their laughs. Teachers likewise need material for their classes, and scholars need material to function as data for their research and to serve as subject matter for their papers and publications.

The humor of Gilman's story revolves around the double meaning of the word material. On the one hand, it refers to physical substance, on the other to communication content. This pun is part of a larger metaphor through which communication is compared to cloth, taletellers are linked to tailors, and text is turned into textile. Across various cultures, stories are *woven* like fabric, *yarns* are spun, accounts *embroidered*, and falsehoods are *manufactured out of whole cloth*. The thrust of this ancient motif, in Gilman's folktale and elsewhere, is to ground the abstract concept of communication in the concreteness of the human lifeworld, to remind us that both form and information are rooted in physical matter. This brings me to the first point I want to make about communication—that our understanding of the process of communication scholarship needs to be grounded in a materialistic conception of the universe.

A materialistic grounding, in turn, means that communication ought to have a scientific basis, insofar as science has provided us with the most reliable means of understanding the material world. This is not to suggest that we all need to be engaged in empirical, quantitative research, but neither should we reject this body of work out of hand. We need not adopt a strict behavioral or social scientific approach to knowledge, but neither should we be ignorant of its conclusions and contributions. And we need not be experts in biology, physics, or mathematics, but we ought to understand the key concepts and theories of the hard sciences. I am not suggesting that we return to positivism, nor to scientism—that is, the compulsion to make all discourse appear scientific (see, for example, Burke, 1945; Postman, 1992; see also Whyte, 1956). I am suggesting that communication scholarship ought to seek consistency with established scientific knowledge.

We can still study the sociology of knowledge and the social construction of reality; in fact, such studies are an important form of reality testing. But we must not forget that even social construction requires raw materials and that scientific knowledge and common-sense reality alike are rooted in our physical existence; they are not simply a result of political decision making. When we think about the idea of social construction in abstract political terms, we tend to exaggerate the ability of human agents to master and control their environment. This is what David Ehrenfeld calls *The Arrogance of Humanism* (1978). When we instead think about social construction in terms of concrete communication, we are more likely to notice and to remember that our situational context provides the materials we use to make our reality, and that our environment shapes and limits what we can build. By the same token, we can be open to the possibility of legitimate spiritual approaches to the study of communication, but again such approaches would still need to take materiality and science into account. After all, the theologians tell us that only God creates *ex nihlo*, out of absolutely nothing. All the rest of us must make do with the materials at hand.

This brings me to my second point, that the study of communication leads naturally to the study of media, and to McLuhan's (1964) famous maxim, "the medium is the message" (p. 7). For what is the common denominator that links these two disparate terms of medium and message? Material! The *material* is the message; it is the *material* that communicators draw upon for their content. And the material is the *medium*; it is the *substance* through which we exchange messages, and the *environment* within which we communicate. We draw upon our material environment, including the technological and the biological, to construct (and deconstruct) our messages and meanings. That is why the medium always precedes the message, just as raw material must be supplied before the finished product can be obtained, just as the physical environment must be in place before life can originate and species evolve, and just as babies must otherwise experiment with making sounds before they can produce meaningful speech.

Kenneth Burke's (1950) notion of common ground can also be understood in terms of media and materiality. Burke argues that communication between two individuals requires a relationship somewhere between absolute difference and absolute commonality. If we were completely the same, identical in all respects, we would have no need to communicate, as one would already know all that the other does. And if we were completely different, with nothing in common, we would be unable to communicate, lacking any basis for shared meaning. Communication can only occur if we begin with some common ground between us, which we can then go on to identify and enlarge. Burke (1945) identifies materialism with the motive of scene in his dramatistic pentad, and *scene* is synonymous with *ground*. Thus, our common ground is in fact the shared scene within which we act, beginning as it does with our mutual existence in the material world. In this sense, our common material ground is the fundamental medium through which we communicate.

Returning to Gilman's (1992) book, I think it crucial to note that the title she gives to her folktale adaptation, *Something From Nothing*, is not entirely accurate. Joseph does not fabricate something out of absolutely nothing. His material is pen and paper, and it is language and experience. He makes this material into something new, and this I would argue is the significance of human communication. Through the magic of sounds and scribbles we alter our environment and create things that never were. We seem to create something from nothing because, as McLuhan (1964) notes, we tend to focus on the content of our messages and ignore the media that we use to communicate. Media function as an invisible environment, giving us the illusion of a nothing out of which comes a something in the form of a message. I should also point out that McLuhan (1964; see also McLuhan, 1995) specifically argued that media should be understood as agents of transformation, and Burke (1950, 1965) discussed the relationship between rhetoric and change; moreover, Susanne K. Langer (1957) wrote about the process of symbolic transformation, and Paul Watzlawick (in Watzlawick, Weakland, & Fisch, 1974) emphasized the link between change and communication. I echo these three seminal scholars in our field in making my third point, that communication is not so much about creation as it is about mutation, and that the process of representation, signification, symbolization, and yes, mediation, is in fact a process of transformation.

As long as it is taken with a grain of salt, the phrase "something from nothing" is a wonderful way to express the power of human communication as an agent of change. Of course, taken literally, it sounds too good to be true, like a sham, a cheat, a con. That is the way Plato (1971, 1973) saw it when he condemned rhetoric as a collection of gimmicks and tricks, suggesting that the study of communication is limited to the cosmetic and the counterfeit, that our field is without subject matter, without substance, without material. In effect, he argued that nothing comes from nothing, and that our field is, in fact, a field about nothing (as *Seinfeld* was a television show about communication). Plato's love for abstract ideas and ideals left no room for the fuzzy logic of rhetoric, let alone the chaos of the human lifeworld. After all, he was part of a philosophical tradition that first invented the concept of permanence as opposed to change, and in this way derived the notion of eternal truth and absolute order. As Robert Logan (2004) has noted, the philosophical tradition that Plato exemplifies rejected such untidy mathematical notions as fractions and infinity, viewing such numbers as horribly unwholesome. And he himself despised the Sophists, the founders of our field, because they saw form as the object of transformation, rather than idealization. The idea of something from nothing would strike Plato as dangerously irrational; likewise, he would not be open to such contemporary notions as chaos, fractal geometry, and complexity. His logic, however dialectical, would not allow for the eco-logic of self-organizing systems, of a system pulling itself up by its own bootstraps (see, for example, Capra, 1996; Gleick, 1987; Kauffman, 1995; Luhmann, 1989; Prigogine & Stengers, 1984; Waldrop, 1992).

I revisit the ancient quarrel between Plato and the Sophists because it shaped and skewed the development of our field. The Sophists understood the centrality of communication, viewing it as the foundation of any worthwhile program of education. Plato all but eliminated communication from his curriculum, and although rhetoric was retrieved by Aristotle, it was relegated to a secondary position where it has remained to this day. Why was Plato's error so powerful? Because all the Sophists could offer were pragmatic approaches to a mundane material reality, whereas the philosophers were selling an idealism with which they constructed a beautiful dream world. In other words, it was the ancient philosophers who were actually building something out of nothing.

I am not sure if we will ever step out of the shadow of the philosophers, but perhaps we might begin with the idea that the study of communication is the study of change, as opposed to permanence. The Sophists were relativists and subjectivists because they recognized the mutability of cultural custom, social organization, and individual perception. They recognized the changing ground of human relationships and adapted themselves accordingly. And as educators, they promised their students that instruction in symbolic form was the surest path to change and growth. We inheritors of the Sophistic tradition commonly refer to communication as a process and a flow—that is, as characterized by change itself. Communication is change, and this, I would suggest, is a tenet that we ought to adopt as a corollary to "One cannot not communicate" (Watzlawick, Bavelas, & Jackson, 1967, p. 51), and a derivative of "the medium is the message."

Symbolic communication is the most radical form of change that we know, coming as close to "something from nothing" as humanly possible. But the material scene that makes up our common ground allows for modifications only moderately less extreme. For example, in Gilman's book, Joseph's act of communication, his writing of "a wonderful story" is only the last in a series of transformations, as the original piece of cloth goes through periodic alteration at the hands of his grandfather. The story begins with the making of a blanket, but the blanket's cloth was made from raw material, which was the product of living organisms, which arose out of a particular physical environment. The universe is a material environment that is characterized by continuous transformation—it is constantly modifying itself. And somehow, despite the tendency of change to move in the direction of disorder and entropy, some of those changes result in increased organization and complexity and ultimately, life. Organisms not only modify themselves to meet the demands of a changing environment, they also transform their environment to make it more favorable to their own survival and prosperity. This process is called ecology. Sometimes organisms alter their environments through the use of technologies and symbolic forms, and this process is called media ecology (Nystrom 1973; Postman, 1970).

Through communication as information, physical systems defy entropy, organize themselves, and become increasingly more complex. Through communication as social action, social systems maintain themselves in space and modify themselves over time. Through communication as a system of meaning, cultures are established and evolve. Through communication as a system of thought, minds are born and grow. Through communication as a system of symbols, we construct worlds and we transcend them, just as Joseph transcended the limitations of needle and thread. We may not escape material reality, but we are able to change and to improve upon our environment and ourselves. The media ecology approach to communication focuses on the means and methods, the techniques and technologies that bring about change. It therefore is concerned with the pragmatics of change, in addition to the substance of transformation. In a human context, change may occur as a result of conscious choice and planning, rather than as a product of automatic processes. But our modifications and manipulations often lead to unanticipated and undesirable changes—this is one of media ecology's primary lessons.

16

ECHO AND NARCISSUS

Having provided you with a sense of myself as a communication scholar, I now want to address the topic of our sense of self in general. And I want to begin by considering a second folktale, one whose theme is also, like *Something from Nothing*, that of transformation. What I am referring to is the myth of Echo and Narcissus, as related by the Roman poet Ovid, in his masterpiece, *Metamorphoses* (1955). The myth is no doubt familiar, so I will only touch on the highlights. Echo was a talkative nymph who used her gift of gab to distract the goddess Juno, allowing her fellow nymphs to escape Juno's wrath. Juno punished Echo by removing her ability to initiate conversation, allowing her only to repeat back whatever she heard. Cursed in this manner, she eventually met Narcissus, a young man so beautiful that everyone he met fell in love with him, including Echo. He was a callous youth, however, and coldly rejected Echo as he did all of his admirers. Broken hearted, the poor nymph faded away until nothing was left of her but her voice—she became the invisible echo that we know as a natural phenomenon. Narcissus was eventually punished by Nemesis, the god of vengeance, who caused Narcissus to see his own image in a pool of water. Not recognizing himself, he was mesmerized by his own beauty. Even after he realized it was only his own reflection, Narcissus could not tear himself away and slowly wasted away until he finally turned into the flower that bears his name.

The story of Echo and Narcissus can be understood in a variety of ways. It is, of course, a story of metamorphosis, of transformation, of change. It is, of course, a nature myth, providing origins for a species of flower and a sonic phenomenon. Obviously, it is also a story about the perils of vanity, infatuation, and unrequited love. And it can be interpreted as a cautionary tale about gender discrimination, with Narcissus representing patriarchy's false consciousness, and Echo sounding a warning about the self-inflicted wounds of feminine passivity and the all-too-real danger of anorexia.

McLuhan (1964) saw in Narcissus a parallel to modern individuals who fall in love with their gadgets, their tools, machines, and media. Just as Narcissus failed to realize that the youth he saw was merely his own reflection, McLuhan argued that by and large we bypass the fact that our technologies are extensions of ourselves; we have become so alienated from our extensions that we do not recognize them as being made in our own image and see them as wholly unrelated to ourselves. Noting that Narcissus and narcosis share the same linguistic root, he wrote of the numbness that we feel in regard to technology and its effects. Technologies become routine, taken for granted, fading into the background. They become an invisible environment, and the numbness that we feel misleads us into perceiving of technology as a nothingness, rather than the something that influences almost every aspect of our lives. Of course, it was Echo who actually became invisible and environmental, in response to the romantic numbness of Narcissus. Even McLuhan, in his commentary on the myth, overlooked poor Echo in his efforts at understanding media.

No one's analysis of Narcissus is better known, however, than that of Sigmund Freud (e.g., 1966). Freud downplayed the case of mistaken identity that triggered the trap set by Nemesis, instead seeing in Narcissus an ego that thinks itself super. Although Freud did not find Narcissus to be quite so compelling or complex as Oedipus, he still named a character disorder after him: narcissism. Narcissists exhibit self-love and a sense of security and superiority entirely out of line with reality; they devalue others or exhibit disinterest in them, while clinging to a "grandiose conception of the self" (Lasch, 1979, p. 84). My treatment of narcissism here does not do justice to the intricacies and debates surrounding this concept. In essence, I simply follow the lead of Christopher Lasch (1979) and use narcissism to refer in a general way to the problem of "too much self."

Freud, like McLuhan, acted as if Echo did not exist and only had eyes for Narcissus. Echo's name did manage to make its way into the psychological literature, though, but through its common meaning (the sound of an "echo"), and only as a somewhat obscure psychological symptom. The term "echolalia" refers to a type of language use in which the speaker repeats back what he or she has heard. A related term is "echopraxia," which refers to the direct imitation of behavior. Echolalia is a normal facet of early language acquisition and also a symptom of various types of brain disorders and disabilities. Here, too, I will not take up all of the specifics of this type of behavior, but rather have enlisted the term to serve as narcissism's counterpart, as a metaphor for the problem of "too little self."

The struggle that I refer to at the beginning of this essay is the struggle to find a balance between too much self and too little. It is, by the same token, a struggle to find a balance between forgetting about others, as narcissists do in their fascination with themselves, and fixating on others, as echolaliacs do as they forfeit their own individuality. The relationship between self and other is essential to the tradition of psychoanalytic commentary practiced by Sigmund Freud (1966), Carl Jung (1969, 1978), Joseph Campbell (1973), Erik Erikson (1950, 1980), Ernest Becker (1971), Norman O. Brown (1985), Francis J. Broucek (1991), and Christopher Lasch (1979); to the symbolic interactionist approach of George Herbert Mead (1934), Kenneth Burke (1945, 1950), Erving Goffman (1959), Eric Berne (1964, 1972), Hugh Dalziel Duncan (1968a, 1968b), Joshua Meyrowitz (1985), and Casey Man Kong Lum (1996); and to the relational perspective of Gregory Bateson (Bateson, 1973, 1978; Ruesch & Bateson, 1968), Edward T. Hall (1959, 1966), Paul Watzlawick (Watzlawick et al, 1967; Watzlawick et al, 1974), R. D. Laing (1965, 1969) and Kenneth Gergen (1991). Underlying these different approaches is the singular notion that we are not born with a sense of self, but rather construct one with the raw material of body and brain, and by means of human communication.

As we learn to use our senses and make sense out of our surroundings, we begin to separate ourselves from our environment and from the individuals with whom we interact. We develop a concept of self as we develop a concept of other, a process that is intimately tied to language acquisition. Language gives us a name and therefore a singular identity. The pronoun "me" provides us with a self that is situated within an environment and is acted upon by that environment. And the pronoun "I" is the perfect expression of the ego acting upon its surroundings. As Ernest Becker (1971) says of "I": "The personal pronoun is the rallying point for self-consciousness, the center of awareness upon which converge all the events to the outside world" (p. 20). First we learn to speak to others, expressing ourselves through words. Then we learn to speak to ourselves, out loud and silently to the form of linguistic thought, the internal monologue. Through such intrapersonal communication we develop self-consciousness. Symbolic communication gives us the ability to become our own material, allowing us to construct a sense of self. It follows, I would argue, that changes in our mode of communication would change the materials and methods of social construction, thereby changing our sense of self.

Echo and Narcissus represent two different extremes in the construction of a sense of self, but they also represent two different modes of sense perception and communication (and as Eric McLuhan, 1998, notes, the two different hemispheres of the brain). As media ecology scholars such as

Marshall McLuhan (1962, 1964, 1995), Harold Innis (1951, 1972), Eric Havelock (1963, 1986), and Walter Ong (1967, 1982) have noted, one of the major divisions in modes of perception and cultural formations is that of the ear and the eye. Echo represents the sense of hearing, communication through sound and the acoustic space that accompanies it. She therefore stands for the sort of media environment that is marked by the absence of literacy and writing, by reliance on speech and song, by emphasis on oral tradition. Such oral cultures lack a storage medium outside of human memory and therefore rely upon repetition to keep knowledge alive. Just as individual memory acts as a neural echo chamber, the collective memory of an oral society functions as an echo system; it is also noteworthy that within one oral culture, that of the Mayans of Guatemala, their wisest storyteller is called the "echoman" (Sanders, 1994, p. 7). Echolalia and echopraxia (in the form of mimesis) facilitate the storage and preservation of information in an oral culture. In contrast to Echo, Narcissus represents the sense of sight, communication through visual imagery and the visual space that it gives rise to. He therefore stands for the type of media environment characterized by the presence of writing systems and literate habits of mind. Like Narcissus, readers become engrossed in the object of their attention, lured into a life of solitary study, trapped by the process of reflection. Writing freezes language, thereby freeing people from the necessity of memorization. Literacy renders the oral tradition obsolescent, and oral cultures have difficulty surviving when they are thrust into competition with literate cultures, just as Echo fades from view after encountering Narcissus.[1]

The interpretations of Ovid's myth as being about sense perception and senses of self are quite complementary. In the same way that Echo represents the extreme of too little self, members of oral cultures have a weak sense of the individual in comparison to literates (Ong, 1967, 1982, 1986; see also Lee, 1959). Collective, tribal identity dominates, as the preservation of knowledge requires a group effort and unanimity. Likewise, conformity and tradition, not novelty and independence, are required for cultural survival. The very mode of aural communication is biased towards the group, as audiences listen as a whole, bound together by the simultaneity of sound; this is in contrast to readers who must read as isolated individuals (Ong, 1982).

Of course, from an oral perspective, members of literate cultures are like Narcissus. They develop too much self. They are freed from the pressures of conformity and tradition and encouraged by this mode of visual communication to view themselves as individuals. Writing makes possible, in Havelock's (1963) phrase, "the separation of the knower from the known" (p. 197), allowing ideas to be assessed objectively, compared and criticized, and individually evaluated; reading, in turn, encourages both empathy and self-consciousness as we intimately encounter one another's thought-worlds (Olson, 1994). Literacy allows us to explore the interior landscape of the mind in a manner heretofore impossible (Ong, 1967, 1982, 1986). Without writing, we would not have the tools to follow the ancient injunction to "know thyself". In *Metamorphoses*, Ovid (1955) relates that a blind soothsayer, when asked by the mother of Narcissus whether her son would live to a ripe old age, replied, "Yes, if he never knows himself" (p. 68). I cannot help but see this an expression of discontent with literate self-absorption. As we express ourselves through writing, we run the risk of falling in love with our own words, sentences, and thoughts as they are laid out before us. This is what Platonic love is really about, as literacy may lead us to adore abstract concepts, such as Plato's ideal forms and the unattainable idealization of romantic love. Writing sets the stage for the cult of individual personality pioneered by Aristotle's student, Alexander the Great (Braudy, 1986), and print in particular made it possible to publicize and immortalize innumerable individual names, from the leaders of government, military, and religion, to authors, scholars, artists, and inventors (Eisenstein, 1980).

Now that we have moved into a post-typographic, postliterate, electronic culture, what has happened to our sense of self? There is at once the fear of a return to echolalia in the form of a mass society in which the individual seeks to "escape from freedom" (Fromm, 1965), gives "obedience to authority" (Milgram, 1974), becomes "the organization man" (Whyte, 1956), is manipulated by "the mind managers" (Schiller, 1973) who use the media for the purpose of "manufacturing consent" (Herman & Chomsky, 1988), and is integrated into a "technological society" (Ellul, 1964) through the methods of "propaganda" (Ellul, 1965). At the same time, there is the fear that we live in a "culture of narcissism" (Lasch, 1979) in which we are members of "the lonely crowd" (Riesman, Denney, & Glazer, 1950), isolated by our "habits of the heart" (Bellah, Madsen, Sullivan, Swidler, & Tipton, 1985) and reduced to either "bowling alone" (Putnam, 2000) or finding some other way of "amusing ourselves to death" (Postman, 1985). And the truth is that both extremes of narcissism and echolalia seem to coexist today, at the expense of a balanced sense of self.

This crisis of the self has gone by many names: R. D. Laing (1965) wrote about the divided self, and we have all heard about the desperate need to find oneself and to find self-esteem. Erik Erikson (1950, 1980) identified the identity crisis, and today we hear all about identity politics (Gitlin, 1995) and identity theft (U. S. Federal Trade Commission, 2000). Media ecologists have noted the blurring of formerly distinct roles such as child and adult (Meyrowitz, 1985; McLuhan, 1964; Postman, 1982) and other forms of identity loss associated with the electronic media (see, for example, Bolter & Grusin, 1999; Carpenter & Heyman, 1970; McLuhan,

1989; Rushing & Frentz, 1995; Sanders, 1994; Turkle, 1995; Wood, 1996); others see such changes as evolutionary rather than revolutionary, the product of an unfolding modernity (e.g., Giddens, 1991; Romanyshyn, 1989; Tuan, 1982). Postmodernists and poststructuralists refer to the identity crisis as the decentering of the subject and sometimes the death of the author, celebrating it for its liberating potential (e.g., Barthes, 1977; Jameson, 1991; Poster, 1990). Kenneth Gergen (1991) writes about the saturated self, in which the individual is segmented into too many selves coexisting without integration; he attributes this multiplication of the self to the proliferation of media of interpersonal communication and finds this form of growth benign, although it certainly can be seen as a variation on the theme of narcissism. Others go so far as to declare us now transhuman (Dewdney, 1998) or posthuman (Hayles, 1999). Cultural conservatives such as William Bennett (1996) promote a notion of character education rooted in nostalgia for the lost sense of a balanced self. They understand as well as anyone that the crisis of the self is a struggle for the self and that our educational institutions represent one of the principal battlegrounds in this conflict. They also turn to religious traditions for salvation because organized religion has traditionally devoted itself to forging collective identities, regulating social behavior, and molding individual consciousness. The religious experience has been concerned with constructing, reconstructing, and/or deconstructing selves, as it has revolved around the relationship between self and the ultimate Other. In the 20th century philosophers such as Jean Paul Sartre and Martin Buber came to speak of the silence of God, which Walter Ong in *The Presence of the Word* (1967) associates with the rise of the mass media and the establishment of the electronic media environment, but God's silence can be seen as another facet of our crisis of identity.

In the end, it is neither Echo nor Narcissus that personifies the electronic media environment. Rather it is Nemesis, the god who avenges Echo by extending and thereby amputating Narcissus.[2] Characterizing the electronic era as the Age of Nemesis would surely be consistent with the criticism of Neil Postman (1982, 1985, 1992), and Jacques Ellul (1964, 1965), among others.

17

AUTISM AND THE STRUGGLE FOR THE SELF

With this in mind, I now want to turn to an example from my personal life. It is neither a folktale, nor a myth, nor a story with a happy ending. Rather, it is the story of my daughter, Sarah, and her disability. In June of 1998, when Sarah was two-and-a-half years old, my wife and I received the diagnosis that Sarah is autistic. We had some concerns about her development during her first year and began to understand that something was seriously wrong during her second year, as she suffered from a series of seizures when she was twenty-one months old, often appeared withdrawn, and failed to develop language normally. She did exhibit echolalia, repeating back words and phrases like "thank you" and "big" without any regard for their meaning, and she showed a remarkable ability to memorize songs such as Raffi's "Baby Beluga" and Barney's "I Love You" refrain. As it turns out, this echolalia is a symptom of autism, although among very young autistic children it can also be a positive indication of their potential for linguistic and cognitive development.[3]

I do not want to dwell on the devastating impact that Sarah's diagnosis of moderate autism had on my family. But, as you no doubt know, reading is one of the coping mechanisms that we literates employ in times of trouble. It is as a parent, and not a scholar, that I read as much as I could on the subject of autism. And yet, as I reviewed the literature, I could not help but notice that what I was learning about this disorder intersected with my own intellectual background in numerous ways. As the name of the syndrome implies, autism is a disorder of the self, and it is a disorder profoundly linked to problems in communication and perception. And although it is a biological condition, the product of a neurological abnormality, present before birth, that affects the development of the brain, no medical tests have yet been developed to test it; instead, diagnosis depends upon behavioral observation. Autism therefore is a fuzzy category, with shifting boundaries. First identified in 1943 by Leo Kanner, it has come to be understood as a spectrum disorder, meaning that there is a continuum between the severest cases, through the mildest, which may go undiagnosed, and perhaps extending into nonautistic normalcy. And it is a syndrome, meaning that it encompasses a wide variety of traits, some of which may or may not be present in any given case, and which may appear in any number of combinations. Autism is referred to as a pervasive developmental disorder, it occurs in males four times as often as it does in females, and it affects approximately half a million people in the United States, with a rate of occurrence somewhere between 1 in 166 and 1 in 1,000.[4]

This disorder is diagnosed by three main criteria. The first has to do with impairments in social interaction; Kanner referred to this as "autistic aloneness" (quoted in Frith, 1989, p.10). There are problems developing relationships, reciprocating emotions, and sharing interests with others, as well as a blindness to nonverbal social cues. The autistic seems lost in his or her own world and an alien in our own. The common ground that typical individuals take for granted is simply not there. The second impairment is in communication, both verbal and nonverbal, and often includes delays in language acquisition or sometimes a complete lack of speech. Moreover, there may be a lack of imaginative play and of interest in narrative. There may also be related problems with the processing of sensory information. At times, the individual may seem impervious to sensory stimulation, not reacting to sounds or to physical pain, whereas at other times he or she may be overly sensitive to certain sensory input. The third criterion is described as "restricted, repetitive, and stereotyped patterns of behavior, interests, or activity" (Siegel, 1996, p. 18). Both simple motions like hand flapping and complex behavioral patterns may be enacted repeatedly. There is a tendency to favor ritual and routine and to behave obsessively and compulsively. Even in mild cases, interests may be pursued with unusual focus and intensity. These symptoms are related to echopraxia, as the behaviors may be learned by imitation; for example, my daughter has been able to pick up and reproduce fairly complex hand maneuvers and dance steps from watching Barney videotapes.

The majority of autistics are categorized as mentally retarded, but of course assessing intelligence is highly problematic when dealing with individuals who may be unable or simply unwilling to speak. Only 20% attain a relatively typical level of intelligence, they are referred to as high functioning (Asperger's Disorder or Syndrome is also considered a form of high-functioning autism). Some autistics have savant skills, highly developed abilities in one specialized area, such as mathematics, computer science, music, art, architecture, mechanics, biology, or simply memorization, visualization, or manual dexterity. These autistic savants are usually well below normal in other areas, however, and autistics in general are particularly handicapped in regards to social and emotional intelligence. The unevenness of autistic intelligence is in part what inspired Howard Gardner's (1983, 1993) theory of multiple intelligences. In his book, *Extraordinary Minds* (1997), he writes:

> When planning their political or religious campaigns or creating works of science or art, extraordinary individuals can focus their attention for many hours at a time, screening out even the most dissonant of stimuli. Such attention is desirable, of course, but it may be akin to autism—a pathological condition in which attention is so focused that the individual is unable ever to engage in normal human intercourse. It is not surprising that the incidence of autism is higher in the families of individuals who perform at a high level in certain academic disciplines, like mathematics, science, and engineering. (p. 134)

Actually, academics of all types seem to have a high incidence of some autistic traits, such as absent-mindedness, intense and single-minded interests, and social impairment (as is apparent to anyone familiar with the ivory tower). This may well have been the case for Albert Einstein, who did not speak until the age of five, had a great deal of difficulty with social interaction, and possessed savant skills in mathematics and visualization. The philosopher Ludwig Wittgenstein also exhibited autistic traits; this adds new shades of meaning to his famous quote, "Whereof one cannot speak, thereof one must be silent" (Wittgenstein, 1922, p. 189), given the mutism characteristic of some autistics and the problems that many of them face in language acquisition.[5] One of the founding fathers of the United States, Thomas Jefferson, may have been mildly autistic, and the same may be true of America's greatest inventor, Thomas Edison, and his modern-day counterpart, Bill Gates.

Along with intellectuals, artists appear likely to have a better than average incidence of autism, as social impairment would not be a factor in solitary creative pursuits, and visual and musical savant skills would be decidedly advantageous. Thus, Vincent Van Gogh's seizures and psychological difficulties may have been the result of the syndrome, and possibly Andy Warhol's antisocial tendencies and love of repetition; among musicians, Béla Bartók and Glenn Gould both exhibited autistic traits. Religion, too, with its elements of repetitive ritual and spiritual isolation, would appeal to high functioning autistics, such as, possibly, the legendary follower of St. Francis, Brother Juniper, as well as the holy fools of Russian Orthodox tradition and the Buddha. This sort of speculation focuses on extraordinary individuals because of their celebrity, and because history tends to ignore the ordinary and the low-functioning alike. One prominent exception, well known in the field of communication, is the 18th century wild boy of Aveyron, the subject of François Truffaut's 1970 film, *L'Enfant Sauvage* (aka *The Wild Child*). A strong case has been made that the original "wild boy" was not raised by wolves, but rather was an autistic child who had been abandoned or run off (Lane, 1977; see also Frith, 1989).

Accounts of autistic individuals can also be found in fictional form. Dustin Hoffman's portrayal of an autistic adult in the 1988 film *Rain Man* is particularly well known, and the recent bestselling novel by Mark Haddon, *The Curious Incident of the Dog in the Night-Time* (2003), takes the reader directly into the interior landscape of the autistic mind. Often unacknowledged is the fact that Tommy, the hero of the 1969 rock opera written by Pete Townsend of The Who, was patterned after autistic children Townsend had observed. Although Tommy's condition is the result of childhood trauma, his symptoms have little to do with repressed memories. Instead, he is unable to hear or see, even though there is nothing wrong with his sensory organs, and he does not speak, even though he is capable of it. Tommy spends his time gazing in the mirror, not out of narcissistic vanity, but because he is lost in his own world; and he displays savant skills of tactile dexterity when placed in front of a pinball machine. Tommy's "amazing journey" actually parallels the delayed development of high-functioning autistics, who as adults gain the ability to communicate something about their experiences. Donna Williams, for example, has written five books about her condition (Williams, 1992, 1994, 1996, 1998, 1999); the following passage is from *Sensing: The Unlost Instinct* (Williams, 1998):

> Up to the age of four, I sensed according to pattern and shifts in pattern. My ability to interpret what I saw was impaired because I took each fragment in without understanding its meaning in the context of its surroundings. I'd see the nostril but lose the nose, see the nose but lose the face, see the fingernail but lose the finger. My ability to interpret what I heard was equally impaired. I heard the intonation but lost the meaning of the words, got a few of the words but lost the sentences. I couldn't consistently process the meaning of my own body messages if I was focusing in on something with my eyes or ears. I didn't know myself in relation to other people because when I focused on processing information about "other," I lost "self," and when I focused on "self," I lost "other." I could either express something in action or make some meaning of some of the information coming in but not both at once. So crossing the room to do something meant I'd probably lose the experience of walking even though my body did it. Speaking, I'd lose the meaning of my own sounds whilst moving. The deaf-blind may have lost their senses; I had my senses but lost the sense. I was meaning deaf, meaning blind. (p. 33)

What Williams describes is a world of fleeting and fragmentary perceptions, an inability to organize sensory data, form gestalts, and construct a
meaningful reality. It was only with difficulty that she was able to build a
world in which she could understand self and other, but not simultaneous-
ly. Either she would shut out her environment and turn inward, or give up
her sense of self and become lost in her perceptions. At least in part, this
stems from an inability to integrate mind and body. As Williams (1998)
later writes (the awkwardness of her prose reflecting the awkwardness of
describing the experience):

> Back then, back in the beginning in the time before mind, "I" was not
> my body nor even considered my selfhood necessarily to exist there.
> There was me and there was the thing others might have called "my
> body" but there was no feeling that this thing belonged to me and the
> concept that it was actually part of me was a very difficult one to grasp
> in more than just theory. (p. 35)

Lacking a sense of her own body, Williams could not fully separate self
from environment and therefore could not create a coherent and integrated conception of her surroundings. We think of perception as being about
the external, but in many ways it begins with the internal, our ability to
perceive and make sense of our bodies, and our boundary with the outside
world. Lacking this most basic form of self-awareness, both meaning-mak-
ing and language acquisition are impaired. Although sight and hearing
dominate our consciousness, the tactile sense is much more basic to our
sense of self, and there are two other body senses we rarely acknowledge.
One is the proprioceptive sense, which tells us about the movement and
position of our joints and muscles. The other is the vestibular sense, our
sense of balance, of gravity, of movement and position in relation to the
earth. Essential to this sense of balance is the inner ear, which perhaps adds
weight to McLuhan's (1964) association of oral cultures with a *balanced*
sensorium. The point here, however, is that both perception and cognition
have a common origin in the self-organization of the nervous system.[6]
    The title of Donna Williams's first book, *Nobody, Nowhere* (1992),
reflects the difficulty she had in establishing a sense of self and the consub-
stantial problem of establishing a meaningful relationship to her environment. What she describes, however, is not a static situation but an ongoing
odyssey, a fact that is reflected in the title of her second book, *Somebody,
Somewhere* (1994). As Oliver Sacks (1995) describes it, the brain is
"dynamic and active, a supremely efficient adaptive system geared for evolution and change, ceaselessly adapting to the needs of the organism—its
need, above all, to construct a coherent self and world, whatever defects or
disorders of brain function befell it" (p. xvii). The self and world that autis-

tics like Williams tend to construct is concrete to an extreme. In other words, they tend not to use abstract, global categories in their thought and perception, instead focusing on the particular, on concrete details.[7] In somewhat different ways, concreteness is a characteristic associated with the mental operations of children (Piaget, 1954), the kind of culture known as "savage" or tribal (Lévi-Strauss, 1966), and individuals with various brain defects and disorders (Sacks, 1987, 1995). Of the latter, Sacks (1987) writes that "their world is vivid, intense, detailed, yet simple, precisely because it is concrete; neither complicated, diluted, nor unified by abstraction" (p. 174). He goes on to argue:

> By a sort of inversion, or subversion, of the natural order of things, concreteness is often seen by neurologists as a wretched thing, beneath consideration, incoherent, regressed. Thus for Kurt Goldstein, the greatest systematiser of his generation, the mind, man's glory, lies wholly in the abstract and categorical, and the effect of brain damage, any and all brain damage, is to cast him out from this high realm into the almost subhuman swamplands of the concrete. If a man loses the 'abstract-categorical attitude' (Goldstein) or 'propositional thought' (Hughlings Jackson), what remains is subhuman, of no moment or interest.
>
> I call this an inversion because the concrete is elemental—it is what makes reality 'real', alive, personal and meaningful. All of this is lost if the concrete is lost. (p. 174)

In other words, the concrete is the basis of human experience—the very term concrete is a material metaphor. Implicit in concrete mental operations is the experience of material reality, of being "close to the human lifeworld" in Ong's (1982, p. 42) memorable phrase. Sacks (1987) suggests that the quality of concreteness "which characterizes the simple . . . gives them their poignant innocence, transparency, completeness and dignity" (p. 174). Abstracting, on the other hand, is a process that takes the individual further and further away from reality, a point central to the general semantics of Alfred Korzybski (1993), S. I Hayakawa (Hayakawa & Hayakawa, 1990), and Wendell Johnson (1946). But the extreme concreteness associated with autism is closely connected to difficulties with language acquisition and language's concomitant capacity for abstraction. Language use for the autistic child may be so concrete that a word learned with a particular individual, in a particular place, and during a particular activity, may not be generalized to other people, places, or situations. Among the most difficult words for autistics to learn to use appropriately are the highly abstract pronouns *I* and *you*; what could be more confusing than a pronoun that refers at one time to oneself, the next time to another? Of course, this may reflect problems in forming a sense of self and other, as well as difficulty in abstracting.

Even savant skills are based on autistic concreteness. Many do quite well at jigsaw puzzles, because they pay close attention to shape rather than picture—in fact, it is just as easy for them to put the pieces together when they are turned upside down. Memorization, which some autistic individuals excel at, is a concrete activity, as Sacks (1995) explains:

> It is characteristic of the savant memory (in whatever sphere—visual, musical, lexical) that it is prodigiously retentive of particulars. The large and the small, the trivial and momentous, may be indifferently mixed, without any sense of salience, of foreground versus background. There is little disposition to generalize from these particulars or to integrate them with each other, causally or historically, or with the self. In such a memory there tends to be an immovable connection of scene and time, of content and context (a so-called concrete-situational or episodic memory)—hence the astounding powers of literal recall so common in autistic savants, along with difficulty extracting the salient features from these particular memories, in order to build a general sense and memory. (p. 200)

Along with memorization, savant skills in visualization also reflect the absence of abstraction. Consider how one such autistic describes her thought processes:

> I think in pictures. Words are like a second language to me. I translate both spoken and written words into full-color movies, complete with sound, which run like a VCR tape in my head. When somebody speaks to me, his words are instantly translated into pictures. Language-based thinkers often find this phenomenon difficult to understand, but in my job as an equipment designer for the livestock industry, visual thinking is a tremendous advantage. (p.19)

This passage was written by Temple Grandin (1995), who holds a PhD in animal science and is on the faculty in that area at Colorado State University. In addition to designing livestock facilities, she has written one book on animal science and two more on her disability (Grandin, 1995; Grandin, & Scariano, 1986). Obviously, visual thinking has its inefficiencies in comparison with language-based thought and does not have the same easy access to abstractions as does thinking with words, but it is probably best understood as a different mode of thought, rather than simply as an inferior, primitive, or undeveloped form of cognition. What Grandin clearly demonstrates is that thoughts are not reducible to words, however close the association between the two for typical individuals. Visual and other forms of nonverbal perception, communication, and mentation are even more basic than language to the making of meaning. It is in this respect that postmodernists such as Fredric Jameson (1972, 1991) and Jean François Lyotard (1984) fall short, mistakenly viewing language as the only game in town, a closed system that serves as our *prison-house*, to use the phrase from Jameson's (1972) book title. This critique is forcefully made by Alexander Durig in *Autism and the Crisis of Meaning* (1996), where he champions Susanne K. Langer (1957) as an antidote to postmodern nihilism:

> The premises of postmodernism hinge heavily on this conviction that language is the medium of meaning, and that it is not capable of formal logical consistency, or guaranteed communicative success, or purity of transmission of knowledge. This is best summed up in Zeno's paradox. Recall how the Greek philosopher said that perfect communication is impossible because every word has to be explained with other words, which have to be explained with other words, ad infinitum. It is an infinite regress; it is all ends against the middle, and there is therefore no absolute base of knowledge or communication possible. This is one of postmodernism's most powerful arguments.
>
> Langer's response is simple, however. Language is not the medium of meaning; meaning is the medium of language. And the fundamental aspect of meaning is symbolic transformation. (p. 168)

Nondiscursive and nonverbal modes of communication, from the visual and iconic to ritual and significant gesture, are pathways to metamorphosis; parallel to discursive and verbal codes, they are alternate methods of translating our perceptions and experiences of material reality into other forms. More importantly, the nondiscursive and nonverbal precede language and serve as the media within which linguistic communication takes form and makes meaning. They constitute the invisible environment that supports linguistic communication, an environment that becomes visible when language acquisition is delayed or disrupted, as is the case for autistics. Typical language development is measured by an increasing ability for abstraction, whereas the nondiscursive and nonverbal are by nature concrete. Moreover, it goes without saying, or at least ought to, that the concrete and material reality of disability (not to mention disease and death) serves as a better context for understanding the human condition than the abstract and immaterial philosophical musings of postmodernists and Platonists alike.[8]

18

THEORY OF MIND

Difficulties processing sensory input, concreteness, and atypical language acquisition all are interrelated with the distinctive quality of autistic alone- ness, social impairment, and what Edgar Schneider in *Discovering My Autism* (1999) calls "the emotional deficit" (p. 94). This is not to say that autistics do not have feelings—they most certainly do. My daughter Sarah is quite capable of throwing temper tantrums, crying in sadness, demon- strating affection and love, or displaying a sense of humor and laughing appropriately (as well as inappropriately). The emotional deficit refers to the subtlety of emotions as a form of social behavior (Duncan, 1968a, 1968b). As Sacks (1995) relates in his discussion of Temple Grandin: "She said that she could understand 'simple, strong, universal' emotions but was stumped by more complex emotions and the games people play. 'Much of the time,' she said, 'I feel like an anthropologist on Mars'" (p. 259). This sense of distance, and the resultant difficulty forming close relationships, is manifested on the most fundamental of levels. For example, seeing eye to eye is one of the most basic forms of relating to others, but autistics like my daughter tend to avoid making eye contact, not out of shyness, but out of meaning blindness.

The simple gesture of pointing at something in one's environment is typically picked up very early in childhood as part of the individual's nat- ural course of development, but for Sarah and many other autistic children, intervention in the form of deliberate instruction is needed or the child may never learn how to point. Pointing implies an awareness of self and other, a shared gaze, a shared attention, a shared meaning. And it is a key step in language acquisition, as we ultimately replace our fingers with words that also "point" to things in our environment. Meaning making is thus linked to empathy, a trait that does not come easily to persons with autism. A lack of empathy does not imply antipathy, however, nor does autistic alienation lead to immoral conduct, as Frith (1989) explains:

> Some of the perceived abnormalities of autistic social behavior can be seen not so much as impairments, but as unusually positive qualities. These qualities can be captured by terms such as innocence, honesty and guilelessness. Autistic people are not adept at deceiving others, nor at impressing others. They are not manipulative or gossipy . . . they are not envious and can give to others gladly. . . . Autistic people may not empathize in the common sense of the word, but neither do they gloat over other people's misfortune. Indeed they can be profoundly upset by the suffering they see, and they can show righteous indignation. (p. 140)

The social, emotional and empathetic deficits of autism all are manifestations of what Frith (1989) believes to be the fundamental impairment of autism: the inability to form a theory of mind—that is, an inability to understand that others have a mind like one's own and a point of view different from one's own. Typical individuals habitually ascribe emotions and motivations to others, and make inferences about others' knowledge and beliefs. Simon Baron-Cohen (1995), a researcher who studied under Frith, refers to what we do as "mindreading" (p. 2). By this he does not mean that we employ extrasensory perception to determine to a certainty what someone else is thinking, although it may appear that way to an autistic individual. Rather, Baron-Cohen points out that we simply employ everyday sense perception to speculate about what others are thinking and planning, with a fair degree of success. Arguing from the perspective of evolutionary psychology, he reasons that, as a species that engages in highly complex social interaction, we have a genetic predisposition towards mindreading.

Along the same lines, Robin Dunbar (1996) argues for the close connection between language and theory of mind, both rooted in the primates' need for social cohesion. Some of the elements of theory of mind are nondiscursive and nonlinguistic, developing during the first two years of normal childhood development; they are also present among autistics and perhaps even among the higher primates (Baron-Cohen, 1995). These elements appear to be a prerequisite for the evolution of language, making possible the nonverbal medium of meaning within which verbal communication takes place. The formation of a complete theory of mind, however, does not occur until the typical individual is already well on the way to language acquisition, sometime after the age of four (Baron-Cohen, 1995). Thus, language and theory of mind appear to be mutually coadaptive systems. From an evolutionary standpoint, apart from the immeasurable value mindreading would hold for a social species, theory of mind also had tremendous survival value because it is an incredibly efficient way to think about any complex system, be it a human being, organism, or the physical environment. Even if it is inaccurate, looking at a thunderstorm anthropomorphically, as a thinking being that throws lightning bolts, is a more efficient way to understand the threatening quality of this meteorological phenomenon (and subsequently respond appropriately to it) than developing complex scientific explanations.

Rather than thinking in terms of mental states and motivations, autistics tend to view others in the most concrete of terms, as objects and behaviors. They may understand many aspects of volition, desire, and intention in others, but have trouble coordinating understandings of self and other as independent consciousnesses that may or may not share attention, awareness, and belief. For example, a common measure of theory of mind is to test for understanding of false belief. In this sort of test, the subject is presented with a story in which characters A and B together hide money inside a box, which is then closed. A then leaves the room, and while he is gone, B removes the money from the box and puts it in his pocket. A then returns, obviously not knowing that the money has been taken by B. The subject knows something that the character A does not know, and he or she is asked where A believes the money to be. Typical individuals who are at least than four years old correctly identify A as holding the false belief that the money is in the box, as do individuals with other mental handicaps such as Down's syndrome with a mental age of four or greater. Most autistics, even those with highly developed language skills, instead credit A with knowing that the money has been moved to B's pocket. In other words, they cannot distinguish between their own knowledge as outside observers and the more limited perspective that A would hold. Baron-Cohen (1995) refers to this syndrome as "mindblindness" (p. xxiii).

Mindblindness is related to both social impairment and difficulties in communication, as much of the common ground that we take for granted is not present. Even when verbal skills are well developed and intelligence high, autistics have difficulty picking up the metacommunicational and relational cues (Watzlawick et al., 1967) that typical individuals take for granted. Nonverbal signals, such as what Baron-Cohen calls (1995) "the language of the eyes" (p. 108), are indecipherable. Consider the following the passage from Dorothy Lee's (1959) anthropological analysis of self-image in Greek culture:

> The organs of highest significance are the eyes. They are the seat of the person. With them, lovers and friends communicate, and they are the pre-eminent medium of enjoyment. Love comes through the eyes, and

the eyes are mentioned the most frequently in the personal poems. "We have not seen you" means "We missed you."

In the folk songs, a beloved's eyes shoot arrows, strike with a poisoned sword, catch a man in a net, they burn the heart or break it into pieces; they lead astray, they bewitch, they destroy. Glances are rarely sweet, and never soft or gentle, in the love dystichs. Here eyes are always black, perhaps because one is apprehensive if they are blue, the color of the evil eye. It is difficult to overestimate the joy of sheer vision. . . . When a long-absent loved one is returning, people congratulate, saying: "Light for your eyes." (p. 145)

As Lee describes it, the language of the eyes overflows with meaning in Greek culture, which is a decidedly visual culture. But even in cultures where it is common to avert one's eyes, there is an art to looking away and a meaningfulness to the averted gaze that is entirely distinct from mind-blindness and the related difficulty processing information communicated through facial expressions that is characteristic of autism. At best, high-functioning individuals like Temple Grandin can try to learn the rules of mental states and social interaction in a highly self-conscious way, as a formal logic that lacks the flexibility, intuitiveness, and spontaneity of typical perception and communication. Lacking a theory of mind may also make it difficult to achieve full self-awareness, given that it would be all but impossible to try to see oneself as others do. Thus, Durig (1996) states that the severity of autism is inversely related to the sense of self. He also points to the similarity between autistic perception and meditation, mysticism and spirituality (which generally involve some form of separation and sublimation of the self); similarly, Durig suggests that mental illness might be better understood as the withdrawal, atrophy, and possibly the annihilation of the self. In other words, autism, meditation, and mental illness all have echolalic qualities. At the same time, autistics may appear to be all self and no other (as the term *autism* implies), unable to recognize that others have beliefs and understandings that differ from one's own; in this sense, they would seem to exhibit a worldview with somewhat akin to infantile narcissism, albeit with significant differences as well. Mindblindness may result in a failure to construct a self, or it may mean that alternate, atypical selves need to be created. For example, typical children engage in role-playing as part of the process of constructing a self, but autistics tend to be impaired in regards to imaginative play. Still, high-functioning individuals may appropriate roles without assimilating them fully or properly, or self-consciously acquire and put on personas as "pseudopersonalities" (Sacks, 1995, p. 266; see also Williams, 1992). Thus, autism can sometimes bear a surface resemblance to schizophrenia (for which it was once mistaken), with its surfeit of selves.

Given the evolutionary advantage of integrated selves equipped with theory of mind, where does autism fit in? Although autism has only been recognized for a little over half a century, I think it reasonable to assume that autistic traits are much more ancient. As Gardner (1983, 1993, 1997) makes clear, traits with high survival value such as various forms of intelligence, along with the ability to maintain focus and concentration, are closely connected to many symptoms of autism. It may well be that autism is, to some degree, too much of a good thing, too extreme a combination of otherwise positive traits.[9] But it is also possible that mindreading is a fairly recent evolutionary development (along with language), and that autistics carry traits that were the norm prior to this development. Their repetitive behaviors and echopraxia, for example, are a form of mimesis, a mode of communication that was dominant before language, according to Merlin Donald (1991). Sacks (1995) makes this connection in his case study of Stephen Wiltshire, an autistic with savant skills in the visual arts:

> Mimesis--itself a power of mind, a way of representing reality with one's body and senses, [is] a uniquely human capacity no less important than . . . language. Merlin Donald, in *Origins of the Modern Mind*, has speculated that mimetic powers of modeling, of inner representation, of a wholly nonverbal and nonconceptual type, may have been the dominant mode of cognition for a million years or more in our immediate predecessor, *Homo erectus*, before the advent of abstract thought and language in *Homo sapiens*. As I watched Stephen sing and mime, I wondered if one might not understand at least some aspects of autism and savantism in terms of the normal development, even hypertrophy, of mimesis-based brain systems, this ancient mode of cognition, coupled with a relative failure in the development of more modern, symbol-based ones. (pp. 240-241)

Along the same lines, perhaps the Neanderthals lacked theory of mind, depending instead on autistic traits such as memory and visualization. Perhaps they disappeared because their mindblindness made them vulnerable to our own ancestors. Or maybe it was the development of mindreading that led to the creative explosion of art and ritual that occurred sometime between 20,000 and 30,000 years ago (Pfeiffer, 1982). Julian Jaynes (1976) posits that self-consciousness (and with it, theory of mind) was an even more recent evolutionary development, simply a matter of a few millennia. No doubt, our ancestors could have survived without mindreading, as have other forms of life. But the introduction of theory of mind, whenever it occurred, may have had a revolutionary impact on our species.

Lacking theory of mind, autistics would be at a decided disadvantage in early human societies, and their social impairment would no doubt collide with oral societies' emphasis on cohesion and conformity. At the same time, the parallels between autism and orality are striking. As previously noted, a concrete mindset is a characteristic shared by members of so-called "savage" or tribal societies, and as Jack Goody (1977) makes clear, such a mindset is a by-product of oral tradition and nonliterate culture. Visual thinking has also been associated with oral cultures (Havelock, 1963; Pfeiffer, 1982), albeit not to the degree of individuals like Temple Grandin. Mimesis, too, continues to function as a powerful mode of communication after the evolution of language, in nonliterate and preliterate societies (Havelock, 1963). Certainly, the autistic would work well with the structure, formality, and emphasis on ritual found in traditional cultures. The type of language use characteristic of higher functioning autistics, "a tendency to verbosity, empty chatter, cliché-ridden and formulaic speech" (Sacks, 1995, p. 245) bears a certain resemblance to orality's own copiousness and reliance on clichés and formulas (Ong, 1982). And there is no doubt that savant skills, and in particular a strong memory, would be highly valued and would probably hold enough survival value to overlook individual idiosyncrasies, and to afford the autistic special status (i.e., shaman).

David R. Olson (1994) suggests that theory of mind is not just a product of language but also of literacy, as it encourages the growth of a more self-conscious self than was previously known. It is also true that the literate mindset allows for abstract thinking on a significantly higher level than the oral mindset (Goody, 1977; Ong, 1982). Therefore, autistic modes of cognition and perception may appear even more alien in a literate society than an oral one. And yet, however oral or even nonlinguistic autistics may seem, we do know that they can thrive in a literate culture and that they have a certain affinity for reading and writing. Whereas autistics are socially impaired, reading and writing is often a private, individualized activity (Havelock, 1963, 1986; McLuhan, 1962; Ong, 1967, 1982, 1986). Whereas autistic savant skills are isolated islands of ability, the written and printed word favors specialization in knowledge and roles (Eisenstein, 1980; Goody, 1977; Innis, 1951, 1972; McLuhan, 1964; Meyrowitiz, 1985; Postman, 1982, 1985). Whereas autistics may perceive the world in fragments, literacy tends to foster fragmentation and analysis as methods of understanding phenomenon and solving problems (Goody, 1977; Logan, 2004; McLuhan, 1962, 1964). Whereas autistics may have difficulty taking in too much information at any one time, literacy favors linear thinking and the "one thing at a time" approach, as we progress from letter to letter, word to word, sentence to sentence, page to page (Carpenter & Heyman, 1970; McLuhan, 1962, 1964; Ong, 1967, 1982).

Similarly, whereas autistics have difficulty taking in sensory data from more than one sensory channel at a time, written communication, in contrast to speech, relies solely on the visual stimuli of the printed or written page (Carpenter & Heyman, 1970; McLuhan, 1962, 1964; Ong, 1967, 1982). And whereas some autistics excel at visual thinking, writing and especially print fosters the development of a visual culture and mentality (Eisenstein, 1980; McLuhan, 1962, 1964; Ong, 1967, 1982). In fact, some autistic children can draw in perspective without training, the most remarkable case being that of Nadia, a three-and-a-half year old savant (see Selfe, 1977). McLuhan (1962, 1964) believed that such abilities are purely a product of alphabetic literacy (see also Romanyshyn, 1989; Wachtel, 1995, in preparation), and it may well be that writing and/or other technologies are needed for the widespread diffusion and adoption of perspective in art. But the basic technique is to draw exactly as one sees, to refrain from any additional processing of sensory data, any additional meaning making. Actually, autistics are naturally capable of a kind of detachment and objectivity that has for long been an ideal of western literate cultures. Along the same lines, autistics tend to ignore context in their communication and behavior, whereas the act of writing by its very nature takes language out of its context of sound and accompanying nonverbal cues and out of the context of social interaction, place, and time (Goody, 1977; Ong, 1982; Postman, 1982, 1985). Literate decontextualization is often associated with abstraction (to abstract is to take something out of a more specific and detailed context), but the experience of autistics shows that it may also involve the removal of an abstract context, leaving behind nothing but the most concrete of elements.

It therefore makes perfect sense that some autistics are hyperlexic— that is, they learn to read at a much younger age than typical children. (This is not to suggest that their reading comprehension is comparable to typical children, nor even measurable.) Some may find typewriters and keyboards to be a more comfortable communication mode than speech, or possibly the only mode they can use, one example being Jasmine Lee O'Neill, a mute autistic savant who authored *Through the Eyes of Aliens: A Book About Autistic People* (1999). The autistic's affinity for the written word is also apparent in one of the more controversial forms of therapy, facilitated communication. Here, adult facilitators assist the autistic in typing on the keyboard, leading them hand over hand in an attempt to overcome difficulties with motor control and coordination. There is a strong possibility that the output of such facilitation might originate with the facilitator rather than the autistic, however. It is for this reason that facilitated communication has been labeled a pseudoscience and charlatanism by some (see, for example, Maurice, 1993a; Siegel, 1996; in contrast, Cohen, 1998, is willing to wait for more evidence before closing the book on facilitated communication). Regardless of the validity and effectiveness of facilitated communication, the literate quality of autism remains.

In our electronic age, autistics encounter an often hostile media environment. From the fluorescent lighting, which many find painful, to the sensory bombardment and information overload, which disrupt the thought processes of us all, our culture offers neither the routine predictability and slow pace of primary orality, nor the quiet concentration of traditional literacy. As one autistic argues, "the way of life of this age is ever more demanding of a certain way of living that is the WORST case of living, for many autistic people, and there are fewer and fewer places to hide, to be sheltered from the media Storms . . . and even the "normal" kid may become mind-fractured into Autism . . . under all the sense stress and overloads!" (Wilson, 2000, no pagination). This comment was posted on *2worlds*, an electronic discussion list set up by and for high-functioning autistics (who object, by the way, to being characterized as disabled, as suffering from a disorder and in need of a cure, rather than simply being different). Electronic media have allowed for greater affiliation and stronger group identity for all manner of social subgroups (Meyrowitz, 1985), including the disabled, as disability studies scholar Simi Linton makes clear in *Claiming Disability: Knowledge and Identity* (1998). Creating a sense of community is particularly difficult among autistics, and many high-functioning individuals instead find a niche in the solitary activity of computer programming. But autistics do feel more comfortable in the company of others who share their mindset than they do with typical individuals and in fact take comfort in identifying and understanding the nature of their difference (Grandin, 1995; Grandin, & Scariano, 1986; Schneider, 1999; Williams, 1992, 1994, 1999). Durig (1996) uses the phrase "culture of autism" (p. 11) to refer to the subculture that encompasses high-functioning autistics, their families, and professionals who work with them (e.g., physicians, therapists, educators). In this regard at least, autistics have been well served by the electronic era's information explosion, as it is only in this period that the syndrome has been recognized and facts about it disseminated, resulting in an increasing public awareness of the disability.[10]

19

CONCLUSION

More and more there is talk today of an epidemic of autism, and it is unclear to what degree this is due to the stresses of our environment, or contaminants and pollutants, or diet and allergies, or infections and vaccinations, or genetic predisposition, or simply improved diagnostic procedures (and it may well be a combination of all of these factors). At present, there is no cure for autism, but many of us in the culture of autism hope that methods of prevention and increasingly more effective interventions might be discovered in the future. There has been some exploration of biological treatments for the disorder, some of which have been helpful, but there have been no major breakthroughs. In lieu of a method to act upon the brain directly, the only course of action is to work through the interface of behavior and the mind—in other words, through therapy and education. Therapy and education do not undo autism, but they can help autistic individuals cope with their environments (and some who are diagnosed with the disability are later mainstreamed and on rare occasions declassified). But not all types of therapy are effective.

In the first decades following the identification of the syndrome, psychoanalytic approaches dominated. Bruno Bettelheim, who laid out such a perspective in *The Empty Fortress: Infantile Autism and the Birth of the Self* (1967), was typical of such practitioners: he manufactured a theory out of whole cloth that blamed mothers for their children's disability and prescribed long-term analysis for both as the way to draw out what he asserted was a normal child hidden behind an autistic shell. Because of this nonsense, parents were consumed by guilt, their life savings were consumed by

psychiatrists' fees, and their children's chances for a better life were consumed by inappropriate and ineffectual (and sometimes harmful) therapies. Bettelheim eventually became the bête noir of the autism community, but despite the fact that Bernard Rimland demonstrated the groundless-
ness of psychoanalytic theories of autism as long ago as 1964, there still are
psychoanalysts who continue this sort of practice today. And because psychoanalysis is considered a medical procedure, health insurance is much
more likely to cover this form of fraud than truly effective therapies, as I
myself found out to my dismay.

Client-centered approaches of the sort championed by the Rogerian
school of psychology proved to be only slightly helpful. It is hard to make
the child the center when the child lacks a center. For this reason, such
approaches have been criticized as a waste of time and money, however
well-meaning they may be. Having been educated at a time when Rogers
and Maslow were in vogue, I was surprised to learn that the only approach
that had any history of helping autistics came from the children of Pavlov
and Skinner, the behavioral school. This approach had been dismissed by
the Freudians for relegating the mind to a black box, vilified by Rogers and
Maslow for reducing human beings to inhuman automatons, and delegit-
imized by Chomsky for failing to account for the complexities of language
acquisition. And yet, as it turns out, operant conditioning and behavior
modification, or what is referred to as Applied Behavior Analysis and the
discrete trial method, held the only hope of helping my daughter. The specific method was pioneered by UCLA psychologist Ivar Lovaas (1981) and
involves breaking down activities into their smallest units. Whereas a complex behavior may be too difficult for the child to grasp, leading the child
to give up in frustration, smaller, simpler units can be successfully learned,
providing the child with a sense of satisfaction and motivation for further
learning. Thus, teaching children to speak would begin with teaching individual phonemes, and teaching children to brush their teeth would involve
teaching the child a series of separate behaviors such as turning on the
water, picking up the toothbrush, wetting the toothbrush,and so forth
(Lovaas, 1981, p. 129). Through a process of discrete trials involving drill
and rewards, each unit of behavior is taught until mastered.

Scientific research indicates that the Lovaas method is effective
(Maurice, 1993b; Smith, Groen, & Wynn, 2000), at least for the high-functioning and for moderately autistic individuals such as my daughter; the
method is particularly effective if the program is begun during early childhood and the intervention is intensive—preferably 30 to 40 hours a week
of one-on-one behavioral treatment. This may seem like too much for a
young child, but the truth is that autistics work best in a highly structured
environment that keeps them engaged with the world. As for the nature of
this behavioral approach, some question whether it turns children into

robots. Based on my own experience I believe that nothing could be further from the truth. The behavioral units may be learned in a mechanical way, but they accumulate into a human whole greater than the sum of its parts, a self. Given the plasticity of the brain during early childhood, this form of therapy is an attempt to work through the interface of human communication and rewire the autistic brain so that development can proceed in a way more closely approximating that of the typical child. It is not so much an attempt to program children as it is to jump start neural self-organization. Additionally, the fact that Helen Keller's teacher, Anne Sullivan, pioneered the technique of discrete trial serves to underscore the humanistic aspect of this approach. The contemporary Lovaas method focuses on language acquisition, cognitive development, and self-help skills, and therefore is probably best supplemented with therapy focusing on emotional development and social interaction, as practiced by Stanley Greenspan, for example (see Greenspan, Wieder, & Simons, 1998). It is also possible to teach high-functioning autistics about mindreading (Howlin, Baron-Cohen, & Hadwin, 1999).

Autism cuts across the extremes of narcissism and echolalia and presents us with a sense of self that is at the same time too little and too much. More than anything else, it is an incomplete sense of self, one cut off from a sense of other. Can autistic individuals develop an integrated sense of self? From what I gather, the raw material is there, but it involves a tremendous struggle to construct a coherent and meaningful sense of the world. Can autistic individuals develop a theory of mind? There is some indication that the answer is yes, but only for some, and only with great difficulty.

As for my daughter, we are fighting to provide her with the best possible life chances, and her teachers are the heroes who are out on the frontlines. And what she herself has taught me is that the self we take for granted is in fact the product of a struggle. It is the most important struggle of our lives, despite the fact that we are largely unaware of it. Through our efforts from early childhood on, we take the raw material we are born with and we build ourselves. And having done so, we continue to transform ourselves. The self is a product of metamorphosis, not a static entity. There are many kinds of selves we can construct with the materials at hand, but they are not all of equal worth. Some may be too easily overwhelmed by others, some too insensitive. Moreover, different media environments tend to favor or discourage different types of selves. As the materials we work with change, our sense of self may also be altered. Thus, for example, we move from oral cultures' tendency to develop too little self to literate cultures' too much self.

Donna Williams writes of how she moved past the stage of "no self, no other," but could exist either as "all self, no other," or "all other, no self." It is only with difficulty that she could develop a "simultaneous sense of self and other". In a similar way, electronic culture seems to oscillate between the extremes of echolalia and narcissism. And I would suggest that on the cultural level this is just as much a disability as it is on the individual level and that our current crisis of the self represents a struggle of the greatest import. It is a struggle over the kinds of selves we want to produce and reproduce.

Ovid's tale of metamorphosis is a tragic one. But the story of Joseph, the tailor's grandson is a human comedy of survival, transformation, and transcendence. It shows us that it is possible to work with the material at hand and make something that never was. We might begin by retrieving oral culture's selflessness, community-mindedness, and the ability to sacrifice oneself for the sake of others. And we could add to it literate culture's self-fullness, its emphasis on individual rights and responsibilities, and the idea of integrity and moral character. Both narcissism and echolalia can be positive traits if exhibited in moderation and balance. Changes in our media environment may have destabilized our culture's established sense of self, but we have the raw materials and the understanding of media and communication necessary to build a new, integrated sense of self. The struggle now falls to us, as parents and as citizens, as scholars and as communicators, and above all, as teachers, to make something from nothing.

NOTES

1. I think it interesting to note that Ovid occupied a peculiar position between the two modes of orality and literacy, as a writer living in a literate society that constituted a small pocket in a largely nonliterate world; moreover, as a poet Ovid idolized the blind bard Homer and emulated the oral tradition that supplied the material for the *Iliad* and the *Odyssey*. It is of course impossible to say whether Ovid was fully conscious of the tension between orality and literacy, let alone aware of its allegorical relationship to this particular portion of his *Metamorphoses*, but it is reasonable to assume that the tale of Echo and Narcissus at least unconsciously reflects these tensions.

2. The reference is to McLuhan's (1964) argument that any given medium or technology, in extending some aspect of the body (or some other attribute), also amputates that organ, much like a prosthetic device; we might also invoke the recent buzzword of the cyborg in this context. Additionally, Echo's revenge corresponds to the tendency of a new medium to retrieve some previously obsolesced element of the past, a tendency that Marshall and Eric McLuhan (1988) declared one of their laws of the media. The important point here is that Nemesis represents something different from either Echo or Narcissus, while in a way connected to both, just as the electronic media retrieves or extends certain qualities of both orality and literacy.

3. I feel compelled to note that despite the fact that seizure disorders are present in one out of four cases of autism (Volkmar, 1989, p. 60), and despite the presence of numerous other symptoms and indicators, the various doctors and therapists who dealt with Sarah kept us in the dark as to this possibility for eight months and more. Only one brave and charitable occupational therapist gave us a hint a few weeks prior to Sarah's examination and diagnosis by a developmental pediatrician. The experience of an unintended conspiracy of silence on the part of health and education professionals is not at all uncommon for parents of autistic children (see, for example, Maurice, 1993a) and is a disservice to both parents and their children. The sooner parents are made aware of the situation, the sooner intervention can begin, and time does make a difference.

4. The facts summarized in this paragraph are taken from a variety of sources. Uta Frith's *Autism: Explaining the Enigma* (1989) is a classic that is intellectually stimulating and displays a great deal of empathy for autistics. Simon Baron-Cohen and Patrick Bolton's *Autism: The Facts* (1993) is an excellent concise guide. Bryna Siegel's *The World of the Autistic Child* (1996) is one of the most comprehensive general introductions, one that offers less optimism about the condition than most other sources. Shirley Cohen's *Targeting Autism* (1998) is the most balanced I have come across, and nearly as complete as Siegel's book. The highly informative websites for the Autism Society of America <http://www.autism-society.org> and The New Jersey Center for Outreach and Services for the Autism Community (COSAC) <http://www.njcosac.org> were also consulted. Additionally, the fact that autism is more common in males than females has led to some theories relating the disorder to gender differences in brain structure (e.g., Baron-Cohen, 2003). As the parent of an autistic girl, I find this argument less than compelling, although it does relate to Leonard Shlain's (1998, 2003) arguments about media ecology and the biology of gender.

5. Consider Wittgenstein's quote in light of the following passages taken from *Through the Eyes of Aliens* by Jasmine Lee O'Neill (1999), a mute autistic savant: "Selective mutism is when the person chooses whom to talk to, and in which situations. . . . Elective mutism is electing to be silent to everyone. Autistics can have periods of either type which last a lifetime, or several years or weeks" (pp. 45-46).

6. Sensory integration and auditory integration therapies are based on these premises, and may be effective supplements to behavioral therapies in improving the cognitive abilities of autistics (see, for example, Kranowitz, 1998; Madaule, 1994; Tomatis, 1996).

7. Alexander Durig (1996) suggests that autistic concreteness amounts to a deficit in inductive reasoning, with high-functioning individuals maintaining normal to superior deductive abilities, whereas low-functioning autistics may have difficulty reasoning deductively as well as inductively.

8. The Sophists, on the other hand, would see in Temple Grandin's visual thinking a process akin to the ancient art of memory described by Frances Yates (1966), in which visualization and memorization are closely allied, a set of mnemonic techniques that culminated in the early modern era's memory theater. In comparison to the memory theater as an artificial mnemonic device, Grandin's comparison of her own thought processes to a VCR suggests a more instinctive and intuitive home theater of memory and mental processing.

9. This would be consistent with McLuhan's (1964; McLuhan & McLuhan, 1988) notion that a medium, when pushed to extremes, flips or reverses into its opposite. Although this law of the media was applied to human inventions alone, media are understood to be extensions of the biological; it therefore may be the case that they follow the same patterns as the biological. Moreover, it may be argued that organisms are themselves media through which genes modify their environments and perpetuate themselves, an argument put forth by Richard Dawkins (1989) in particular.

10. I note with some degree of pride that my wife, Barbara Strate, was instrumental in starting up an electronic discussion list for parents of autistic children in northern New Jersey. Her MOSAIC list (an acronym for Mothers' Onward Search for Autism Interventions and Causation), which is run through Yahoo! Groups (originally egroups), has had an enormous impact on the culture of autism in our region, and has served as a model for other communities. Previously, parents had struggled in isolation to obtain needed services, or more often were unaware of the services to which they were entitled. Now, parents are empowered by becoming well informed and organized through an e-mail subscription (this is especially significant given that the heavy demands of dealing with an autistic child make physical attendance at support groups all but impossible).

REFERENCES

Abram, D. (1996). *The spell of the sensuous: Perception and language in a more-than-human world.* New York: Pantheon.

ADILKNO [The Foundation for the Advancement of Illegal Knowledge]. (1994). *Cracking the movement: Squatting beyond the media* (L. Martz, Trans.). Brooklyn, NY: Autonomedia.

Adorno, T.W. (1973). *Negative dialectics* (E.B. Ashton, Trans.). New York: Seabury Press.

Albrecht, R. (2004). *Mediating the muse: A communications approach to music, media, and cultural change.* Cresskill, NJ: Hampton Press.

Altheide, D. L. (1976). *Creating reality: How TV news distorts events.* Beverly Hills, CA: Sage.

Altheide, D. L. (1985). *Media power.* Beverly Hills: Sage.

Altheide, D. L. (1995). *An ecology of communication: Cultural formats of control.* New York: Aldine de Gruyter.

Altheide, D. L. (2002). *Creating fear: News and the construction of crisis.* New York: Aldine de Gruyter.

Altheide, D. L., & Snow, R. P. (1979). *Media logic.* Beverly Hills: Sage.

Altheide, D. L., & Snow, R. P. (1991). *Media worlds in the postjournalism era.* New York: Aldine de Gruyter.

Ames, A., & Dewey, J. (1960). *The morning notes of Adelbert Ames, Jr.: Including a correspondence with John Dewey* (H. Cantril, Ed.). New Brunswick: Rutgers University Press.

Aristotle. (1954). *The rhetoric and the poetics of Aristotle* (W. R. Roberts & I. Bywater, Trans.). New York: The Modern Library.

Aristotle. (1969). *Physics* (H. G. Apostle, Trans.). Bloomington: University of Indiana Press.

Arquilla, J., & Ronfeldt, D. F. (1996). *The advent of netwar.* Santa Monica, CA: Rand.

Arquilla, J., & Ronfeldt, D. F. (Eds.). (1997). *In Athena's camp: Preparing for conflict in the information age.* Santa Monica, CA: Rand.

135

Arquilla, J., & Ronfeldt, D. F. (1999). *The emergence of noopolitik: Toward an American information strategy.* Santa Monica, CA: Rand.

Arquilla, J., & Ronfeldt, D. F. (2000). *Swarming and the future of conflict.* Santa Monica, CA: Rand.

Arquilla, J., & Ronfeldt, D. F. (Eds.). (2001). *Networks and netwars: The future of terror, crime, and militancy.* Santa Monica, CA: Rand.

Barnes, S. B. (2001). *Online connections: Internet interpersonal relationships.* Cresskill, NJ: Hampton Press.

Barnes, S. B. (2003). *Computer-mediated communication: Human-to-human communication across the Internet.* Boston: Allyn & Bacon.

Barnes, S. B., & Strate, L. (1996). The educational implications of the computer: A media ecology critique. *New Jersey Journal of Communication, 4*(2), 180-208.

Barnhurst, K. G., & Nerone, J. C. (2001). *The form of news: A history.* New York Guilford.

Baron-Cohen, S. (1995). *Mindblindness: An essay on autism and theory of mind.* Cambridge, MA: MIT Press.

Baron-Cohen, S. (2003). *The essential difference: The truth about the male and female brain.* New York: Basic Books.

Baron-Cohen, S., & Bolton, P. (1993). *Autism: The facts.* Oxford: Oxford University Press.

Barry, A. M (1997). *Visual intelligence: Perception, image, and manipulation in visual communication.* Albany: State University of New York Press.

Barthes, R. (1977). *Image, music, text* (S. Heath, Trans.). New York: Hill and Wang.

Bateson, G. (1972). *Steps to an ecology of mind: Collected essays in anthropology, psychiatry, evolution, and epistemology.* Chicago: University of Chicago Press.

Bateson, G. (1973). *Steps to an ecology of mind.* New York: Ballantine.

Bateson, G. (1978). *Mind and nature: A necessary unity.* New York: Dutton.

Bateson, G. (2002). *Mind and nature: A necessary unity.* Cresskill, NJ: Hampton Press.

Baudrillard, J. (1981). *For a critique of the political economy of the sign* (C. Levin, Trans.). St. Louis, MO: Telos Press.

Baudrillard, J. (1983). *Simulations* (P. Foss, P. Patton, & P. Beitchman, Trans.). New York: Semiotext(e).

Baudrillard, J. (1994). *Simulacra and simulation* (S. F. Glaser, Trans.). Ann Arbor: University of Michigan Press.

Becker, E. (1971). *The birth and death of meaning: An interdisciplinary perspective on the problem of man* (2nd ed.). New York: The Free Press.

Bellah, R. N., Madsen, R., Sullivan, W. M., Swidler, A., & Tipton, S. M. (1985). *Habits of the heart: Individualism and commitment in American life.* New York: Perennial Library.

Beniger, J. R. (1986). *The control revolution: Technological and economic origins of the information society.* Cambridge, MA: Harvard University Press.

Benjamin, W. (1968). *Illuminations* (H. Zohn, Trans.). New York: Harcourt, Brace & World.

Bennett, W. J. (Ed.). (1996). *The book of virtues for young people: A treasury of great moral stories.* Parsippany, NJ: Silver Burdett Press

Berne, E. (1964). *Games people play.* New York: Grove.

Berne, E. (1972). *What do you say after you say hello?* New York: Grove.

Bertalanffy, L. v. (1967). *Robots, men, and minds: Psychology in the modern world.* New York: G. Braziller.

Bertalanffy, L. v. (1969). *General system theory: Foundations, development, applications.* New York: G. Braziller.

Bettelheim, B. (1967). *The empty fortress: Infantile autism and the birth of the self.* New York: Free Press.

Birdwhistell, R. L. (1970). *Kinesics and context: Essays on body motion communication.* Philadelphia: University of Pennsylvania Press.

Bishop, J., & Prins, H. (2003). *Oh what a blow that phantom gave me!* [video]. (Available from Media Generation, 8378 Faust Ave., West Hills, CA, 91304).

Blackmore, S. J. (1999). *The meme machine.* London: Oxford University Press.

Bolter, J. D. (1984). *Turing's man: Western culture in the computer age.* Chapel Hill: University of North Carolina Press.

Bolter, J. D. (1991). *Writing space: The computer, hypertext, and the history of writing.* Hillsdale, NJ: Lawrence Erlbaum Associates.

Bolter, J. D. (2001). *Writing space: Computers, hypertext, and the remediation of print* (2nd ed.). Mahwah, NJ: Lawrence Erlbaum Associates.

Bolter, J. D., & Grusin, R. (1999). *Remediation: Understanding new media.* Cambridge, MA: MIT Press.

Boorstin, D. J. (1962). *The image: Or what happened to the American dream.* New York: Atheneum.

Boorstin, D. J. (1978a). *The image: A guide to pseudo-events in America.* New York: Atheneum.

Boorstin, D. J. (1978b). *The republic of technology: Reflections on our future community.* New York: Harper & Row.

Boorstin, D. J. (1983). *The discoverers.* New York: Random House.

Boorstin, D. J. (1984). *Books in our future: A report from the Librarian of Congress to the Congress.* Washington, DC: Library of Congress.

Boorstin, D. J. (1992). *The creators: A history of the heroes of imagination.* New York: Random House.

Boorstin, D. J. (1998). *The seekers: The story of man's continuing quest to understand his world.* New York: Random House.

Braudy, L. (1986). *The frenzy of renown: Fame and its history.* New York: Oxford University Press.

Brodie, R. (1996). *Virus of the mind: The new science of the meme.* Seattle, WA: Integral Press.

Brown, N. O. (1985). *Life against death: The psychoanalytical meaning of history* (2nd ed.). Hanover, NH: Wesleyan University Press.

Broucek, F. J. (1991). *Shame and the self.* New York: Guilford Press.

Buber, M. (1970). *I and Thou* (W. Kaufmann, Trans.). New York: Charles Scribner's Sons.

Burke, K. (1945). *A grammar of motives.* Berkeley: University of California Press.

Burke, K. (1950). *A rhetoric of motives.* Berkeley: University of California Press.

Burke, K. (1965). *Permanence and change: An anatomy of purpose* (2nd rev. ed.). Indianapolis: Bobbs-Merrill.

Campbell, J. (1973). *The hero with a thousand faces.* Princeton: Princeton University Press.

Campbell, J. (1982). *Grammatical man: Information, entropy, language, and life*. New York: Simon & Schuster

Capra, F. (1975). *The Tao of physics: An exploration of the parallels between modern physics and eastern mysticism*. New York: Shambhala.

Capra, F. (1982). *The turning point: Science, society, and the rising culture*. New York: Simon & Schuster.

Capra, F. (1996). *The web of life: A new scientific understanding of living systems*. New York: Anchor Books.

Capra, F. (2002). *The hidden connections: Integrating the biological, cognitive, and social dimensions of life into a science of sustainability*. New York: Doubleday.

Carey, J. W. (1989). *Communication as culture: Essays on media and society*. Boston: Unwin Hyman.

Carey, J. W. (1997). *James Carey: A critical reader* (E. S. Munson & C. A. Warren, Eds.). Minneapolis: University of Minnesota Press.

Carpenter, E. (1973). *Oh, what a blow that phantom gave me!* New York: Holt, Rinehart & Winston.

Carpenter, E., & Heyman, K. (1970). *They became what they beheld*. New York: Outerbridge and Dienstfrey.

Carpenter, E., & McLuhan, M. (1960). *Explorations in communication*. Boston: Beacon Press.

Cassidy, M. (2004). *Bookends: The changing media environment of American classrooms*. Cresskill, NJ: Hampton Press.

Cavell, R. (2002). *McLuhan in space: A cultural geography*. Toronto: University of Toronto Press.

Chase, S. (1938). *The tyranny of words*. New York: Harcourt, Brace.

Chaytor, H. J. (1950). *From script to print: An introduction to medieval vernacular literature*. Cambridge: W. Heffer.

Chesebro, J. W., & Bonsall, D.G. (1989). *Computer-mediated communication: Human relationships in a computerized world*. Tuscaloosa: University of Alabama Press.

Chesebro, J. W., & Bertelsen, D. A. (1996). *Analyzing media: Communication technologies as symbolic and cognitive systems*. New York: Guilford Press.

Chomsky, N. (1972). *Language and mind*. New York: Harcourt Brace Jovanovich.

Christians, C. G. (1976). *Jacques Ellul and democracy's "vital information" premise*. Lexington, KY: Association for Education in Journalism.

Christians, C. G., & Van Hook, J. M. (Eds.). (1981). *Jacques Ellul: Interpretive essays*. Urbana: University of Illinois Press.

Cohen S. (1998). *Targeting autism: What we know, don't know, and can do to help young children with autism and related disorders*. Berkeley: University of California Press.

Couch, C. J. (1984). *Constructing civilizations*. Greenwich, CT: JAI Press.

Couch, C. J. (1989). *Social processes and relationships: A formal approach*. Dix Hills, NY: General Hall.

Couch, C. J. (1996). *Information technologies and social orders* (D. R. Maines & S.-L. Chen, Eds.). New York: Aldine de Gruyter.

Crowley, D. J., & Heyer, P. (Eds.). (1991). *Communication in history: Technology, culture, society* (1st ed.). New York: Longman.

Crowley, D. J., & Heyer, P. (Eds.). (1995). *Communication in history: Technology, culture, society* (2nd ed.). White Plains, NY: Longman.

Crowley, D. J., & Heyer, P. (Eds.). (1999). *Communication in history: Technology, culture, society* (3rd ed.). New York: Longman.

Crowley, D. J., & Heyer, P. (Eds.). (2003). *Communication in history: Technology, culture, society* (4th ed.). Boston: Allyn & Bacon.

Curtis, J. M. (1978). *Culture as polyphony: An essay on the nature of paradigms.* Columbia: University of Missouri Press.

Curtis, J. M. (1987). *Rock eras: Interpretations of music and society, 1954-1984.* Bowling Green, OH: Bowling Green State University Popular Press.

Czitrom, D. J. (1983). *Media and the American mind: From Morse to McLuhan.* Chapel Hill: University of North Carolina Press.

Dale, S. (1996). *McLuhan's children: The Greenpeace message and the media.* Toronto: Between the Lines.

Damasio, A. R. (1994). *Descartes' error: Emotion, reason, and the human brain.* New York: Putnam.

Damasio, A. R. (1999). *The feeling of what happens: Body and emotion in the making of consciousness.* New York: Harcourt Brace.

Damasio, A. R. (2003). *Looking for Spinoza: Joy, sorrow, and the feeling brain.* Orlando, FL: Harcourt.

Dance, F. E. X. (Ed.). (1967). *Human communication theory: Original essays.* New York: Holt, Rinehart & Winston.

Dance, F. E. X. (Ed.). (1982). *Human communication theory: Comparative essays.* New York: Harper & Row.

Dance, F. E. X., & Larson, C. E. (1976). *The functions of human communication: A theoretical approach.* New York: Holt, Rinehart & Winston.

Danet, B. (2001). *Cyberpl@y: Communicating online.* New York: Berg.

Dawkins, R. (1989). *The selfish gene.* London: Oxford University Press.

Debray, R. (1981). *Teachers, writers, celebrities: The intellectuals of modern France* (D. Macey, Trans.). London: NLB.

Debray, R. (1996). *Media manifestos: On the technological transmission of cultural forms* (E. Rauth, Trans.). New York: Verso.

Debray, R. (2000). *Transmitting culture* (E. Rauth, Trans.). New York: Columbia University Press.

de Kerckhove, D. (1995). *The skin of culture: Investigating the new electronic reality.* Toronto: Sommerville.

de Kerckhove, D. (1997). *Connected intelligence: The arrival of the web society.* Toronto: Sommerville.

de Kerckhove, D. (2001). *The architecture of intelligence.* Boston: Birkhauser.

Deibert, R. J. (1997). *Parchment, printing, and hypermedia: Communication in world order transformation.* New York: Columbia University Press.

DeLuca, K. M. (1999). *Image politics: The new rhetoric of environmental activism.* New York: Guilford Press.

Derrida, J. (1973). *Speech and phenomena: And other essays on Husserl's theory of signs* (D. B. Allison, Trans.). Evanston: Northwestern University Press.

Derrida, J. (1976). *Of grammatology* (G. C. Spivak, Trans.). Baltimore: Johns Hopkins University Press.

Derrida, J. (1978). *Writing and difference* (A. Bass, Trans.). Chicago: University of Chicago Press.

Dewdney, C. (1998). *Last flesh: Life in the transhuman era*. Toronto: HarperCollins.

Donald, M. (1991). *Origins of the modern mind: Three stages in the evolution of culture and cognition*. Cambridge, MA: Harvard University Press.

Drucker, P. F. (1942). *The future of industrial man*. New Brunswick, NJ: Transaction.

Drucker, P. F. (1946). *The concept of the corporation*. New Brunswick, NJ: Transaction.

Drucker, P. F. (1959). *Landmarks of tomorrow*. New Brunswick, NJ: Transaction.

Drucker, P. F. (1968). *The age of discontinuity: Guidelines to our changing society*. New Brunswick, NJ: Transaction.

Drucker, P. F. (1970). *Technology, management & society*. New York: Harper & Row.

Drucker, P. F. (1979). *Adventures of a bystander*. New York: Harper & Row.

Drucker, P. F. (1989). *The new realities: In government and politics, in economics and business, in society and world view*. New York: Harper & Row.

Drucker, P. F. (1993). *Post-capitalist society*. New York: Harperbusiness.

Drucker, P. F. (2000). *The ecological vision: Reflections on the American condition*. New Brunswick, NJ: Transaction.

Drucker, S. J., & Cathcart R. (Eds.). (1994). *American heroes in a media age*. Cresskill, NJ: Hampton Press.

Drucker, S. J., & Gumpert, G. (Eds.). (1997). *Voices in the street: Explorations in gender, media, and public space*. Cresskill, NJ: Hampton Press.

Drucker, S. J., & Gumpert, G. (Eds.). (1999). *Real law @ virtual space: Communication regulation in cyberspace*. Cresskill, NJ: Hampton Press.

Dunbar, R. (1996). *Grooming, gossip, and the evolution of language*. Cambridge, MA: Harvard University Press.

Duncan, H. D. (1968a). *Communication and social order*. London: Oxford University Press.

Duncan, H. D. (1968b). *Symbols in society*. New York: Oxford University Press.

Durig, A. (1996). *Autism and the crisis of meaning*. Albany: State University of New York Press.

Eastham, S. (1990). *The media matrix: Deepening the context of communication studies*. Lanham, MD: University Press of America.

Eastham., S. (2003). *Biotech time-bomb: How genetic engineering could irreversibly change the world*. Ponsonby, New Zealand: RSVP.

Edelman, G. M. (1987). *Neural Darwinism: The theory of neuronal group selection*. New York: Basic Books.

Edelman, G. M. (1992). *Bright air, brilliant fire: On the matter of the mind*. New York: Basic Books.

Ehrenfeld, D. (1978). *The arrogance of humanism*. Oxford: Oxford University Press.

Einstein, A. (1954). *Relativity, the special and the general theory: A popular exposition* (Rev. ed., R.W. Lawson, Trans.). London: Methuen.

Eisenstein, E. L. (1979). *The printing press as an agent of change: Communications and cultural transformations in early modern Europe* (2 vols.). New York: Cambridge University Press.

Eisenstein, E. L. (1980). *The printing press as an agent of change*. New York: Cambridge University Press.

Eisenstein, E. L. (1983). *The printing revolution in early modern Europe*. New York: Cambridge University Press.

Ellul, J. (1951). *The presence of the kingdom* (O. Wyon, Trans.). Philadelphia: Westminster..

Ellul, J. (1964). *The technological society* (J. Wilkinson, Trans.). New York: Knopf.

Ellul, J. (1965). *Propaganda: The formation of men's attitudes* (K. Kellen & J. Lerner, Trans.). New York: Vintage.

Ellul, J. (1967). *The political illusion* (K. Kellen, Trans.). New York: Vintage.

Ellul, J. (1970). *The meaning of the city* (D. Pardee, Trans.). Grand Rapids, MI: Eerdmans.

Ellul, J. (1976). *The ethics of freedom* (G. W. Bromiley, Trans.). Grand Rapids, MI: Eerdmans.

Ellul, J. (1980). *The technological system* (J. Neugroschel, Trans.). New York: Continuum.

Ellul, J. (1981). *Perspectives on our age: Jacques Ellul speaks on his life and work* (W. H. Vanderburg, Ed., J. Neugroschel, Trans.). New York: Seabury.

Ellul, J. (1982). *In season, out of season: An introduction to the thought of Jacques Ellul: Interviews by Madeleine Garrigou-Lagrange* (L. K. Niles, Trans.). San Francisco: Harper and Row.

Ellul, J. (1985). *The humiliation of the word* (J. M. Hanks, Trans.). Grand Rapids, MI: Eerdmans.

Ellul, J. (1990). *The technological bluff* (G. W. Bromiley, Trans.). Grand Rapids, MI: Eerdmans.

Ellul, J. (1991). *Anarchy and Christianity* (G. W. Bromiley, Trans.). Grand Rapids, MI: Eerdmans.

Ellul, J. (1997). *Sources and trajectories: Eight early articles by Jacques Ellul that set the stage* (M. J. Dawn, Trans. and Ed.). Grand Rapids, MI: Eerdmans.

Ellul, J. (1998). *Jacques Ellul on religion, technology, and politics: Conversations with Patrick Troude-Chastenet* (J. M. France, Trans.). Atlanta: Scholars Press.

Erikson, E. H. (1950). *Childhood and society*. New York: W. W. Norton.

Erikson, E. H. (1980). *Identity and the life cycle*. New York: W. W. Norton.

Esté, A. (1997). *Cultura replicante: El orden semiocentrista*. Barcelona: Editorial Gedisa.

Farrell, T. J. (2000). *Walter Ong's contribution to cultural studies: Phenomenology and I-thou communication*. Cresskill, NJ: Hampton Press.

Febvre, L., & Martin, H.-J. (1976). *The coming of the book: The impact of printing, 1450-1800* (D. Gerard, Trans.). London: Verso.

Forsdale, L. (1981). *Perspectives on communication*. Reading, MA: Addison-Wesley.

Foucault, M. (1971). *The order of things: An archeology of the human sciences*. New York: Pantheon Books.

Foucault, M. (1972). *The archeology of knowledge* (A. M. Sheridan Smith, Trans.). New York: Pantheon Books.

Foucault, M. (1977). *Discipline and punish: The birth of the prison* (A. Sheridan, Trans.). New York: Pantheon Books.

Fraim, J. (2003). *Battle of symbols: Global dynamics of advertising, entertainment, and media*. Einsiedeln, Switzerland: Daimon.

Freud, S. (1961). *The future of an illusion* (J. Strachey, Trans.). New York: W. W. Norton.

Freud, S. (1962). *Civilization and its discontents* (J. Strachey, Trans.). New York: W. W. Norton.

Freud, S. (1966). *Introductory lectures on psychoanalysis* (J. Strachey, Trans.). New York: W. W. Norton.

Frith, U. (1989). *Autism: Explaining the enigma.* Oxford: Blackwell.

Fromm, E. (1965). *Escape from freedom.* New York: Avon Books.

Fry, K. (2003). *Constructing the heartland: Television news and natural disaster.* Cresskill, NJ: Hampton Press.

Fuller, R. B. (1971). *Operating manual for spaceship earth.* New York: E.P. Dutton.

Fuller, R. B., Agel, J., & Fiore, Q. (1970). *I seem to be a verb.* New York: Bantam.

Fuller, R. B., & Applewhite, E. J. (1975). *Synergetics: Explorations in the geometry of thinking.* New York: Macmillan.

Gabler, N. (1998). *Life the movie: How entertainment conquered reality.* New York: Knopf.

Gardner, H. (1983). *Frames of mind: The theory of multiple intelligences.* New York: BasicBooks.

Gardner, H. (1993). *Multiple intelligences: The theory in practice.* New York: BasicBooks.

Gardner, H. (1997). *Extraordinary minds: Portraits of exceptional individuals and an examination of our own extraordinariness.* New York: BasicBooks.

Geddes, P. (1904). *City development: A study of parks, gardens and culture institutes: A report to the Carnegie Dunfermline Trust.* Edinburgh: Geddes and Colleagues.

Geddes, P. (1915). *Cities in evolution: An introduction to the town planning movement and to the study of civics.* London: Williams and Norgate.

Gelb, I. J. (1963). *A study of writing* (rev. ed.). Chicago: University of Chicago Press.

Gencarelli, T. F.. (2000). The intellectual roots of media ecology in the thought and work of Neil Postman. *The New Jersey Journal of Communication 8*(1), 91-103.

Genosko, G. (1999). *McLuhan and Baudrillard: Masters of implosion.* London: Routledge.

Gergen, K. J. (1991). *The saturated self: Dilemmas of identity in contemporary life.* New York: BasicBooks.

Gibson, S. B., & Oviedo, O. O. (Eds.). (2000). *The emerging cyberculture: Literacy, paradigm, and paradox.* Cresskill, NJ: Hampton Press.

Giddens, A. (1991). *Modernity and self-identity: Self and society in the late modern age.* Stanford, CA: Stanford University Press.

Giedion, S. (1947). *Space, time and architecture: The growth of a new tradition.* Cambridge, MA: Harvard University Press.

Giedion, S. (1948). *Mechanization takes command: A contribution to anonymous history.* New York: Oxford University Press.

Gilman, P. (1992). *Something from nothing.* New York: Scholastic.

Gitlin, T. (1995). *The twilight of common dreams: Why America is wracked by culture wars.* New York: Metropolitan Books.

Gleick, J. (1987). *Chaos: Making a new science.* New York: Viking Penguin.

Goffman, E. (1959). *The presentation of self in everyday life*. Garden City, NY: Anchor Books.

Goffman, E. (1961). *Asylums: Essays on the social situation of mental patients and other inmates*. Garden City, NY: Anchor Books.

Goffman, E. (1963). *Behavior in public places: Notes on the social organization of gatherings*. New York: Free Press.

Goffman, E. (1967). *Interaction ritual: Essays on face-to-face behavior*. Garden City, NY: Anchor Books.

Goffman, E. (1974). *Frame analysis: An essay on the organization of experience*. New York: Harper & Row.

Goffman, E. (1979). *Gender advertisements*. New York: Harper & Row.

Goffman, E. (1981). *Forms of talk*. Philadelphia: University of Pennsylvania Press.

Gombrich, E. H. (1960). *Art and illusion: A study in the psychology of pictorial representation*. New York: Pantheon.

Gombrich, E. H. (1984). *The sense of order: A study in the psychology of decorative art*. London: Phaidon.

Goody, J. (1968). (Ed.). *Literacy in traditional societies*. Cambridge, UK: Cambridge University Press.

Goody, J. (1977). *The domestication of the savage mind*. Cambridge, UK: Cambridge University Press.

Goody, J. (1986). *The logic of writing and the organization of society*. Cambridge, UK: Cambridge University Press.

Goody, J. (1987). *The interface between the written and the oral*. Cambridge, UK: Cambridge University Press.

Goody, J. (2000). *The power of the written tradition*. Cambridge, UK: Cambridge University Press.

Gordon, W. T. (1997). *Marshall McLuhan: Escape into understanding*. New York: Basic Books.

Gozzi, R. Jr. (1990). *New words and a changing American culture*. Columbia: University of South Carolina Press.

Gozzi, R. Jr. (1999). *The power of metaphor in the age of electronic media*. Cresskill, NJ: Hampton Press.

Grandin, T. (1995). *Thinking in pictures and other reports from my life with autism*. New York: Random House.

Grandin, T., & Scariano, M. M. (1986). *Emergence: Labeled autistic*. Novato, CA: Arena Press.

Greenspan, S. I., Wieder, S., & Simons, R. (1998). *The child with special needs: Encouraging intellectual and emotional growth*. Reading, MA: Addison-Westey.

Gregory, R. L. (1970). *The intelligent eye*. New York: McGraw-Hill.

Gregory, R. L. (1973). *Eye and brain: The psychology of seeing* (2nd ed.). New York: McGraw-Hill.

Gronbeck. B. E., Farrell, T. J., & Soukup, P. A. (Eds.). (1991). *Media, consciousness, and culture: Explorations of Walter Ong's thought*. Newbury Park, CA: Sage.

Grosswiler, P. (1998). *Method is the message: Rethinking McLuhan through critical theory*. Montreal: Black Rose Books.

Gumpert, G. (1987). *Talking tombstones and other tales of the media age*. New York: Oxford University Press.

Gumpert, G., & Cathcart, R. (Eds.). (1979). *Inter/media: Interpersonal communication in a media world.* New York: Oxford University Press.

Gumpert, G., & Cathcart, R. (Eds.). (1982). *Inter/media: Interpersonal communication in a media world* (2nd ed.). New York: Oxford University Press.

Gumpert, G., & Cathcart, R. (Eds.). (1986). *Inter/media: Interpersonal communication in a media world* (3rd ed.). New York: Oxford University Press.

Gumpert, G., & Drucker, S. J. (Eds.). (1998). *The huddled masses: Communication and immigration.* Cresskill, NJ: Hampton Press.

Gumpert, G., & Drucker, S. J. (Eds.). (2002). *Take me out to the ballgame: Communicating baseball.* Cresskill, NJ: Hampton Press.

Gumpert, G., & Fish, S. L. (1990). *Talking to strangers: Mediated therapeutic communication.* Norwood, NJ: Ablex.

Haddon, M. (2003). *The curious incident of the dog in the night-time.* New York: Doubleday.

Hall, E. T. (1959). *The silent language.* Garden City, NY: Doubleday.

Hall, E. T. (1966). *The hidden dimension.* Garden City, NY: Doubleday.

Hall, E. T. (1976). *Beyond culture.* Garden City, NY: Anchor Press.

Hall, E. T. (1983). *The dance of life: The other dimension of time.* Garden City, NY: Anchor Press.

Havelock, E. A. (1950). *The crucifixion of intellectual man.* Boston: Beacon Press.

Havelock, E.A. (1963). *Preface to Plato.* Cambridge, MA: The Belknap Press of Harvard University Press.

Havelock, E.A. (1976). *Origins of western literacy.* Toronto: The Ontario Institute for Studies in Education.

Havelock, E.A. (1978). *The Greek concept of justice: From its shadow in Homer to its substance in Plato.* Cambridge, MA: Harvard University Press.

Havelock, E. A. (1982a). *Harold Innis: A memoir.* Toronto: Harold Innis Foundation.

Havelock, E.A. (1982b). *The literate revolution in Greece and its cultural consequences.* Princeton, NJ: Princeton University Press.

Havelock, E.A. (1986). *The muse learns to write: Reflections on orality and literacy from antiquity to the present.* New Haven, CT: Yale University Press.

Havelock, E. A., & Hershbell, J. P. (Eds.). (1978). *Communication arts in the ancient world.* New York: Hastings House.

Hawking, S. W. (1998). *A brief history of time* (rev. ed.). New York: Bantam Books.

Hayakawa, S. I., & Hayakawa, A. R. (1990). *Language in thought and action* (5th ed.). San Diego: Harcourt Brace.

Hayles, N. K. (1999). *How we became posthuman: Virtual bodies in cybernetics, literature, and informatics.* Chicago: University of Chicago Press.

Hayles, N. K. (2002). *Writing machines.* Cambridge, MA: MIT Press.

Heidegger, M. (1973). *The question concerning technology and other essays* (W. Lovitt, Trans.). New York: Harper & Row.

Heim, M. (1987). *Electric language: A philosophical study of word processing.* New Haven: Yale University Press.

Heim, M. (1993). *The metaphysics of virtual reality.* New York: Oxford University Press.

Heisenberg, W. (1958). *Physics and philosophy: The revolution in modern science.* Amherst, NY: Prometheus Books.

Herman, E. S., & Chomsky, N. (1988). *Manufacturing consent: The political economy of the mass media.* New York: Pantheon.

Heyer, P. (1988). *Communications and history: Theories of media, knowledge, and civilization.* New York: Greenwood Press.

Heyer, P. (2003). *Harold Innis.* Lanham, MD: Rowman & Littlefield.

Hobart, M. E., & Schiffman, Z. S. (1998). *Information ages: Literacy, numeracy, and the computer revolution.* Baltimore: John Hopkins University Press.

Hofstadter, D. R. (1979). *Gödel, Escher, Bach: An eternal golden braid.* New York: Basic Books.

Howlin, P., Baron-Cohen, S., & Hadwin, J. (1999). *Teaching children with autism to mind-read: A practical guide.* Chichester: John Wiley & Sons.

Huizinga, J. (1955). *Homo ludens: A study of the play element in culture.* Boston: Beacon.

Hunt, A. W. (2003). *The vanishing word: The veneration of visual imagery in the postmodern world.* Wheaton, IL: Crossway Books.

Ihde, D. (1973). *Sense and significance.* Pittsburgh: Duquesne University Press.

Ihde, D. (1976). *Listening and voice: A phenomenology of sound.* Athens: Ohio University Press.

Ihde, D. (1979). *Technics and praxis.* Boston: D. Reidel.

Ihde, D. (1983). *Existential technics.* Albany: State University of New York Press.

Ihde, D. (1990). *Technology and the lifeworld: From garden to earth.* Bloomington: Indiana University Press.

Ihde, D. (1991). *Instrumental realism: The interface between philosophy of science and philosophy of technology.* Bloomington: Indiana University Press.

Ihde, D. (1998). *Expanding hermeneutics: Visualism in science.* Evanston, IL: Northwestern University Press.

Ihde, D. (2002). *Bodies in technology.* Minneapolis: University of Minnesota Press.

Illich, I. (1971). *Deschooling society.* New York: Harper Colophon.

Illich, I. (1973). *Tools for conviviality.* New York: Harper & Row.

Illich, I. (1974). *Energy and equity.* New York: Harper & Row.

Illich, I. (1975). *Medical nemesis: The expropriation of health.* London: Calder & Boyars.

Illich, I. (1977) *Disabling professions.* London: M. Boyars.

Illich, I. (1985). *H2O and the waters of forgetfulness: Reflections on the historicity of "stuff."* Dallas: Dallas Institute of Humanities and Culture.

Illich, I., & Sanders, B. (1989). *ABC: The alphabetization of the popular mind.* New York: Vintage.

Innis, H. A. (1949). *The press: A neglected factor in the economic history of the twentieth century.* London: Oxford University Press.

Innis, H. A. (1951). *The bias of communication.* Toronto: University of Toronto Press.

Innis, H. A. (1972). *Empire and communications* (rev. ed., M. Q. Innis, Ed.). Toronto: University of Toronto Press.

Innis, H. A. (1980). *The idea file of Harold Innis* (W. Christian, Ed.). Toronto: University of Toronto Press.

Innis, H. A. (2004). *Changing concepts of time.* Lanham, MD: Rowman & Littlefield.

Jameson, F. (1972). *The prison-house of language: A critical account of structuralism and Russian formalism.* Princeton: Princeton University Press.

Jameson, F. (1991). *Postmodernism, or, the cultural logic of late capitalism*. Durham, NC: Duke University Press.

Jaynes, J. (1976). *The origin of consciousness in the breakdown of the bicameral mind*. Boston: Houghton Mifflin.

Jensen, J. (1990). *Redeeming modernity: Contradictions in media criticism*. Newbury Park, CA: Sage.

Johnson, M. (1987). *The body in the mind: The bodily basis of meaning, imagination, and reason*. Chicago: University of Chicago Press.

Johnson, S. (1997). *Interface culture: How new technology transforms the way we create and communicate*. San Francisco: HarperEdge.

Johnson, S. (2001). *Emergence: The connected lives of ants, brains, cities, and software*. New York: Scribner.

Johnson, W. (1946). *People in quandries: The semantics of personal adjustment*. New York: Harper & Row.

Jones, S. (1992). *Rock formation: Music, technology, and mass communication*. Newbury Park, CA: Sage.

Jung, C. G. (1969). *The archetypes and the collective unconscious* (R. F. C. Hull, Trans.). Princeton: Princeton University Press

Jung, C. G. (1978). *Aion: Researches into the phenomenology of the self* (R. F. C. Hull, Trans.). Princeton: Princeton University Press

Katsh, M. E. (1989). *The electronic media and the transformation of law*. New York: Oxford University Press.

Katsh, M. E. (1995). *Law in a digital world*. New York: Oxford University Press.

Kaufer, D. S., & Carley, K. M. (1993). *Communication at a distance: The influence of print on sociocutural organization and change*. Hillsdale, NJ: Erlbaum.

Kauffman, S. A. (1993). *The origins of order: Self-organization and selection in evolution*. New York: Oxford University Press.

Kauffman, S. A. (1995). *At home in the universe: The search for the laws of self-organization and complexity*. New York: Oxford University Press.

Kauffman, S. A. (2000). *Investigations*. New York: Oxford University Press.

Kelly, K. (1994). *Out of control: The rise of neo-biological civilization*. Reading, MA: Addison-Wesley.

Kittler, F. A. (1990). *Discourse networks 1800/1900* (M. Metteer with C. Cullens, Trans.). Stanford: Stanford University Press.

Kittler, F. A. (1997). *Literature, media, information systems: Essays* (J. Johnston, Ed.). Amsterdam: GB Arts International.

Kittler, F. A. (1999). *Gramophone, film, typewriter* (G. Winthrop-Young & M. Wutz, Trans.). Stanford: Stanford University Press.

Korzybski, A. (1993). *Science and sanity: An introduction to non-Aristotelian systems and general semantics* (5th ed.). Englewood, NJ: The International Non-Aristotelian Library/Institute of General Semantics.

Kozol, J. (1986). *Illiterate America*. New York: New American Library.

Kranowitz, C. S. (1998). *The out of sync child: Recognizing and coping with sensory integration dysfunction*. New York: Perigee.

Kroker, A. (1984). *Technology and the Canadian mind: Innis/McLuhan/Grant*. New York: St. Martin's Press.

Kroker, A. (1993). *Spasm: Virtual reality, android music, and electric flesh.* New York: St. Martin's Press.

Kroker, A., & Cook, D. (1987). *The postmodern scene: Excremental culture and hyper-aesthetics.* New York: St. Martin's Press.

Kroker, A., & Kroker, M. (Eds.). (1997). *Digital delirium.* New York: St. Martin's Press.

Kuhns, W. (1969). *Environmental man.* New York: Harper & Row.

Kuhns, W. (1971). *The post-industrial prophets: Interpretations of technology.* New York: Weybright & Talley.

Laing, R. D. (1965). *The divided self: An existential study in sanity and madness.* Harmondsworth: Penguin.

Laing, R. D. (1969). *Self and others* (2nd ed.). Harmondsworth: Penguin.

Lakoff, G. (1987). *Women, fire, and dangerous things: What categories reveal about the mind.* Chicago: University of Chicago Press.

Lakoff, G., & Johnson, M. (1980). *Metaphors we live by.* Chicago: University of Chicago Press.

Lakoff, G., & Johnson, M. (1989). *More than cool reason: A field guide to poetic metaphor.* Chicago: University of Chicago Press.

Lakoff, G., & Johnson, M. (1999). *Philosophy in the flesh: The embodied mind and its challenge to Western thought.* New York: Basic Books.

Landes, D. S. (2000). *Revolution in time: Clocks and the making of the modern world* (rev. & enlarged ed.). Cambridge, MA: Harvard University Press.

Landow, G. P. (1992). *Hypertext: The convergence of contemporary critical theory and technology.* Baltimore: John Hopkins University Press.

Landow, G. P. (1997). *Hypertext 2.0: The convergence of contemporary critical theory and technology.* Baltimore: Johns Hopkins University Press.

Lane, H. (1977). *The wild boy of Aveyron.* Cambridge, MA: Harvard University Press.

Langer, S. K. K. (1953). *Feeling and form: A theory of art.* New York: Scribner.

Langer, S. K. K. (1957). *Philosophy in a new key: A study in the symbolism of reason, rite and art* (3rd ed.). Cambridge, MA: Harvard University Press.

Langer, S. K. K. (1967). *Mind: An essay on human feeling* (Vol. 1). Baltimore: Johns Hopkins Press.

Langer, S. K. K. (1972). *Mind: An essay on human feeling* (Vol. 2). Baltimore: Johns Hopkins Press.

Langer, S. K. K. (1982). *Mind: An essay on human feeling* (Vol. 3). Baltimore: Johns Hopkins Press.

Lanham, R.A. (1993). *The electronic word: Democracy, technology, and the arts.* Chicago: University of Chicago Press.

Lasch, C. (1979). *The culture of narcissism: American life in an age of diminishing expectations.* New York: W. W. Norton.

Lasch, C. (1991). *The true and only heaven: Progress and its critics.* New York: W. W. Norton.

Lasch, C. (1995). *The revolt of the elites: And the betrayal of democracy.* New York: W. W. Norton.

Laszlo, E. (1972). *The systems view of the world: The natural philosophy of the new developments in the sciences.* New York: G. Braziller.

Laszlo, E. (1996). *The systems view of the world: A holistic vision for our time.* Cresskill, NJ: Hampton Press.

Lee, D. (1959). *Freedom and culture.* Englewood Cliffs, NJ: Prentice-Hall.

Lee, D. (1976). *Valuing the self: What we can learn from other cultures.* Englewood Cliffs, NJ: Prentice-Hall.

Leverette, M. (2003). *Professional wrestling: The myth, the mat, and American popular culture.* Lewiston, NY: Edwin Mellen Press.

Levinson, P. (Ed.). (1982). *In pursuit of truth: Essays on the philosophy of Karl Popper on the occasion of his 80th birthday.* Atlantic Highlands, NJ: Humanities Press.

Levinson, P. (1988). *Mind at large: Knowing in the technological age.* Greenwich, CT: JAI Press.

Levinson, P. (1992). *Electronic chronicles: Columns of the changes in our time.* San Francisco: Anamnesis Press.

Levinson, P. (1995). *Learning cyberspace: Essays on the evolution of media and the new education.* San Francisco: Anamnesis Press.

Levinson, P. (1997). *The soft edge: A natural history and future of the information revolution.* London & New York: Routledge.

Levinson, P. (1999). *Digital McLuhan: A guide to the information millennium.* London & New York: Routledge.

Levinson, P. (2000). McLuhan and media ecology. *Proceedings of the Media Ecology Association 1,* 17-22. [Electronic version, retrieved April 27, 2004 from http://www.media-ecology.org/publications/proceedings/v1/McLuhan_and_media_ecology.html]

Levinson, P. (2003). *Realspace: The fate of physical presence in the digital age, on and off planet.* London & New York: Routledge.

Levinson, P. (2004). *Cellphone: The story of the world's most mobile medium, and how it has transformed everything.* New York: Palgrave Macmillan.

Lévi-Strauss, C. (1966). *The savage mind.* Chicago: University of Chicago Press.

Lévi-Strauss, C. (1967). *Structural anthropology* (C. Jacobson & B. G. Schoepf, Trans.). Garden City, NY: Anchor Books.

Lévi-Strauss, C. (1969). *The raw and the cooked* (J. Weightman & D. Weightman, Trans.). New York: Harper & Row.

Linton, S. (1998). *Claiming disability: Knowledge and identity.* New York: New York University Press.

Logan, R.K. (1986). *The alphabet effect: The impact of the phonetic alphabet on the development of Western civilization.* New York: William Morrow.

Logan, R. K. (1997). *The fifth language: Learning a living in the computer age.* Toronto: Stoddard.

Logan, R. K. (2000). *The sixth language: Learning a living in the Internet age.* Toronto: Stoddard.

Logan, R. K. (2004). *The alphabet effect: A media ecology understanding of the making of western civilization.* Cresskill, NJ: Hampton Press.

Lord, A. B. (1960). *The singer of tales.* Cambridge, MA: Harvard University Press.

Lovaas, O. I. (1981). *Teaching developmentally disabled children: The ME book.* Austin, TX: Pro-Ed.

Luhmann, N. (1982). *The differentiation of society* (S. Holmes & C. Larmore, Trans.). New York: Columbia University Press.

Luhmann, N. (1989). *Ecological communication* (J. Bednarz, Jr., Trans.). Chicago: University of Chicago Press.

Luhmann, N. (1995). *Social systems* (J. Bednarz, Jr. with D. Baecker, Trans.). Stanford: Stanford University Press.

Luhmann, N. (2000a). *Art as a social system* (E. M. Knodt, Trans.). Stanford: Stanford University Press.

Luhmann, N. (2000b). *The reality of the mass media* (K. Cross, Trans.). Stanford: Stanford University Press.

Lule, J. (2001). *Daily news, eternal stories: The mythological role of journalism.* New York: Guilford Press.

Lum, C. M. K. (1996). *In search of a voice: Karaoke and the construction of identity in Chinese America.* Mahwah, NJ: Erlbaum.

Lum, C. M. K. (Ed.). (2006). *Perspectives on culture, technology, and communication: The media ecology tradition.* Cresskill, NJ: Hampton Press.

Lupton, E. (1993). *Mechanical brides: Women and machines from home to office.* New York: Cooper Hewitt National Museum of Design Smithsonian Institution & Princeton Architectural Press.

Luriia, A. R. (1981). *Language and cognition* (J. Y. Wertsch, Trans.). Washington, DC: V. H. Winston.

Lyotard, J.-F. (1984). *The postmodern condition: A report on knowledge* (G. Bennington & B. Massumi, Trans.). Minneapolis: University of Minnesota Press.

Lyotard, J.-F. (1991). *The inhuman: Reflections on time* (G. Bennington & R. Bowlby, Trans.). Stanford: Stanford University Press.

Madaule, P. (1994). *When listening comes alive: A guide to effective learning and communication* (2nd ed.). Norval, ON: Moulin.

Mander, J. (1978). *Four arguments for the elimination of television.* New York: Morrow.

Mander, J. (1991). *In the absence of the sacred: The failure of technology and the survival of the Indian nations.* San Francisco: Sierra Club Books.

Manovich, L. (2001). *The language of new media.* Cambridge, MA: MIT Press.

Marchand, P. (1989). *Marshall McLuhan: The medium and the messenger.* New York: Ticknor & Fields.

Martin, H.-J. (1994). *The history and power of writing* (L.G. Cochrane, Trans.). Chicago: University of Chicago Press.

Marvin, C. (1988). *When old technologies were new: Thinking about electric communication in the late nineteenth century.* New York: Oxford University Press.

Marx, K. (1967). *Capital: A critique of political economy* (F. Engels, Ed., S. Moore & E. Aveling, Trans.). New York: International.

Marx, K., & Engels, F. (1972). *The German ideology* (C. J. Arthur, Ed.). New York: International.

Maturana, H. R., & Varela, F. J. (1980). *Autopoiesis and cognition: The realization of the living.* Boston: D. Reidel.

Maturana, H. R., & Varela, F. J. (1992). *The tree of knowledge: The biological roots of human understanding* (rev. ed., R. Paolucci, Trans.). Boston: Shambhala.

Maurice, C. (1993a). *Let me hear your voice: A family's triumph over autism.* New York: Fawcett Columbine.

Maurice, C. (Ed.). (1993b). *Behavioral intervention for young children with autism: A manual for parents and professionals*. Austin, TX: Pro-Ed.

McCloud, S. (1993). *Understanding comics: The invisible art*. New York: Paradox Press.

McCloud, S. (2000). *Reinventing comics*. New York: Paradox Press.

McLuhan, E. (1997). *The role of thunder in Finnegans Wake*. Toronto: University of Toronto Press.

McLuhan, E. (1998). *Electric language: Understanding the message*. New York: Buzz Books.

McLuhan, M. (1960). *Report on project in understanding new media*. Washington, DC: U.S. Department of Health.

McLuhan, M. (1962). *The Gutenberg galaxy: The making of typographic man*. Toronto: University of Toronto Press.

McLuhan, M. (1964). *Understanding media: The extensions of man*. New York: McGraw Hill.

McLuhan, M. (1969). *The interior landscape: The literary criticism of Marshall McLuhan, 1943-1962* (E. McNamara, Ed.). New York: McGraw-Hill.

McLuhan, M. (1970). *Culture is our business*. New York: McGraw-Hill.

McLuhan, M. (1987). *The letters of Marshall McLuhan* (M. Molinaro, C. McLuhan, & W. Toye, Eds.). Toronto: Oxford University Press.

McLuhan, M. (1989). Violence of the media. In G. Sanderson & F. Macdonald (Eds.), *Marshall McLuhan: The man and his message* (pp. 92-98). Golden, CO: Fulcrum.

McLuhan, M. (1995). *Essential McLuhan* (E. McLuhan & F. Zingrone, Eds.). New York: Basic Books.

McLuhan, M. (1997). *Media research: Technology, art, communication* (M. A. Moos, Ed.). Amsterdam: G+B Arts International.

McLuhan, M. (1999). *The medium and the light: Reflections on religion* (E. McLuhan & J. Szklarek, Eds.). Toronto: Stoddart.

McLuhan, M. (2002). *The mechanical bride: Folklore of industrial man*. Corte Madera, CA: Gingko Press. (Original work published 1951)

McLuhan, M. (2003a). *Understanding media: The extensions of man* (Critical Ed., W. T. Gordon, Ed.). (Original work published 1964)

McLuhan, M. (2003b). *Understanding me: Lectures and interviews* (S. McLuhan & D. Staines, Eds.). Cambridge, MA: MIT Press.

McLuhan, M., & Carson, D. (2004). *The book of probes* (E. McLuhan & W. Kuhns, Eds.). Corte Madera, CA: Ginko Press.

McLuhan, M., & Fiore, Q. (1967). *The medium is the massage: An inventory of effects*. Corte Madera, CA: Gingko Press

McLuhan, M., & Fiore, Q. (1968). *War and peace in the global village: An inventory of some of the current spastic situations that could be eliminated by more feedforward*. Corte Madera, CA: Gingko Press

McLuhan, M., & McLuhan, E. (1988). *Laws of media: The new science*. Toronto: University of Toronto Press.

McLuhan, M., & Nevitt, B. (1972). *Take today: The executive as dropout*. New York: Harcourt Brace Jovanovich.

McLuhan, M., & Parker, H. (1968). *Through the vanishing point: Space in poetry and painting.* New York: Harper & Row.

McLuhan, M., & Parker, H. (1969). *Counterblast.* New York: Harcourt, Brace & World.

McLuhan, M., & Powers, B. R. (1989). *The global village: Transformations in world life and media in the twenty-first century.* New York: Oxford University Press.

McLuhan, M., & Watson, W. (1970). *From cliché to archetype.* New York: Viking Press.

McLuhan-Ortved, S. (Producer), & Wolfe, T. (Writer). (1996). *The video McLuhan* [Video]. (Available from Video McLuhan Inc., 73 Sighthill Avenue, Toronto Ontario M4T 2H1 Canada)

McMahon, K. (Director), & Sobelman, D. (Writer). (2002). *McLuhan's Wake* [Video]. (Available from National Film Board of Canada Library, 22-D Hollywood Avenue, Ho-Ho-Kus, New Jersey, 07423)

McWhorter, J. (2003). *Doing our own thing: The degradation of language and music and why we should, like, care.* New York: Gotham.

Mead, G. H. (1934). *Mind, self and society from the standpoint of a social behaviorist* (C. W. Morris, Ed.). Chicago: University of Chicago Press.

Meyrowitz, J. (1985). *No sense of place: The impact of electronic media on social behavior.* New York: Oxford University Press.

Milgram, S. (1974). *Obedience to authority: An experimental view.* New York: Harper & Row.

Milgram, S. (1992). *The individual in a social world: Essays and experiments* (2nd ed., J. Sabini & M. Silver, Eds.). New York: McGraw Hill.

Milgram, S. & Shotland, R. L. (1973). *Television and antisocial behavior: Field experiments.* New York: Academic Press.

Miller, D. L. (1989). *Lewis Mumford: A life.* New York: Weidenfeld & Nicolson.

Mitcham, C. (1994). *Thinking through technology: The path between engineering and philosophy.* Chicago: University of Chicago Press.

Mitchell, W. J. (1992). *The reconfigured eye: Visual truth in the post-photographic era.* Cambridge, MA: MIT Press.

Mitchell, W. J. (1995). *City of bits: Space, place, and the infobahn.* Cambridge, MA: MIT Press.

Mitchell, W. J. (1999). *e-topia: "Urban life, Jim—but not as we know it."* Cambridge, MA: MIT Press.

Mitchell, W. J. (2003). *Me++: The cyborg self and the networked city.* Cambridge, MA: MIT Press.

Mitroff, I. I., & Bennis, W. G. (1989). *The unreality industry: The deliberate manufacturing of falsehood and what it is doing to our lives.* New York: Oxford University Press.

Mumford, L. (1924). *Sticks and stones: A study of American architecture and civilization.* New York: Boni and Liveright.

Mumford, L. (1926). *The golden day: A study in American experience and culture.* New York: Boni and Liveright.

Mumford, L. (1929). *Herman Melville.* New York: Harcourt Brace.

Mumford, L. (1931). *The brown decades: A study of the arts in America, 1865-1895.* New York: Harcourt Brace.

Mumford, L. (1934). *Technics and civilization.* New York: Harcourt Brace.

Mumford, L. (1938). *The culture of cities.* New York: Harcourt, Brace.

Mumford, L. (1941). *The South in architecture.* New York: Harcourt, Brace.

Mumford, L. (1944). *The condition of man.* New York: Harcourt, Brace.

Mumford, L. (1945). *City development.* New York: Harcourt, Brace.

Mumford, L. (1952). *Art and technics.* New York: Columbia University Press.

Mumford, L. (1954). *In the name of sanity.* New York: Harcourt, Brace.

Mumford, L. (1956a). *From the ground up.* New York: Harcourt, Brace.

Mumford, L. (1956b). *The transformations of man.* New York: Harper & Bros.

Mumford, L. (1961). *The city in history: Its origins, its transformations, and its prospects.* New York: Harcourt Brace and World.

Mumford, L. (1963). *The highway and the city.* New York: Harcourt Brace and World.

Mumford, L. (1967). *The myth of the machine: I. Technics and human development.* New York: Harcourt Brace and World.

Mumford, L. (1968). *The urban prospect.* New York: Harcourt Brace and World.

Mumford, L. (1970). *The myth of the machine: II. The pentagon of power.* New York: Harcourt Brace Jovanovich.

Nevitt, B. (1982). *The communication ecology: Re-presentation versus replica.* Toronto: Butterworths.

Newton, J. H. (2000). *The burden of visual truth: The role of photojournalism in mediating reality.* Mahwah, NJ: Lawrence Erlbaum Associates.

Novak, F. G., Jr. (Ed). (1995). *Lewis Mumford and Patrick Geddes: The correspondence.* London: Routledge.

Nystrom, C. (1973). Towards a science of media ecology: The formulation of integrated conceptual paradigms for the study of human communication systems (Doctoral dissertation, New York University, 1973). *Dissertation Abstracts International, 34,* 7800.

Ogden, C. K., & Richards, I. A. (1923). *The meaning of meaning: A study of the influence of language upon thought and of the science of symbolism.* New York: Harcourt, Brace.

Olson, D. R. (1994). *The world on paper: The conceptual and cognitive implications of writing and reading.* Cambridge, UK: Cambridge University Press.

Olson, D. R., & Torrance N. (Eds.). (1991). *Literacy and orality.* Cambridge: Cambridge University Press.

O'Neill, J. L. (1999). *Through the eyes of aliens: A book about autistic people.* London: Jessica Kingsley.

O'Neill, M. J. (1993). *The roar of the crowd: How television and people power are changing the world.* New York: Times Books.

Ong, W. J. (1958). *Ramus, method, and the decay of dialogue: From the art of discourse to the art of reason.* Cambridge, MA: Harvard University Press.

Ong, W. J. (1962). *The barbarian within: And other fugitive essays and studies.* New York: Macmillan.

Ong, W. J. (1967a). *In the human grain: Further explorations of contemporary culture.* New York: Macmillan.

Ong, W. J. (1967b). *The presence of the word: Some prolegomena for cultural and religious history.* Minneapolis: University of Minnesota Press.

Ong, W. J. (Ed.). (1968). *Knowledge and the future of man*. New York: Holt, Rinehart, & Winston.

Ong, W. J. (1971). *Rhetoric, romance, and technology: Studies in the interaction of expression and culture*. Ithaca, NY: Cornell University Press.

Ong, W.J. (1977). *Interfaces of the word: Studies in the evolution of consciousness and culture*. Ithaca, NY: Cornell University Press.

Ong, W. J. (1981). *Fighting for life: Contest, sexuality, and consciousness*. Ithaca, NY: Cornell University Press.

Ong, W. J. (1982). *Orality and literacy: The technologizing of the word*. London: Methuen.

Ong, W. J. (1986). *Hopkins, the self, and God*. Toronto: University of Toronto Press.

Ong, W. J. (1992-1999). *Faith and contexts* (4 vols., T. J. Farrell & P. A. Soukup, Eds.). Atlanta: Scholars Press.

Ong, W. J. (2002a). *An Ong reader: Challenges for further inquiry* (T. J. Farrell & P. A. Soukup, Eds.). Cresskill, NJ: Hampton Press.

Ong, W. J. (2002b). Ecology and some of its future. *Explorations in Media Ecology 1*(1), 5-11.

Ovid. (1955). *Metamorphoses* (R. Humphries, Trans.). Bloomington: Indiana University Press.

Paglia, C. (1990). *Sexual personae: Art and decadence from Nefertiti to Emily Dickinson*. New Haven, CT: Yale University Press.

Paglia, C. (1991). *Sex, art, and American culture: Essays*. New York: Vintage Books.

Paglia, C. (1994). *Vamps and tramps: New essays*. New York: Vintage Books.

Paglia, C. (1998). *The birds*. London: BFI.

Paglia, C. (2002). The North American intellectual tradition. *Explorations in Media Ecology 1*(1), 21-30.

Parry, M. (1971). *The making of Homeric verse: The collected papers of Milman Parry* (A. Parry, Ed.). Oxford: Clarendon Press.

Patterson, G. (1990). *History and communications: Harold Innis, Marshall McLuhan, and the interpretation of history*. Toronto: University of Toronto Press.

Pawlowski, C. (2000). *Glued to the tube: The threat of television addiction to today's family*. Naperville, IL: Sourcebooks.

Peirce, C. S. (1991). *Peirce on signs: Writing on semiotic*. Chapel Hill: University of North Carolina Press.

Perkinson, H. (1991). *Getting better: Television and moral progress*. New Brunswick, NJ: Transaction.

Perkinson, H. (1995). *How things got better: Speech, writing, printing, and cultural change*. Westport, CT: Bergin & Garvey.

Perkinson, H. (1996). *No safety in numbers: How the computer quantified everything and made people risk-aversive*. Cresskill, NJ: Hampton Press.

Pfeiffer, J. E. (1982). *The creative explosion: An inquiry into the origins of art and religion*. New York: Harper & Row.

Piaget, J. (1954). *The construction of reality in the child* (M. Cook, Trans.). New York: Basic Books.

Piscitelli, A. (1998). *Post/televisión: Ecología de los medios en la era de internet*. Buenos Aires: Paidós Contextos.

Plato. (1971). *Gorgias* (W. Hamilton, Trans.). London: Penguin.

Plato. (1973). *Phaedrus and Letters VII and VIII* (W. Hamilton, Trans.). New York: Penguin.

Poster, M. (1990). *The mode of information: Poststructuralism and social context.* Chicago: University of Chicago Press.

Poster, M. (1995). *The second media age.* Cambridge, MA: Polity Press.

Postman, N. (1961). *Television and the teaching of English.* New York: Appleton-Century-Crofts.

Postman, N. (1970). The reformed English curriculum. In A.C. Eurich (Ed.), *High school 1980: The shape of the future in American secondary education* (pp. 160-168). New York: Pitman.

Postman, N. (1976). *Crazy talk, stupid talk.* New York: Delacorte.

Postman, N. (1979). *Teaching as a conserving activity.* New York: Delacorte.

Postman, N. (1982). *The disappearance of childhood.* New York: Delacorte.

Postman, N. (1985). *Amusing ourselves to death: Public discourse in the age of show business.* New York: Viking.

Postman, N. (1988). *Conscientious objections: Stirring up trouble about language, technology, and education.* New York: Alfred A. Knopf.

Postman, N. (1992). *Technopoly: The surrender of culture to technology.* New York: Alfred A. Knopf.

Postman, N. (1995). *The end of education: Redefining the value of school.* New York: Alfred A. Knopf.

Postman, N. (1999). *Building a bridge to the eighteenth century: How the past can improve our future.* New York: Alfred A. Knopf.

Postman, N. (2000). The humanism of media ecology. *Proceedings of the Media Ecology Association 1,* 10-16 [Electronic version, retrieved April 27, 2004 from http://www.media-ecology.org/publications/proceedings/v1/humanism_of_media_ecology.html]

Postman, N., Nystrom, C., Strate, L., & Weingartner, C. (1987). *Myths, men, and beer: An analysis of beer commercials on broadcast television, 1987.* Falls Church, VA: American Automobile Association Foundation for Traffic Safety.

Postman, N., & Powers, S. (1992). *How to watch TV news.* New York: Penguin Books.

Postman, N., & Weingartner, C. (1966). *Linguistics: A revolution in teaching.* New York: Delta.

Postman, N., & Weingartner, C. (1969). *Teaching as a subversive activity.* New York: Delta.

Postman, N., & Weingartner, C. (1971). *The soft revolution: A student handbook for turning schools around.* New York: Delacorte.

Postman, N., & Weingartner, C. (1973). *The school book: For people who want to know what all the hollering is about.* New York: Delacorte.

Prigogine, I., & Stengers, I. (1984). *Order out of chaos: Man's new dialogue with nature.* New York: Bantam.

Prigogine, I., & Stengers, I. (1997). *The end of certainty: Time, chaos, and the new laws of nature.* New York: Free Press.

Putnam, R. D. (2000). *Bowling alone: The collapse and revival of American community.* New York: Simon & Schuster.

Rheingold, H. (1985). *Tools for thought: The people and ideas behind the next computer revolution.* New York: Simon & Schuster.

Rheingold, H. (1988). *They have a word for it: A lighthearted lexicon of untranslatable words and phrases.* Louisville, KY: Sarabande Books.

Rheingold, H. (1991). *Virtual reality.* New York: Summit Books.

Rheingold, H. (1993). *The virtual community: Home-steading on the electronic frontier.* Reading, MA: Addison Wesley.

Rheingold, H. (2003). *Smart mobs: The next social revolution.* Cambridge, MA: Perseus.

Richards, I. A. (1929). *Practical criticism: A study of literary judgment.* New York: Harcourt, Brace.

Richards, I. A. (1936), *The philosophy of rhetoric.* New York: Oxford University Press.

Riesman, D., Denney, R., & Glazer, N. (1950). *The lonely crowd: A study of the changing American character.* New Haven: Yale University Press.

Rifkin, J. (1987). *Time wars: The primary conflict in human history.* New York: H. Holt.

Rifkin, J. (1992). *Beyond beef: The rise and fall of cattle culture.* New York: Dutton.

Rifkin, J. (1995). *The end of work: The decline of the global labor force and the dawn of the post-market era.* New York: Putnam.

Rifkin, J. (1998). *The biotech century: Harnessing the gene and remaking the world.* New York: Putnam.

Rifkin, J. (2000). *The age of access: The new culture of hypercapitalism, where all of life is a paid-for experience.* New York: Putnam.

Rifkin, J. (2002). *The hydrogen economy: The creation of the worldwide energy web and the redistribution of power on earth.* New York: Putnam.

Rimland, B. (1964). *Infantile autism: The syndrome and its implications for a neural theory of behavior.* New York: Appleton-Century-Crofts.

Ripmaster, T. (1978). *The ecology of history: Commentary on history and historiography.* Washington, DC: University Press of America.

Romanyshyn, R. D. (1989). *Technology as symptom and dream.* London: Routledge.

Ronfeldt, D. F. (1998). *The Zapatista "social netwar" in Mexico.* Santa Monica, CA: Rand.

Rosen, J. (1999). *What are journalists for?* New Haven: Yale University Press.

Rothenberg, D. (1993). *Hand's end: Technology and the limits of nature.* Berkeley: University of California Press.

Roszak, T. (1994). *The cult of information: A neo-Luddite treatise on high-tech, artificial intelligence, and the true art of thinking* (2nd ed.). Berkeley: The University of California Press.

Ruesch, J., & Bateson, G. (1951). *Communication: The social matrix of psychiatry.* New York: Norton.

Rushing, J. H., & Frentz, T. S. (1995). *Projecting the shadow: The cyborg hero in American film.* Chicago: University of Chicago Press.

Rushkoff, D. (1994a). *Cyberia: Life in the trenches of hyperspace.* New York: HarperCollins.

Rushkoff, D. (1994b). *Media virus! Hidden agendas in popular culture.* New York: Ballantine.

Rushkoff, D. (1996). *Playing the future: What we can learn from digital kids.* San Francisco: HarperCollins.

Rushkoff, D. (1999). *Coercion: Why we listen to what 'they' say.* New York: Riverhead.

Rushkoff, D. (2003a). *Nothing sacred: The truth about Judaism.* New York: Crown.

Rushkoff, D. (2003b). *Open source democracy.* London: Demos.

Ryan, P. (1974). *Cybernetics of the sacred.* Garden City, NY: Anchor.

Ryan, P. (1993). *Video mind, earth mind: Art, communications, and ecology.* New York: Peter Lang.

Sacks, O. (1987). *The man who mistook his wife for a hat and other clinical tales.* New York: Perennial Library.

Sacks, O. (1995). *An anthropologist on Mars.* New York: Random House.

Sanders, B. (1994). *A is for ox: Violence, electronic media, and the silencing of the written word.* New York: Pantheon Books.

Sanderson, G., & Macdonald, F. (Eds.). (1989). *McLuhan: The man and his message.* Goldon, CO: Fulcrum.

Sapir, E. (1921). *Language: An introduction to the study of speech.* New York: Harcourt Brace Jovanovich.

Saussure F. d. (1983). *Course in general linguistics* (C. Bally & A. Sechehaye with A. Riedlinger, Eds., R. Harris. Trans.). LaSalle, IL: Open Court.

Schafer, R. M. (1977). *The tuning of the world.* New York: Alfred A. Knopf.

Schiller, H. I. (1973). *The mind managers.* Boston: Beacon Press.

Schlossberg, E. (1998). *Interactive excellence: Defining and developing new standards for the twenty-first century.* New York: Ballantine.

Schmandt-Besserat, D. (1978). *An archaic recording system and the origin of writing.* Malibu, CA: Undena.

Schmandt-Besserat, D. (1979). *Early technologies.* Malibu, CA: Undena.

Schmandt-Besserat, D. (1986). The origins of writing: An archeologist's perspective. *Written Communications 3,* 31-45.

Schmandt-Besserat, D. (1992). *Before writing: From counting to cuneiform* (2 vols.). Austin: University of Texas Press.

Schmandt-Besserat, D. (1996). *How writing came about.* Austin: University of Texas Press.

Schneider, E. (1999). *Discovering my autism: Apologia pro vita sua* (with apologies to Cardinal Newman). London: Jessica Kingsley.

Schwartz, T. (1974). *The responsive chord.* Garden City, NY: Anchor Books.

Schwartz, T. (1981). *Media: The second god.* New York: Random House.

Selfe, L. (1977). *A case of extraordinary drawing ability in an autistic child.* London: Academic Press.

Shannon, C. E., & Weaver, W. (1949). *The mathematical theory of communication.* Urbana: University of Illinois Press.

Shenk, D. (1997). *Data smog: Surviving the information glut.* San Francisco: HarperEdge.

Shenk, D. (1999). *The end of patience: Cautionary notes on the information revolution.* Bloomington: Indiana University Press.

Shlain, L. (1991). *Art and physics: Parallel visions in space, time, and light.* New York: Morrow.

Shlain, L. (1998). *The alphabet versus the goddess: The conflict between word and image.* New York: Viking.

Shlain, L. (2003). *Sex, time and power: How women's sexuality shaped human evolution*. New York: Viking.

Siegel, B. (1996). *The world of the autistic child: Understanding and treating autistic spectrum disorders*. New York: Oxford University Press.

Slouka, M. (1996). *War of the worlds: Cyberspace and the high-tech assault on reality*. New York: Basic.

Smith, A. (1980a). *The geopolitics of information: How western culture dominates the world*. New York: Oxford University Press.

Smith, A. (1980b). *Goodbye, Gutenberg: The newspaper revolution of the 1980s*. New York: Oxford University Press.

Smith, A. (1993). *Books to bytes: Knowledge and information in the postmodern era*. London: British Film Institute.

Smith, A. (1996). *Software for the self: Culture and technology*. New York: Oxford University Press.

Smith, T., Groen, A. D., & Wynn, J. W. (2000). Randomized trial of intensive early intervention for children with pervasive developmental disorder. *American Journal on Mental Retardation, 105*(4), 269-285.

Snow, R. P. (1983). *Creating media culture*. Newbury Park, CA: Sage.

Sontag, S. (1977). *On photography*. New York: Farrar, Straus & Giroux.

Sontag, S. (2003). *Regarding the pain of others*. New York: Farrar, Straus & Giroux.

Stamps, J. (1995). *Unthinking modernity: Innis, McLuhan, and the Frankfurt School*. Montreal & Kingston: McGill-Queens University Press.

Steinberg, S. H. (1996). *Five hundred years of printing* (rev. ed., J. Trevitt, Ed.). New Castle, DE: Oak Knoll Press.

Stephens, M. (1988). *A history of news: From the drum to the satellite*. New York: Viking.

Stephens, M. (1998). *The rise of the image, the fall of the word*. New York: Oxford University Press.

Strate, L. (1994). Post(modern)man, Or Neil Postman as a postmodernist. *ETC.: A Review of General Semantics, 51*(2), 159-170.

Strate, L. (2000). Narcissism and echolalia: Sense and the struggle for self. *Speech Communication Annual, 14,* 14-62.

Strate, L. (2003a). Neil Postman, defender of the word. *ETC.: A Review of General Semantics, 60*(4), 341-350.

Strate, L. (2003b). Something from nothing: Seeking a sense of self. *ETC: A Review of General Semantics, 60*(1), 4-21.

Strate, L. (2004). A media ecology review. *Communication Research Trends, 23*(2), 2-48.

Strate, L., Jacobson, R. L,. & Gibson, S. B. (Eds.). (1996). *Communication and cyberspace: Social interaction in an electronic environment*. Cresskill, NJ: Hampton Press.

Strate, L., Jacobson, R. L,. & Gibson, S. B. (Eds.). (2003). *Communication and cyberspace: Social interaction in an electronic environment* (2nd ed.). Cresskill, NJ: Hampton Press.

Strate, L., & Lum, C. M. K. (2000). Lewis Mumford and the ecology of technics. *The New Jersey Journal of Communication, 8*(1), 56-78.

Strate, L., & Wachtel, E. A. (2005). Introduction. In L. Strate & E. Wachtel (Eds.), *The legacy of McLuhan* (pp. 1-21). Cresskill, NJ: Hampton Press.

Strate, L., & Wachtel, E. A. (2005). *The legacy of McLuhan.* Cresskill, NJ: Hampton Press.

Strogatz, S. (2003). *Sync: The emerging science of spontaneous order.* New York: Hyperion.

Tabbi, J., & Wutz, M. (Eds.). (1997). *Reading matters: Narrative in the new media ecology.* Ithaca: Cornell University Press.

Talbott, S. (1995). *The future does not compute.* Sebastopol, CA: O'Reilly & Associates.

Tenner, E. (1996). *Why things bite back: Technology and the revenge of unintended consequences.* New York: Knopf.

Tenner, E. (2003). *Our own devices: The past and future of body technology.* New York: Knopf.

Thaler, P. (1994). *The watchful eye: American justice in the age of the television trial.* Westport, CT: Praeger.

Thaler, P. (1997). *The spectacle: Media and the making of the O.J. Simpson story.* Westport, CT: Praeger.

Theall, D. F. (1971). *The medium is the rear view mirror.* Montreal: McGill-Queens University Press.

Theall, D. F. (1995). *Beyond the word: Reconstructing sense in the Joyce era of technology, culture, and communication.* Toronto: University of Toronto Press.

Theall, D. F. (1997). *James Joyce's techno-poetics.* Toronto: University of Toronto Press.

Theall, D. F. (2001). *The virtual Marshall McLuhan.* Montreal & Kingston: McGill-Queens University Press..

Tomatis, A. (1996). *The ear and language.* Norval, ON: Moulin.

Tuan, Y.-F. (1982). *Segmented worlds and self: Group life and individual consciousness.* Minneapolis: University of Minnesota Press.

Turkle, S. (1984). *The second self: Computers and the human spirit.* New York: Simon and Schuster.

Turkle, S. (1995). *Life on the screen: Identity in the age of the Internet.* New York: Simon and Schuster.

U. S. Federal Trade Commission. (2000). *ID theft: When bad things happen to your good name* [on-line]. Available: http://www.consumer.gov/idtheft/

Veblen, T. (1899). *The theory of the leisure class: An economic study of institutions.* New York; MacMillan.

Veblen, T. (1921). *The engineers and the price system.* New York, B.W. Huebsch.

Virilio, P. (1986). *Speed and politics: An essay on dromology* (M. Polizzotti, Trans.). New York: Semiotext(e).

Virilio, P. (1991). *The lost dimension* (D. Moshenberg, Trans.). New York: Semiotext(e).

Virilio, P. (1997). *Open sky* (J. Rose, Trans.). London: Verso.

Volkmar, F. R. (1989). Medical problems, treatments, and professionals. In M. D. Powers (Ed.), *Children with autism: A parents' guide* (pp. 55-77). Bethesda, MD: Woodbine House.

Vygotsky, L. S. (1986). *Thought and language* (rev. ed., A. Kozulin, Trans. & Ed.). Cambridge, MA: MIT Press.

Wachtel, E. (1995). To an eye in a fixed position: Glass, art, and vision. In J. C. Pitt (Ed.), *New directions in the philosophy of technology* (pp.41-61). Amsterdam: Kluwer.

Wachtel, E. (in preparation). *From cave walls to computer screens: The interplay of art, technology, and perception.* Cresskill, NJ: Hampton Press.

Waite, C. K. (2003). *Mediation and the communication matrix.* New York: Peter Lang.

Waldrop, M.M. (1992). *Complexity: The emerging science at the edge of order and chaos.* New York: Simon & Schuster.

Warren, C. A., & Vavrus, M. D. (Eds.). (2002). *American cultural studies.* Urbana: University of Illinois Press.

Wasser, F. (2001). *Veni, vidi, video: The Hollywood empire and the VCR.* Austin: University of Texas Press.

Watts, D. J. (2003). *Six degrees: The science of a connected age.* New York: Norton.

Watzlawick, P. (1976). *How real is real?: Confusion, disinformation, communication.* New York: Random House.

Watzlawick, P. (1983). *The situation is hopeless, but not serious* (The pursuit of unhappiness). New York: Norton.

Watzlawick, P. (1988). *Ultra-solutions: Or, how to fail most successfully.* New York: Norton.

Watzlawick, P. (1990). *Münchhausen's pigtail: Or, psychotherapy & "reality": Essays and lectures.* New York: Norton.

Watzlawick, P., Bavelas, J. B., & Jackson, D. D. (1967). *Pragmatics of human communication: A study of interactional patterns, pathologies, and paradoxes.* New York: W. W. Norton.

Watzlawick, P., Weakland, J., & Fisch, R. (1974). *Change: Principles of problem formation and problem resolution.* New York: W. W. Norton.

Weeks, D. L., & Hoogestraat, J. (Eds.). (1998). *Time, memory, and the verbal arts: Essay's on Walter Ong's thought.* Cranbury, NJ: Susquehanna University Press.

Weizenbaum, J. (1976). *Computer power and human reason.* San Francisco: W.H. Freeman.

Welch, K. E. (1999). *Electric rhetoric: Classical rhetoric, oralism, and a new literacy.* Cambridge, MA: MIT Press.

White, Lynn, Jr. (1962). *Medieval technology and social change.* Oxford: Clarendon Press.

White, Lynn, Jr. (1978). *Medieval religion and technology: Collected essays.* Berkeley: University of California Press.

Whitehead, A. N., & Russell, B. (1925-1927). *Principia mathematica* (2nd ed., 3 vols.). Cambridge, UK: The University Press.

Whorf, B. L. (1956). *Language, thought, and reality.* Cambridge, MA: MIT Press.

Whyte, W. H., Jr. (1956). *The organization man.* New York: Touchstone.

Wiener, N. (1950). *The human use of human beings: Cybernetics and society.* Boston: Houghton Mifflin.

Wiener, N. (1961). *Cybernetics: Or control and communication in the machine and animal.* Boston: Houghton Mifflin.

Wiener, N. (1964). *God and golem, Inc.: A comment on certain points where cybernetics impinges on religion.* Cambridge, MA: MIT Press.

Williams, D. (1992). *Nobody, nowhere: The extraordinary autobiography of an autistic.* New York: Times Books.

Williams, D. (1994). *Somebody, somewhere: Breaking free from the world of autism.* New York: Times Books.

Williams, D. (1996). *Autism: An inside-out approach.* London: Jessica Kingsley.

Williams, D. (1998). *Autism and sensing: The unlost instinct.* London: Jessica Kingsley.

Williams, D. (1999). *Like colour to the blind: Soul searching and soul finding.* London: Jessica Kingsley.

Wilson, F. (2000, August 29). Why is there so much autism in kids today?! *2worlds Listserv* [on-line]. Available: http://groups.yahoo.com/group/2worlds/message/79

Winner, L. (1977). *Autonomous technology: Technics-out-of-control as a theme in political thought.* Cambridge, MA: MIT Press.

Winner, L. (1986). *The whale and the reactor: A search for limits in an age of high technology.* Chicago: University of Chicago Press.

Winner, L. (1992). *Democracy in a technological society.* Boston: Kluwer.

Wittgenstein, L. (1922). *Tractatus logico-philosophicus* (C. K. Ogden, Trans.). London: Routledge.

Wittgenstein, L. (1961). *Tractatus logico-philosophicus* (D. F. Pears & B. F. McGuinness, Trans.). London: Routledge.

Wittgenstein, L. (1963). *Philosophical investigations* (G. E. M. Anscombe, Trans.). Oxford: Basil Blackwell.

Wood, D. N. (1996). *Post-intellectualism and the decline of democracy: The failure of reason and responsibility in the twentieth century.* Westport, CT: Praeger.

Wood, D. N. (2003). *The unraveling of the West: The rise of postmodernism and the decline of democracy.* Westport, CT: Praeger.

Yates, F. A. (1966). *The art of memory.* Chicago: University of Chicago Press.

Youngkin, B. R. *The contributions of Walter J. Ong to the study of rhetoric: History and metaphor.* Lewiston, NY: Mellen University Press.

Zingrone, F. (2001). *The media symplex: At the edge of meaning in the age of chaos.* Cresskill, NJ: Hampton.

AUTHOR INDEX

A

Abram, D., 42, *135*
ADILKNO, 19, *135*
Adorno, T.W., 3, *135*
Agel, J., 24, 75, *135*, *142*
Albrecht, R., 42, *135*
Altheide, D.L., 62, *135*
Ames, A., 89, *135*
Applewhite, E.J., 3, 75, *135*, *142*
Aristotle, 80, *135*
Arquilla, J., 78, *135*, *136*

B

Barnes, S.B., 10, 57, 77, *136*
Barnhurst, K.G., 29, *136*
Baron-Cohen, S., 120, 121, 129, 132, *136*, *145*
Barry, A.M., 48, *136*
Barthes, R., 110, *136*
Bateson, G., 2, 59, 60, 61, 107, *136*, *155*
Baudrillard, J., 34, 48, *136*

Bavelas, J.B., 61, 82, 83, 102, 107, 121, *136*, *159*
Becker, E., 107, *136*
Bellah, R.N., 109, *136*
Beniger, J.R., 75, *136*
Benjamin, W., 48, *136*
Bennett, W.J., 110, *136*
Bennis, W.G., 48, *136*, *151*
Berne, E., 107, *136*
Bertalanffy, L.v., 63, 83, *137*
Bertelsen, D.A., 57, *137*, *138*
Bettelheim, B., 127, *137*
Birdwhistell, R.L., 59, *137*
Bishop, J., 31, *137*
Blackmore, S.J., 60, *137*
Bolter, J.D., 33, 43, 71, 88, 109, *137*
Bolton, P., 132, *136*, *137*
Bonsall, D.G., 57, *138*
Boorstin, D.J., 2, 47, 48, 71, 88, *137*
Braudy, L., 109, *137*

Brodie, R., 60, *137*
Broucek, F.J., 107, *137*
Brown, N.O., 107, *137*
Buber, M., 91, *137*
Burke, K., 100, 101, 107, *137*

C

Campbell, J., 63, 80, 107, *137*, *138*
Capra, F., 64, 102, *138*
Carey, J.W., 19, 28, 29, 58, 65, 66,
    70, *138*
Carley, K.M. 47, *138*, *146*
Carpenter, E., 22, 31, 32, 51, 88,
    109, 124, 125, *138*
Carson, D., 25, *150*
Cassidy, M., 77, *138*
Cathcart, R., 48, 57, *138*, *140*, *144*
Cavell, R., 25, *138*
Chase, S., 82, *138*
Chaytor, H.J., 46, *138*
Chesebro, J.W., 57, *138*
Chomsky, N., 86, 109, *138*, *145*
Christians, C.G., 74, *138*
Cohen, S., 125, 132, *138*
Cook, D., 34, *138*, *147*
Couch, C.J., 62, *138*
Crowley, D., 19, *138*
Curtis, J.M., 32, *139*
Czitrom, D.J., 30, *139*

D

Dale, S., 26, *139*
Damasio, A.R., 90, *139*
Dance, F.E.X., 87, *139*
Danet, B., 43, *139*
Dawkins, R., 60, 133, *139*
de Kerckhove, D., 32, *139*
Debray, R., 19, 87, 88, *139*
Deibert, R.J., 47, *139*
DeLuca, K.M., 48, *139*
Denney, R., 109, *139*, *155*
Derrida, J., 46, 87, *139*, *140*
Dewdney, C., 110, *140*
Dewey, J., 89, *135*, *140*

Donald, M., 45, 123, *140*
Drucker, P.F., 75-76, *140*
Drucker, S., 48, 57, *140*, 144
Dunbar, R., 45, 120, *140*
Duncan, H.D., 59, 107, 119, *140*
Durig, A., 84, 118, 122, 126, 133,
    140

E

Eastham, S., 71, *140*
Edelman, G.M., 90, *140*
Ehrenfeld, D., 100, *140*
Einstein, A., 91, *140*
Eisenstein, E.L., 46, 47, 48, 109,
    124, 125, *140*
Ellul, J., 22, 73, 74, 109, 110, *141*
Engels, F., 71, *141*, *149*
Erikson, E.H., 107, 109, *141*
Esté, A., 82, *141*

F

Farrell, T.J., 37, 91, *141*, *143*
Febvre, L., 46, *141*
Fiore, Q., 24, 75, 81, *141*, *142*, *150*
Fisch, R., 61, 101, 107, *159*
Fish, S.L., 57, *141*, *144*
Forsdale, L., 86, *141*
Foucault, M., 87, *141*
Fraim, J., 86, *141*
Frentz, T.S., 89, 110, *155*
Freud, S., 89, 106, 107, *142*
Frith, U., 112, 114, 120, 132, *142*
Fromm, E., 109, *142*
Fry, K., 77, *142*
Fuller, R.B., 3, 75, *142*

G

Gabler, N., 48, 77, *142*
Gardner, H., 84, 112, 123, *142*
Geddes, P., 70, *142*
Gelb, I.J., 46, *142*
Gencarelli, T.F., 53, *142*
Genosko, G., 26, *142*
Gergen, K.J., 107, 110, *142*
Gibson, S.B., 43, 57, *142*, *157*

Giddens, A., 110, *142*
Giedion, S., 71, *142*
Gilman, P., 95, 99, 101, *142*
Gitlin, T., 109, *142*
Glazer, N., 109, *142, 155*
Gleick, J., 102, *142*
Goffman, E., 59, 60, 107, *143*
Gombrich, E.H., 89, *143*
Goody, J., 19, 41, 42, 124, 125, *143*
Gordon, W.T., 25, *143*
Gozzi, R., 86, *143*
Grandin, T., 117, 126, *143*
Greenspan, S.I., 129, *143*
Gregory, R.L., 89, *143*
Groen, A.D., 128, *143, 157*
Gronbeck, B.E., 37, *143*
Grosswiler, P., 25, *143*
Grusin, R., 33, 43, 88, 109, *137, 143*
Gumpert, G., 48, 57, *140, 143, 144*

H

Haddon, M., 114, *144*
Hadwin, J., 129, 90, 107, *144, 145*
Hall, E.T., 57, 58, 59, *144*
Havelock, E.A., 28, 39, 40, 108, 124, *144*
Hawking, S.W., 91, *144*
Hayakawa, A.R., 82, 116, *144*
Hayakawa, S.I., 82, 116, *144*
Hayles, N.K., 64, 75, 110, *144*
Heidegger, M., 78, *144*
Heim, M., 43, *144*
Heisenberg, W., *144*
Herman, E.S., 109, *145*
Hershbell, J.P., 40, *144*
Heyer, P., 19, 28, 29, *138, 139, 145*
Heyman, K., 31, 109, 124, 125, *138*
Hobart, M.E., 49, *145*
Hofsadter, D.R., 82, *145*
Hoogestraat, J., 37, *145, 159*

Howlin, P., 129, *145*
Huizinga, J., 89, *145*
Hunt, A.W., 49, 77, *145*

I

Ihde, D., 78, *145*
Illich, I., 76, *145*
Innis, H. A., 3, 27, 28, 41, 48, 71, 108, 124, *145*
Jackson, D.D., 61, 82, 83, 102, 107, 121, *145, 159*
Jacobson, R.L., 57, *145, 157*
Jameson, F., 110, 118, *145, 146*
Jaynes, J., 123, *146*
Jensen, J., 30, 53, *146*
Johnson, M., 86, *146, 147*
Johnson, S., 64, *146*
Johnson, W., 82, 116, *146*
Jones, S., 29, 48, *146*
Jung, C.G., 107, *146*

K

Katsh, M.E., 43, *146*
Kaufer, D.S., 47, *146*
Kauffman, S.A., 64, 102, *146*
Kelly, K., 78, *146*
Kittler, F.A., 47, *146*
Korzybski, A., 3, 82, 116, *146*
Kozol, J., 47, *146*
Kranowitz, C.S., 132, *146*
Kroker, A., *29, 34, 146*
Kroker, M., 34, *147*
Kuhns, W., 18, 19, 25, 29, 65, 66, 73, 74, 75, *147*

L

Laing, R.D., 107, 109, *147*
Lakoff, G., 86, *147*
Landes, D.S., 71, *147*
Landow, G.P., 43, *147*
Lane, H., 114, *147*
Langer, S.K.K., 83, 84, 101, 118, *147*
Lanham, R.A., 43, *147*
Larson, C.E., 87, *139, 147*

Lasch, C., 48, 49, 106, 107, 109,
   147
Laszlo, E., 63, *147*, *148*
Lee, D., 42, 85, 108, 121, *148*
Leverette, M., 86, *148*
Levinson, P., 21, 25, 56, *148*
Lévi-Strass, C., 87, 116, *148*
Linton, S., 126, *148*
Logan, R.K., 32, 64, 102, 124, *148*
Lord, A.B., 41, *148*
Lovaas, O.I., 128, *148*
Luhmann, N., 63, 102, *148*, *149*
Lule, J., 77, *149*
Lum, C.M.K., 4, 10, 65, 77, 107,
   149, *157*
Lupton, E., 33, *149*
Luriia, A.R., 87, *149*
Lyotard, J.-F., 76, 118, *149*

M

Macdonald, F., 24, *156*
Madaule, P., 132, *149*
Madsen, R., 109, *136*
Maines, D.R., *149*
Mander, J., 76, *149*
Manovich, L., 88, *149*
Marchand, P., 25, *149*
Martin, H.-J., 46, *141*, *149*
Marvin, C., 29, *149*
Marx, K., 71, *149*
Maturana, H.R., 63, *149*
Maurice, C., 125, 128, 132, *149*,
   150
McCloud, S., 33, 48, 49, *150*
McLuhan, E., 24, 25, 32, 81, 107,
   131, 133, *150*
McLuhan, M., 4, 17, 18, 21, 22,
   23, 24, 25, 26, 29, 31, 32, 35,
   36, 51, 52, 66, 71, 80, 81, 88,
   100, 101, 106, 108, 109, 110,
   115, 124, 125, 131, 133, *138*,
   150, *151*
McLuhan-Ortved, S., 25, *151*
McMahon, K., 25, *151*

McWhorter, J., 86, *151*
Mead, G.H., 59, 107, *151*
Meyrowitz, J., 19, 60, 62, 65, 107,
   109, 124, 125, *151*, *152*
Milgram, S., 61, 109, *151*
Miller, D.L., 65, 70, *151*
Mitcham, C., 78, *151*
Mitchell, W.J., 71, *151*
Mitroff, I.I., 48, *151*
Mumford, L., 65, 66, 67, 68, 69,
   70, 73, *151*, *152*

N

Nerone, J.C., 29, *136*
Nevitt, B., 24, 29, 32, *150*, *152*
Newton, J.H., 48, 49, *152*
Novak, F.G., 70, *152*
Nystrom, C., 4, 52, 61, 65, 103,
   152, *154*

O

O'Neill, J.L., 125, 132, *152*
O'Neill, M.J., 47, *152*
Ogden, C.K., 3, 81, *152*
Olson, D.R., 42, 109, 124, *152*
Ong, W.J., 10, 16, 19, 19, 20, 29,
   35, 36, 37, 52, 81, 91, 108, 109,
   110, 116, 124, 125, *152*, *153*
Ovid, 103, 109, *153*
Oviedo, O.O., 43, *142*

P

Paglia, C., 2, 19, 20, 88, 89, *153*
Parker, H., 24, *151*
Parry, M., 41, *153*
Patterson, G., 29, *153*
Pawlowski, C., 77, *153*
Peirce, C.S., 82, *153*
Perkinson, H.J., 2, 56, *153*
Pfeiffer, J.E., 45, 123, 124, *153*
Piaget, J., 116, *153*
Piscitelli, A., 47, *153*
Plato, 80, 101, *153*, *154*
Poster, M., 110, *154*

Postman, N., 4, 10, 15, 16, 17, 18, 19, 22, 43, 51, 52, 53, 71, 77, 81, 92, 100, 103, 109, 110, 124, 125, *154*
Powers, B.R., 24, *151*
Powers, S., 52, *154*
Prigogine, I., 63-64, 102, *154*
Prins, H., 31, *137*
Putnam, R.D., 109, *154*

R

Rheingold, H., 78, 85, *154, 155*
Richards, I. A., 3, 81, *152, 155*
Riesman, D., 109, *155*
Rifkin, J., 76, *155*
Rimland, B., 128, *155*
Ripmaster, T., 48, *155*
Romanyshyn, R.D., 33, 110, 125, *155*
Ronfeldt, D.F., 78, *135, 136, 155*
Rosen, J., 77, *155*
Roszak, T., 77, *155*
Rothenberg, D., 78, *155*
Ruesch, J., 61, 107, *155*
Rushing, J.H., 89, 110, *155*
Rushkoff, D., 60, 78, *155, 156*
Russell, B., 82, *159*
Ryan, P., 32, 82, *156*

S

Sacks, O., 116, 117, 119, 122, 123, 124, *156*
Sanders, B., 76, 108, 110, *145, 156*
Sanderson, G., 24, *156*
Sapir, E., 84, *156*
Saussure, F.d., 88, *156*
Scariano, M., 117, 126, *143*
Schafer, R.M., 33, *156*
Schiffman, Z.S., 49, *145*
Schiller, H.I., 109, *156*
Schlossberg, E., 33, *156*
Schmandt-Besserat, D., 46, *156*
Schneider, E., 119, 126, *156*
Schwartz, T., 29, 32, *156*

Selfe, L., 125, *156*
Shannon, C.E., 60, 75, *156*
Shenk, D., 77, *156*
Shlain, L., 33, 132, *156, 157*
Shotland, R.L., 61, *151*
Siegel, B., 112, 125, 132, *157*
Simons, R., 129, *143*
Slouka, M., 77, *157*
Smith, A., 47, *157*
Smith, T., 128, *157*
Snow, R.P., 62, *135, 157*
Sobelman, D., 25, *151*
Sontag, S., 48, 49, *157*
Soukup, P.A., 10, 37, *143*
Stamps, J., 29, 48, 70, *157*
Steinberg, S.H., 46, *157*
Stengers, I., 63-64, 102, *154*
Stephens, M., 47, 48, 77, *157*
Strate, L., 10, 26, 52, 53, 57, 65, *136, 154, 157*
Strogatz, S., 64, *158*
Sullivan, W.M., 109, *136*
Swidler, A., 109, *136*

T

Tabbi, J., 19, *158*
Talbott, S., 77, *158*
Tenner, E., 76, *158*
Thaler, P., 77, *158*
Theall, D.F., 26, 33, 81, *158*
Tipton, S.M., 109, *136*
Tomatis, A., 132, *158*
Torrance, N., 42, *152*
Tuan, Y.-F., 110, *158*
Turkle, S., 77, 110, *158*

U

U.S. Federal Trade Commission, 109, *158*

V

Van Hook J.M., 74, *138*
Varela, F.J., 63, *149*
Vavrus, M.D., 29, *159*
Veblen, T., 70, 71, *158*

Virilio. P., 34, *158*
Volkmar, F.R., 132, *158*
Vygotsky, L.S., 87, *159*

W

Wachtel, E.A., 10, 26, 125, *158,*
159
Waite, C.K., 42, *159*
Waldrop, M.M., 102, *159*
Warren, C.A., 29, *159*
Wasser, F., 29, *159*
Watson, W., 24, 80, *151*
Watts, D.J., 64, *159*
Watzlawick, P., 61, 82, 83, 101,
102, 107, 121, *159*
Weakland, J., 61, 101, 107, *159*
Weaver, W., 60, 75, *156*
Weeks, D.L., 37, *159*
Weingartner, C., 18, 51, 52, *154*
Weizenbaum. J., 77, *159*
Welch, K.E., 42, *159*
White, L., 71, *159*

Whitehead, A.N., 82, *159*
Whorf, B.L., 85, *159*
Whyte, W.H., 100, 109, *159*
Wieder, S., 129, *143*
Wiener, N., 60, 63, 75, *159, 160*
Williams, D., 114, 115, 122, 126,
160
Wilson, F., 126, *160*
Winner, L., 76, *160*
Wittgenstein, L., 82, 112, *160*
Wolfe, T., 25, *151*
Wood, D.N., 76, 100, *160*
Wutz, M., 19, *158*
Wynn, J.W., 128, *156*

Y

Yates, F.A., 45, 133, *160*
Youngkin, B.R., 37, *160*

Z

Zingrone, F., 25, 32, 64, *160*

SUBJECT INDEX

A

abstraction, 2, 40, 42, 77, 83, 86, 100, 102, 109, 116, 118, 124, 125
access, 28, 59-60, 62, 76
accounting, 42, 45-46,
acoustic, 22, 33, 35, 88, 108, *see also* sound
acoustic ecology, 32
advertising, 22, 31, 33, 60, 74
Aeschylus, 40
aesthetics, 40, 67, 69
agitation, propaganda of, 74
agrarian life, 17
agricultural revolution, 68
Alexander the Great, 109
aliteracy, 47
alphabet, 22, 32, 33, 36, 39, 46, 76, 125
American culture, 22, 29-30, 36-37, 48, 53, 86, 89, *see also* United States

American cultural studies, 5, 19, 29-30, 74
amputation, 23, 110, 131 n. 2,
analogical coding, 56, 83
analysis, 124
anthropotropic view, 56
anthropology, 31, 41-42, 57-58, 60, 70, 85-87, 119, 121
Apollo, Apollonian, 88-89
Applied Behavior Analysis, 128-129
Arabia, 46, *see* also Semites
archeology, 45
archetype, *see* cliché and archetype
architecture, 23, 57, 58, 65, 67, 71, 74-75, 113
art, 17, 25, 26, 32, 33, 42, 43, 45, 48, 63, 65, 66, 67, 71, 74, 77, 83-85, 88-90, 109, 113, 123, 125
art history, 88-89
artificial intelligence, 60

Asperger's Disorder or Syndrome, 112
assembly line, 22, 75
Attic playwrights, 40
audience, 32, 33
aura, 48
authenticity, 48-49
authority, 61, 62, 109
autism, 6-9, 84, 111-130, 132-133
  ns. 3-10
automobile, 23
autopoiesis, 63, *see also* emergence,
  self-organization

B

back region, 59, 62
balance, 15, 28, 35, 63, 66, 95,
  107, 109, 110, 115, 130
barriers, *see* access
baseball, 57
Basic English, 80
Bellamy, Edward, 80
behavioral school of psychology,
  128
Benedictine monks, 66
Bible, 79-80
binary coding, binary opposition,
  61, 63, 87
biography, 25, 28
biology, 15, 37, 42, 58-59, 60-61,
  64, 66, 67, 69, 70, 75, 78, 88-
  90, 91, 100, 111, 113, 127, 132
  n. 4, 133 n. 9, *see also* life
blowback, 4, *see also* effects
body, 45, 78, 83, 86, 87, 90, 107,
  114-115, 123
book, 46, 47, 58
brain, 24, 33, 64, 69, 87, 89-90,
  106, 107, 111, 115-116, 123,
  129
broadcasting, 60, 77, *see also* radio,
  television
Bronx, 95
business, *see* management
Butler, Samuel, 80

C

Canada, 29, 95
capitalism, 22, 67, 71, 75
categorizing, 2, 86
Catholicism, 16, 25, 36-37, *see also*
  Christianity
cause, 80
cave art, cave painting, 45
celebrity, 48, 88, 113-114
cell phone, *see* mobile telephone
Cervantes, Miguel de, 80
change, 3, 48, 61, 71, 101-103,
  105, 107, 110, 115, 118, 129-
  130, *see also* material transformation, symbolic transformation
chaos, 63-64, 89, 102
Chicago School, 4, 59, 70, *see also*
  University of Chicago
childhood, children, 52, 62, 95, 99,
  116, 119-120, 122, 125, 127-
  129, 133 n. 10
chirography, *see* scribal culture,
  scribal era
Christianity, 19, 37, 47, 74, 77, 88,
  see also Catholicism,
  Evangelical, French Reformed
  Church, Protestant Reformation
cities, 57, 64, 65, 67-68, 70, 71, *see*
  also urban studies
class, 70
classics, 39, 43,
clay envelopes, 46
clay tablets, 27
clay tokens, 46
cliché and archetype, 24, 28
client-centered therapy, 128
clocks, 23, 66-67, 71
closed system, 16, 118
clothing, 23, 58, 95-97, 99
cognition, 36, 42, 63, 87, 90, 111,
  117, 123, 124, 129, 132 n. 6,
coins, 46, *see also* money
Columbia University, 51, 55, 67

comedy, 88
comics, 22, 33, 49
common ground, 101, 103, 112, 121
communication, 1, 3, 6, 16, 17, 18, 19, 23, 24, 25, 27, 28, 29, 32, 35-37, 40, 42, 45, 47, 48, 51-53, 56-61, 63, 65, 66, 69, 70, 75, 81, 82, 85-87, 89, 95, 99-103, 105, 107, 108, 112, 117-118, 121, 122, 125, 129, 130
communication about communication, 61, *see also* metacommunication
communication ecology, 32
Communication Research Trends, 9-10
communication studies, 6, 26, 27, 29, 47, 55-64, 74, 100-103
community, 29, 39, 68, 78, 126, 133 n. 10
complexity, 32, 63-64, 75, 102, 103
computer, 32, 33, 34, 37, 43, 47, 49, 56, 61, 62, 64, 71, 73, 77, 78, 82, 126
computer-mediated communication, 43, 57, 82
computer science, 60, 112-113
concreteness, 2, 40, 99, 100, 116-117, 118, 121, 124, 125, 133 n. 7
consciousness, 16, 35-37, 41, 87, 89, 90, 107, 110, 115, 123, 124
conservatism, 110
consumerism, 49, 78
containers, 68-69, 71
content, 17, 22, 32, 34-35, 41, 51, 61, 66, 82, 99, 101
content level, 61
context, 2, 37, 42, 59, 60, 82, 100, 117, 125
control revolution, 75
cool medium, *see* hot and cool media

Copernican revolution, 47
copy, copies, 4, 36
corporate America, 22
corporation, 75-76
cosmology, 37, 91-92
creation, creativity, 79, 86, 99, 100-101, 123
crime, 78
cultural studies, 25, 26, 37, 61, *see also* American cultural studies
cultural geography, 25
cultural history, 35, 37, 45
culture, 15, 19, 22, 23, 24, 27, 28, 29, 31, 32, 33, 35-37, 40, 41, 42, 43, 45, 51, 53, 58-59, 60, 62, 65, 66, 76, 78, 85-89, 102, 103, 108-110, 123-126, 129-130
culture is communication, 58
culture of autism, 126, 127
cuneiform, 46
Curious Incident of the Dog in the Night-Time, 114
cyberculture, 78
cybernetics, 32, 60, 61, 63, 66, 75
cyberspace, 56, 57
cyborg, 71, 89, 131 n. 2,

D

Dagwood Bumstead, 22
Daisy commercial, 31
dance, 83
death, 22
decentering, decentralization, 63, 66, 110
deconstruction, 43, 46
defining technology, 71
democracy, 47, 48, 74, 76-77, 78, 89
descriptive research, 2
dialectic, dialectics, 2-3, 16, 25, 40, 102
dialogic, 3
dialogue, 5

difference, 1-4, 63, 101, 126
differences that make a difference,
     2, 60
differentiation, 63
digital coding, 61, 83
digital media, technology, 25, 33,
     34, 37, 42-43, 49, 56
Dionysus, Dionysian, 88-89
disability, 106, 111, 126, 127
disaster, 77
discourse, 74, 100
discrete trial method, 128-129
discursive symbolism, 83, 118
dissipative systems, 63-64
documentary, 25, 31
Down's syndrome, 121
dramatism, 101

E

e-mail, 62, 133 n. 10
Echo, 6, 105-110, 131 n. 1, 131 n.
     2
echolalia, 6, 8, 95, 106-110, 111,
     122, 129-130
echopraxia, 106, 108, 112, 123
ecologic, 3, 102
ecological approach, ecological
     concern, 16, 28, 61-62, 71, 91-
     92
ecological age, 91-92
ecological communication, 63
ecological history, 6, 65
ecological holism, 47
ecology, 5, 15, 18, 22, 24, 32, 33,
     36, 60, 64, 65-66, 70, 73, 76,
     77, 78, 91-92, 103
ecology of communication, 62
ecology of history, 49
ecology of human culture, 70
ecology of images, 49
ecology of mind, 60
ecology of sense, 33
economics, 27, 28, 29, 42, 56, 60,
     63, 70-71, 75, 76, 82

education, 18, 19, 22, 23, 28, 35,
     39-40, 51-53, 55, 56, 63, 74, 76,
     77, 92, 99, 102, 110, 127, 128-
     129, 132 n. 3,
effects, 4, 17, 19, 24, 36, 42, 76,
     78, 103, 106
efficiency, 73-74
efficient cause, 80
egalitarianism, 2, 56
Egypt, 27, 28, 80
electronic age, 17, 23, 66, 70, 109,
     126, 130
electronic media, electronic tech-
     nologies, 17, 23, 24, 32, 33, 34,
     35, 36, 42-43, 47, 49, 51-53, 56,
     57, 62-63, 66, 75, 76, 77, 86,
     126, 131 n. 2,
Ellul, Jacques, 6, 73-78, 110
emergence, 63-64, 66, 83, *see also*
     self-organization, system(s)
emotion, 17, 18, 83, 89, 90, 112,
     119-120, 129
empire, 28, 47
encoding, 55-56, *see also* analogical
     coding, digital coding, symbol,
     symbolic communication
energy, 66, 76, 88
English, *see* literature, literary
     studies, literary theory
Enlightenment, 53
entropy, 2, 103
environment, 15, 16, 17, 18, 22,
     36, 56, 57, 58-59, 61, 62, 63,
     65, 66, 73, 82, 84-85, 92, 100,
     101, 103, 106, 107, 115, 118,
     127, 128, 133 n. 9
environmentalism, 49, 76
eotechnic phase, 66
*ETC: A Review of General
     Semantics*, 9, 52
ethics, 74
ethnography, 2, 77
Evangelical, 77

evolution, 15, 16-17, 36, 37, 45, 47, 56, 58-59, 60, 64, 65-66, 70, 88, 103, 110, 115, 120-121, 122, 124
evolutionary psychology, 120
Exodus, 80
Explorations, 22, 31
Explorations in Media Ecology, 10, 19
extensions, 23, 58-59, 66, 81, 110, 131 n. 2, 133 n. 9
exteriority, 36
eye contact, 119, 121-122

F

face-to-face communication, 57, 62, 87
facial expressions, 122
fallibalism, 55
falsification, 2, 55
family, family communication, 61, 77
feedback, 75
feeling, *see* emotion
field (as term and metaphor), 4-5, 22
film, *see* motion picture, photography
final cause, 80
Finnegans Wake, *see* Joyce, James
fire, 87
fluorescent lighting, 126
folk art, folk culture, folk tale, 43, 70, 95, 99, 101, 105, 122
Fordham University, 12, 25, 31, 32
formal cause, 80
formal communication, 58, 86
forms, 48, 79-90, 99, 102, 109
formulas, 39
Forsdale, Louis, 55, 86
fractal geometry, 102
fragmentation, 124
France, 88, *see also* French Reformed Church

Frankfurt School, 4, 25, 29, 48
French Reformed Church, 74, *see also* Christianity
Freudianism, 2, 89, 106, 127-128
front region, 59
future, futurism, 3, 19, 36, 65, 75, 77

G

galaxy, 22
games, 23, 34, 57, 82, 86, 119
gender, 33, 36, 56, 57, 60, 62, 68, 88-89, 106, 132 n. 4
general semantics, 9, 52, 82-83, 116, *see also ETC: A Review of General Semantics*
general system(s), *see* system(s)
generalizing, 2, 5, 29, 117
Genesis, 79
genetic engineering, 71, 76
geodesic dome, 75
geopolitics, 47
glasses, 58
global village, 23, 24, 75
God, 79, 100, 110
goddess worship, 33
Gospel of John, 79
government, 42, 74, 76, 109
grammar, 3, 51, 63
grammatology, 46, 87
graphic revolution, 48
Greece, 28, 33, 37, 39-41, 46, 121-122
Greenpeace, 26, 49
group theory, 61

H

Harvard University, 35
heavy and light media, 27, 28
hero, 41, 48, 88
Hesiod, 40
hierarchies, 62
high context cultures, 59

history, 2, 3, 16, 19, 22, 26, 27-28,
   29, 37, 41, 42, 45-49, 55, 65-70,
   73, 76, 77, see also media
   history
Homer, 39-41, 131n. 1
Hopi, 85
Hopkins, Gerard Manley, 35, 36
horizontal propaganda, 74
hot and cool media, 23, 58
housing, see architecture
human, 45, 61, 66, 68-70, 74, 87,
   89, 92, 118, 123
human agency, 55, 100
human culture, 70
humanism, 92, 100
Huxley, Aldous, 80
hyperlexic, 125
hypermedia, 47, see also hypertext
hypermediacy, 34
hyperreal, 49
hypertext, 20, 33, 43, see also
   hypermedia

I

I-Thou, 37, 91
icon, 82, 118
iconoclasm, 80
identity, 47, 109-110, 126, see also
   self
ideology, 59, 71, 73
idols, 79-80, 89
illiteracy, 47
image, 16, 48-49, 52, 74, 77, 79,
   80, 108
immediacy, 34
immigration, 57
impact, see effects
index, 82
India, 46
individualism, 36, 61, 78, 107, 108,
   109, 130
industrial age, industrial revolution,
   17, 65, 66-67, 75
informal communication, 58

information, 28, 37, 47, 53, 56, 60,
   62, 63, 71, 75, 77, 78, 89, 99,
   103, 108, 112, 124
information explosion, 15, 126
information overload, 53, 77, 126
information systems, 17, 62, 75, 90
information theory, 60, 63, 75
innovation, 24, 29, 32, 45, 48, 53,
   56, 76, 80
Innis, Harold, 5, 27-30, 39, 41, 47,
   57, 70, 71, 74, 108
Institute of General Semantics, 9
institutions, 42, 53, 63
integration, propaganda of, 74
intelligence, 32, 60, 82, 112, 113,
   121, 123
interaction, 3, 18, 33, 42, 57, 63,
   77, 112, 120, 125, 129
intercultural communication, 31,
   59, 85-86
interface, 36, 37, 42, 64, 129
interiority, 36
inter/media, 57, 87, see also interpersonal media, mediated interpersonal communication
international communications,
   international relations, 47, 81
International Society for General
   Semantics, 9
internet, 32, 47, 56, 77, 78
interpersonal communication, 52,
   56-57, 62-63
interpersonal media, 57, 110, see
   also interpersonal media,
   mediated interpersonal communication
intrapersonal communication, 107,
   110
Israel, 28, 33, 46, see also Judaism,
   Semites

J

Jews, Jewish culture, see Israel,
   Judaism, Semites

journalism, 26, 29, 47, 48, 52, 62, 77, *see also* newspapers, public journalism
Joyce, James, 32, 81
Judaism, 16, 37, 78, 79-80, 95, *see also* Israel, Semites
Jungian psychology, 37, 89
justice, 40, 42-43, 77, *see also* law

K

keyboard, 125
kinesics, 45, 59, 118
knowledge, 28, 35, 36, 39, 40, 47, 56, 59, 63, 69, 75, 80, 87, 100, 108, 118, 120, 124, 126

L

law, legal system, 26, 42-43, 57, 63, 77, *see also* justice
laws of media, 24, 25, 32, 46, 131 n. 2, 133 n. 9
language, languages, 3, 6, 18, 23, 24, 27, 28, 32, 36, 42, 43, 45, 51, 58, 61, 64, 67, 69, 79, 81-87, 88, 101, 106, 107, 108, 111, 112, 113, 115-118, 119, 120, 121, 124, 128, 129
liberalism, 49
life, 15, 64, 66, 100, 103, 123, *see also* biology
light, 79, 88
light media, *see* heavy and light media
linear, lineal, linearity, 20, 32, 42, 46, 83, 124
linguistic relativism, 84-86, *see also* Sapir-Whorf Hypothesis
linguistics, 16, 51-52, 70, 81, 84
lists, 43
literacy, 16, 24, 33, 35-36, 40, 41-43, 47, 52, 59, 62, 76, 79, 86, 88, 108, 111, 124-126, 129, 130, 131 n. 1, 131 n. 2

literature, literary studies, literary theory 24, 26, 36, 41, 46, 47, 51, 67, 80-82, 84-89, 109
lithography, 48
logic, 3, 62, 82-83, 89, 102, 118, 122
love, 106, 109, 121
low context cultures, 59

M

machine, 17, 33, 64, 65, 68-70, 75, 106, *see also* mechanization
machine ideology, 58, 66
magazines, 22
management, 24, 75-76
margins, marginalization, 28, 48
Marx, Karl; Marxism, 2, 25, 48, 70-71
mass communication, 29, 47, 56-57
mass media, 23, 26, 63, 110
mass production, 22
mass society, 109
Massachusetts Institute of Technology, 60
material, materialism, 27, 58, 66, 83, 84, 88, 99-103, 107, 116, 118, 129, 130
material cause, 80
material transformation, 6, 99-103
mathematics, 83, 100, 102, 112, *see also* number
mathematical theory of communication, 60
Mayans, 108
McLuhan, Marshall, 4, 5, 16-20, 21-26, 27-30, 31-34, 35-36, 39, 41, 46, 47, 49, 51, 52, 55, 56, 58, 62, 65, 66, 69, 71, 74, 76, 77, 81, 82, 86, 88, 90, 91-92, 100, 106, 108
meaning, 3, 32, 81-84, 100, 101, 103, 114-115, 118, 119-120, 125, 131 n. 2, 133 n. 9

meaning of meaning, 3, 81
mechanical reproduction, 36, 48
mechanization, 17, 21-22, 24, 57,
   66-67, 71, *see also* machine
media, 3, 4, 15, 16, 17-18, 21, 23,
   24, 27, 28, 32, 35, 36, 42, 45,
   47, 53, 55, 57, 61, 62, 64, 65,
   66, 82, 84, 86, 87, 100, 101,
   106, 110, 118, 130, 133 n. 9
media activism, 49, 70, 77
media ecology, characteristics, 2, 3
   definitions and descriptions, 15,
      17-18, 23, 60, 103
   as a field, 4-5, 6, 7, 9-10, 16-20,
      21, 22, 31, 45, 55, 61-62, 65,
      67, 79-80, 83, 92
   as praxis, 18
   scholarship, 25, 27, 28-30, 32,
      35, 36, 37, 39, 40, 42, 47, 49,
      52, 57, 61-64, 65, 107-10871,
      75, 77, 83, 84, 86, 87-88, 91-
      92, 132 n. 4
Media Ecology Association, 10, 11-
   12, 19
Media Ecology Book Series, 10
Media Ecology Graduate Program,
   8-9, 11-12, 18, *see also* New
   York University
Media Ecology Review, 9
media environment, 4, 23, 40, 47,
   53, 56, 62, 78, 86, 108, 126,
   129, 130
media epistemology, 52
media events, 48
media evolution, *see* evolution
media history, 5, 19, 27-28, 45-49,
   55-56, 63
media production, 31-32
media theory, 19, *see also* medium
   theory
media virus, 60, 78, *see also* meme
mediated communication, 87

mediated interpersonal communication, 57, 110, *see also*
   inter/media
mediation, 3, 4, 34, 42, 45, 87, 88,
   91, 101
medicine, 76, 111, 128, 132 n. 3,
medieval, medievalism, 22, 47, 71
mediology, 19, 87-88
medium, 2, 4, 5, 15, 18, 23, 24, 28,
   32, 34, 39, 48, 49, 51, 55, 56,
   59, 60, 61, 63, 65, 66, 76, 79,
   80, 81, 82, 83-85, 86, 87, 88,
   90, 92, 95, 100, 101, 118, 120,
   121, 131 n. 2, 133 n. 9
medium is the message, 17, 23, 58,
   62, 84, 100, 102
medium theory, 19, 47, 62, 65
megamachine, 69-70
meme, 60, 78
memory, 32, 36, 37, 39-40, 45, 80,
   108, 111, 113, 114, 117, 123,
   124, 133 n. 8
memory theater, 45, 133 n. 8
Mental Research Institute (Palo
   Alto), 61, *see also* Palo Alto
   Group
Mesopotamia, 27, 28, 45-46
message, messages, 2, 4, 18, 32, 41,
   52, 63, 82, 100, 101
metacommunication , 121, *see also*
   communication about communication
metaphor, 4-5, 15, 23, 32, 37, 52,
   77, 81, 82, 86, 99, 107, 116
meter, 39, 41
military, 28,109, *see also* war,
   weapons
mimesis, mimetic stage, 45, 108,
   123, 124
mind, 59, 60-61, 84, 87, 103, 109,
   115, 127, *see also* theory of
   mind
mindblindness, 121-123

minority groups, 62
mnemonics, 36, 45, 133 n. 8
mobile telephone, 56, 78
modernity, modernism, 22, 29, 30, 46-47, 53
money, 23, 58, *see also* coins
monochronic time, 57
monologic, 3, 4
monopoly of knowledge, 28, *see also* access
moral progress, 56
moral theology, 92
morality, 120, 130
MOSAIC, 133 n. 10
Moses, 80
motion picture, 17, 29, 31, 33, 34, 47, 48, 49, 77, 88, 89, *see also* documentary
Mumford, Lewis, 6, 55, 57, 65-71, 74
Museum, 33
music, 29, 32-33, 42, 49, 61, 83, 113
myth, 40, 53, 86, 87, 105

N

narcissism, 6, 8, 95, 106-110, 114, 118, 122, 129-130
Narcissus, 6, 48-49, 105-110, 131 n. 1, 131 n. 2,
narcosis, 106
narrative, 53, 112
National Association of Educational Broadcasters, 23
National Council of Teachers of English, 17, 51
nationalism, 29, 46, 47
nature, 40, 61, 73, 78, 87, 105
Navajo, 85
Nazi Germany, 70
Neanderthals, 123
negative dialectics, 3
Nemesis, 105, 106, 110, 131 n. 2,
neologism, 86

neotechnic phase, 66, 70
nervous system, 89-90, 111, 115, 129, *see also* brain
network, 5, 20, 60, 64, 71, 73, 78, 92
neural networks, 60
New Criticism, 81
New Guinea, 31
new media, 26, 43, *see also* cyber-space, digital media, internet, mobile telephone, online communication
New York City, 16, 19, 25, 31, 51
New York School, 4, 6, 55-62, 83
New York Society for General Semantics, 9
New York State Communication Association, 6-9, 12
New York University, 8, 11-12, 16, 18, 55, *see also* Media Ecology Graduate Program
New Yorker, 67
news, *see* journalism
newspapers, 22, 47
non-Aristotelian, 82-83, *see also* general semantics
nondiscursive modes, 118, 120, *see also* presentational symbolism
nonlinear, 32, 33, 83
nonverbal communication, 58-59, 61, 84, 111, 117, 118, 120, 121, 123, 125
North American intellectual tradition, 19
numbers, numerals, 23, 46, 56, 61, 69, 84
numbing, 23, 106

O

obedience to authority, 61
obsessive, 88, 112
Oedipus, 106
one cannot not communicate, 61, 102

Ong, Walter, 4, 5, 8, 10, 11, 15-20, 25, 35-37, 39, 41, 47, 52, 77, 88, 91-92, 108
online communications, 25, 43, 57, 77
open source, 78
open system, 20
open-system awareness, 16-17, 20, 92
oral tradition, 4-5, 28, 40, 108, 124, 131 n. 1, *see also* primary orality, oralism, orality, residual orality
oralism, 42
orality, 16, 24, 33, 35-36, 39-41, 47, 53, 57, 59, 76, 78, 79, 108, 115, 123-124, 129, 130, 131 n. 1, 131 n. 2, *see also* oral tradition, oralism, orality-literacy studies, primary orality, residual orality, secondary orality
orality-literacy studies, 5-6, 16, 19, 35-37, 39-43, 45, 52, 85
order, 63-64, 89, 102
organic ideology, 59, 66, 70
Orwell, George, 80
other, 2, 107, 110, 114-115, 119, 121, 129-130
Ovid, 105, 109, 130, 131 n. 1,

P

paganism, 88-89
painting, 24
paleotechnic phase, 66, 67, 70
Palo Alto Group, 60-61
paper, 28, 42, 101
papyrus, 27, 28
parchment, 47
paralogic, 3
particularism, 2, 3, 29, 60
pentad, 101
perception, 1, 17, 24, 48, 49, 51-52, 66, 71, 78, 83, 89-90, 102, 107-108, 115-118, 120, 122,

124, *see also* phenomenology, senses
perfection, 49
performance, 59-60
permanence, 102
personalism, 35, 70, 92
persuasion, 78, 80, *see also* propaganda
pervasive developmental disorder, 112
phenomenology, 16, 22, 36, 37, 42, 78, *see also* perception, senses
philosophy, 2, 24, 39-40, 52, 55-56, 70, 75, 78, 80, 81-82, 83-84, 86, 90, 91-92, 102, 110, 118
photography, 31, 48, 49, 71, 81
physics, 33, 63, 64, 80, 91, 100
pictures, 61
pinball, 104
Plato, Platonism, 2, 5, 6, 39-40, 80, 101-102, 109, 118
play, 43, 59-60, 67, 89, 92, 112, 122
Playboy, 25
poetry, 24, 35, 36, 39-41, 83, 105, 121, 131 n.1,
pointing, 119-120
political economy, 28, 29, 71
political propaganda, 74
political science, politics, 2, 15, 26, 28, 29, 31, 40, 42, 47, 49, 52, 56, 62, 63, 74, 75, 76, 78, 100, 113
polychronic time, 57
popular culture, 22, 32
positivism, 100
posthuman, 64, 75, 110
post-industrial, 18-19, 29, 65, 73, 75
post-intellectualism, 76
Postman, Neil, 4, 5, 8, 9, 10, 11, 15-20, 39, 51-53, 55, 74, 77, 83, 86, 91-92, 110

postliterate, 108
postmodern, postmodernism, 25, 29, 34, 43, 47, 49, 53, 56, 63, 76, 110, 118
poststructuralism, 26, 29, 43, 62, 87, 110
post-typographic, 109
power, 59, 62, 69-70, 87
pragmatism, 20, 61, 82, 102, 103
praxis, 78
prehistoric, 45
present, 3
presentational symbolism, 83, *see also* nondiscursive modes
pre-Socratics, 40
press, 28
primary orality, 35, 41, 42, 126, *see also* oral tradition, oralism, orality, orality-literacy studies
print, 16, 22, 28, 33, 35, 36, 46-47, 48, 51-53, 56, 57, 60, 62, 66, 125, *see also* engraving
probes, 2, 24, 25
professionalism, 76, 132 n. 3,
progress, 49, 55-56, 88
Prometheus, 40
propaganda, 73-74, 78, 109, *see also* persuasion
proposition, 83
Protestant Reformation, 47
proxemics, 57
Psalm of David (115th), 79-80
pseudo-event, 48
psychoanalysis, psychiatry, 49, 60, 89, 106, 107, 127-128, *see also* Freud, Jungian psychology
psychology, psychotherapy, 33, 36, 57, 60-61, 82, 89, 106, 127-129
public journalism, 77
public opinion, 74
public relations, 48
public space, 57

Q
Queens College, 56
R
race, 56
radio, 17, 18, 48, 86, *see also* broadcasting
Rain Man, 114
Ramus, Peter, 35
rationality, 74, 83, 90
reading, 42, 82, 108-109, 124
reality, 32, 48-49, 55, 61, 62, 63, 81, 83, 100, 102, 103, 106, 115, 116, 118, *see also* worldview
receiver, 2
recursion, 82
relational communication, 61, 106, 121
relationship level, 61
relationships, 2, 3, 15, 28, 37, 55, 61-63, 82, 91-92, 101, 102, 107, 110, 111
relativism, 102
religion, religious studies, 25, 36, 42, 52, 70, 73, 74, 75, 78, 109, 110, 113
remediation, 33-34, 43, 88
Renaissance, 47, 77
residual orality, 36, 88
resonance, 32
rhetoric, 2, 3, 24, 36, 37, 42, 49, 80, 81-82, 86, 92, 101, 102
risk, risk aversion, 2, 4, 56
ritual, 83, 112, 118, 123, 124
ritual view, 29
roads, 23, 70
Rogerian therapy, 128
roles, 59-60, 62-63, 89, 99, 122, 124
romance, 36
Rome, 28, 46, 105

S

sacred, 32, 76, *see also* religion,
   spirituality
St. Louis, 16
Saint Louis University, 16, 35, 36
Sapir-Whorf Hypothesis, Sapir-
   Whorf-Korzybski Hypothesis,
Sapir-Whorf-Lee Hypothesis, 85-
   86
Sapir-Whorf-Korzybski-Ames-
   Einstein-Heisenberg-
   Wittgenstein-McLuhan-Et Al.
   Hypothesis, 51, 91
saturated self, 110
savant, 22, 112, 113-114, 117, 123,
   124
schizophrenia, 122
science, 28, 40, 46, 47, 61, 64, 67,
   73, 75, 78, 82, 99-100, 113, 121
science fiction, 89
scientism, 100
screen, 42, 77
scribal culture, scribal era, 22, 35,
   36, 46
sculpture, 83
Second Commandment, 80
secondary orality, 35, 36, 42
Seinfeld, 102
self, 2, 6, 8, 34, 42, 47, 48-49, 59,
   62-63, 77, 85, 89, 95, 105-110,
   111, 114-116, 119, 121-123,
   124, 129-130, *see also* identity
self-organization, 63, 102, 103,
   115, 129, *see also* emergence,
   system(s)
self-referential, self-reflexive, 34,
   63, 82
semantic environment, 83
semantics, 52, 60
semiology, semiotics, 32, 67, 82, 88
Semites, 39
sender, 2

senses, 2, 3-4, 22, 23, 33, 35, 48,
   52, 66, 71,78, 81, 83, 89-90,
   108, 112, 114-115, 119, 120,
   123, 124, 125, 126, 132 n. 6, *see
   also* perception, phenomenology
Serbo-Croatia, 41
sex, 33, 68, 88-89, *see also* gender
Shakespeare, William, 80
Shelley, Mary, 80
Sherlock Holmes, 22
sight, 32, *see also* visual communication, visual thinking, visualism
signs, 82
signification, 4, 87, 88, 101
signified, 82
signifier, 82
silence, 82, 88, 110, 132 n. 3, 132
   n. 5
similarity, 2, 3
Simpson, O. J., 77
simulation, 49
singer of tales, 41
situations, 59-60, 62
Small World Theorem, 64
social construction, 61, 63, 100,
   103, 107
social ecology, 76
social organization, 15, 23, 42, 47,
   59, 63, 68, 78, 102, 103
social science, 62, 100
social space, 57, 60
socialism, 71
sociological propaganda, 74
sociology, 29, 42, 59-60, 63, 70,
   73-75, 100
Socrates, 80
something from nothing, 6, 9, 95-
   97, 99-103, 105, 130
song, 39, 41, 108
Sophists, 102, 133 n. 8
sound, 32, 35, 79, 88, 100, 101,
   108, *see also* acoustic
sound recording, 31, 33, 47, 48, 49

Soviet Union, 70
space, 3, 24, 25, 27, 28, 29, 43, 49,
    56, 57-58, 60, 71, 90, 103, 108
space bias, 28
spaceship earth, 75
specialization, 22, 76, 92, 124
speech, spoken word, 23, 35, 36,
    37, 56, 60, 69, 79, 80, 82, 87,
    99, 100, 107, 108, 112, 114,
    125
Speech Communication Annual, 7-9
speech pathology, 82
spirituality, 36, 42, 100, 122, *see*
    also religion, sacred
staples, 27
status, 88
steam powered printing press, 48
Strate, Barbara, 133 n. 10
structure, 17, 87
structuralism, 87
subject, 63, 110
subjectivism, 102
Sullivan, Anne, 129
Sumerians, 46, *see also*
    Mesopotamia
surveillance, 87
survival, 17, 60
symbol, symbol systems, 17, 28,
    59, 69, 81- 84, 86, 101, 103,
    123
symbolic communication, symbolic
    form, 6, 27, 45, 52, 81-84, 87,
    102-103, 107, *see also* encoding
symbolic ecology, 83
symbolic interaction, 59-60, 62,
    89, 107
symbolic transformation, 101, 118
synergy, 66, 75
system(s), system(s) theory, 18, 19,
    24, 36, 60-64, 66, 73, 75, 80,
    82, 83, 89, 102, 103, *see also*
    cybernetics

T

Taoism, 64
technical communication, 58
technical syncretism, 66
technics, 6, 65-71, 78, 89
technique, la technique, 17, 18, 22,
    66, 73-74, 75, 78, 80, 103
technocracy, 53
technologic, 3
technological determinism, 76
technological evolution, *see*
    evolution
technological network, 73
technological society, 22, 73-74,
    86, 109, *see also* technopoly
technological studies, 6, 19, 53, 65-
    71, 73-78
technological system, 73
technology, technologies, 3, 15, 16,
    17, 18, 19, 23, 24, 27, 28, 29,32,
    33, 36, 39, 42, 45, 48, 49, 53,
    55, 56, 58, 62-63, 65-71, 73-78,
    80, 81, 87, 88, 89, 90, 100, 103,
    106, 125, 131 n. 2,
    as autonomous, 73, 76, 78
    as self-augmenting, 73
technopoly, 22, 53, 76, *see also*
    technological society
technorealism, 77
telecommunications, 28, 29
telegraph, 29
telephone, 17, 58, 81
telescope, 47, 81
television, 17, 18, 23, 34, 47, 48,
    51-52, 56, 58, 61, 62, 76, 77,
    86, 102, *see also* broadcasting
tensegrity, 3, 75
terrorism, 78
tetrad, *see* laws of media
Thamus, 80
theocracy, 47
theology, 37, 74, 100, *see also*
    moral theology

theory, 4
theory group, 4
theory of logical types, 82
theory of mind, 6, 120-124, 129
theory of multiple intelligences, 84,
    113
Theuth, 80
thought, 15, 18, 32, 35, 82, 84, 86-
    87, 103, 107,109, 116-117, 126
time, 3, 27, 28, 29, 37, 49, 57-58,
    66, 71, 76, 91, 103, 125
time bias, 3, 28
time binding, 3
time zone, 29
Tommy (The Who), 114
tools, 17, 53, 58, 66, 67, 68, 69, 76
Toronto, 16, 19
Toronto School, 4, 5, 19, 29, 31-
    34, 39, 41
tourism, 48
Tower of Babel, 80
tragedy, 88
transactions, 18
transformation, *see* change,
    material transformation,
    symbolic transformation
transhuman, 110
transportation, 28, 56, 58, 70
transportation view, 29, 32
tribal culture, tribalism, 31, 39, 68,
    108, 116, 124
trivium, 3
typewriter, 47, 125
typography, *see* print

U

United States, 70, 77, *see also*
    American culture
universalism, 2, 3, 42, 60, 87
universe, 15-16, 64, 91-92, 99, 103
universe of discourse, 2
University of Chicago, 27, *see also*
    Chicago School

University of Toronto, 27, 31, 32,
    39, 40, *see also* Toronto School
U. S. Department of Health, 23
urban studies, 57, 67, 70

V

values, 17, 18
VCR, 29
verbal communication, 37, 58, 74,
    84, 112, 118, 120
vernacular, 46
vertical propaganda, 74
video art, 32, 82
violence, 76
virtual community, 78
virtual reality, 34, 43, 78
visual communication, 33, 45, 49,
    71, 77, 108, 118, 122, 123, 124-
    125
visual thinking, 117, 123, 124-125,
    133 n. 8
visualism, 4, 22, 33, 35, 77, 78, 87,
    88, 108
voyeur, 89

W

war, 24, 78, *see also* military
weapons, 23, 58, 68, 70
web, website, 33, 34
wild boy of Aveyron, 114
word, 16, 35-37, 49, 52, 74, 77,
    79, 84
word processing, 33, 43
world order, 47
worldview, 23, 73, 84, 86, *see also*
    reality
wrestling, 86
writing, 16, 33, 35, 36, 40, 41-43,
    45-46, 56, 64, 69, 75, 76, 80,
    87, 101, 103, 108-109, 124-125

Y

youth culture, 78

CPSIA information can be obtained at www.ICGtesting.com
Printed in the USA
BVOW05s1638200915

418706BV00001B/15/P